Global Environme Governance

uthampton

More than 20 years after the Bruntland Commission report, *Our Common Future*, we have yet to secure the basis for a serious approach to global environmental governance. The failed 2002 World Summit on Sustainable Development showed the need for a new approach to globalization and sustainability.

Taking a critical perspective, rooted in political economy, regulation theory, and post-sovereign international relations, this book explores questions concerning the governance of environmental sustainability in a globalizing economy. With contributions from leading international scholars, the book offers a comprehensive framework on globalization, governance, and sustainability, and examines institutional mechanisms and arrangements to achieve sustainable environmental governance. The book:

- considers current failures in the framework of global environmental governance
- addresses the problematic relationship between sustainability and globalization
- explores controversies of development and environment that have led to new processes of institution building
- examines the marketization of environmental policymaking; stakeholder politics and environmental policymaking; socio-economic justice; the political origins of sustainable consumption; the role of transnational actors; and processes of multi-level global governance.

This book will be of interest to students and researchers of political science, international studies, political economy, and environmental studies.

Jacob Park is Assistant Professor of Business Strategy and Sustainability at Green Mountain College, Vermont, USA.

Ken Conca is Professor of Government and Politics at the University of Maryland, USA.

Matthias Finger is Professor of Management of Network Industries at the Swiss Federal Institute of Technology (EPFL), Lausanne, Switzerland.

Environmental Politics / Routledge Research in Environmental Politics

Edited by Matthew Paterson, *University of Ottawa*

Over recent years environmental politics has moved from a peripheral interest to a central concern within the discipline of politics. This series aims to reinforce this trend through the publication of books that investigate the nature of contemporary environmental politics and show the centrality of environmental politics to the study of politics per se. The series understands politics in a broad sense and books will focus on mainstream issues such as the policy process and new social movements as well as emerging areas such as cultural politics and political economy. Books in the series will analyse contemporary political practices with regards to the environment and/or explore possible future directions for the "greening" of contemporary politics. The series will be of interest not only to academics and students working in the environmental field, but will also demand to be read within the broader discipline.

The series consists of two strands:

Environmental Politics addresses the needs of students and teachers, and the titles will be published in paperback and hardback. Titles include:

Global Warming and Global Politics
Matthew Paterson

Politics and the Environment
James Connelly and Graham Smith

International Relations Theory and Ecological Thought
Towards synthesis
Eric Laferrière and Peter Stoett

Planning Sustainability
Edited by Michael Kenny and James Meadowcroft

Deliberative Democracy and the Environment
Graham Smith

EU Enlargement and the Environment
Institutional change and environmental policy in Central and Eastern Europe
Edited by JoAnn Carmin and Stacy D. VanDeveer

The Crisis of Global Environmental Governance
Towards a new political economy of sustainability
Edited by Jacob Park, Ken Conca and Matthias Finger

Routledge Research in Environmental Politics presents innovative new research intended for high-level specialist readership. These titles are published in hardback only and include:

The Crisis of Global Environmental Governance

Towards a new political economy of sustainability

Edited by
Jacob Park, Ken Conca
and Matthias Finger

Routledge
Taylor & Francis Group

LONDON AND NEW YORK

First published 2008
by Routledge
2 Park Square, Milton Park, Abingdon, Oxon OX14 4RN

Simultaneously published in the USA and Canada
by Routledge
270 Madison Avenue, New York, NY 10016

Transferred to Digital Printing 2008

Routledge is an imprint of the Taylor & Francis Group, an informa business.

© 2008 Jacob Park, Ken Conca and Matthias Finger election and
editorial matter; individual contributors, their contributions

Typeset in Times New Roman by
Taylor & Francis Books
Printed and bound in Great Britain by
TJI Digital, Padstow, Cornwall

British Library Cataloguing in Publication Data
A catalogue record for this book is available from the British Library

Library of Congress Cataloging in Publication Data
The crisis of global environmental governance : towards a new political
  economy of sustainability / edited by Jacob Park, Ken Conca and
  Matthias Finger.
    p. cm. – (Environmental politics)
  Includes bibliographical references and index.
  1. Sustainable development. 2. Globalization. I. Park, Jacob. II. Conca,
  Ken. III. Finger, Matthias.
  HC79.E5C729 2008
338.9'27–dc22   2007038788

ISBN 978-0-415-44919-9 (hbk)
ISBN 978-0-415-44920-5 (pbk)
ISBN 978-0-203-92910-0 (ebk)

Contents

Contributors

Henri Acselrad is Professor at the Institute for Urban and Regional Research and Planning of the Federal University of Rio de Janeiro and researcher at the Brazilian National Council for Scientific Development. He is editor of *Revista Brasileira de Estudos Urbanos e Regionais* and earned his PhD in Economics at the University of Paris I (Panthéon-Sorbonne), France. He writes on environmental conflicts and planning and is the co-organizer (with Bruce Stiftel and Vanessa Watson) of the Dialogues in Urban and Regional Planning, volume 2 (Routledge, 2006). He was a member of the group of 16 authors of The Jo' Burg Memo for the World Summit 2002 on Sustainable Development, published by the Heinrich Böll Foundation.

Saleem H. Ali is Associate Professor of Environmental Studies at the University of Vermont's Rubenstein School of Natural Resources, and a member of the adjunct faculty of Brown University's Watson Institute for International Studies. His research focuses on the causes and consequences of environmental conflicts and how ecological factors can promote peace. He has also been on the visiting faculty for the United Nations University for Peace (Costa Rica). He is the author of *Mining, the Environment and Indigenous Development Conflicts* (University of Arizona Press, 2003) and editor of *Peace Parks: Conservation and Conflict Resolution* (MIT Press, 2007). Dr. Ali is also a member of the expert advisory group on environmental conflicts for the United Nations Environment Programme and the World Conservation Union's Taskforce on Transboundary Conservation. He has also been involved in promoting environmental education in madrassahs (Islamic religious schools) and using techniques from environmental planning to study the rise of these institutions in Pakistan. Dr. Ali received his doctorate in Environmental Planning from MIT, a Master's in environmental studies from Yale, and a Bachelor's in chemistry from Tufts.

Ulrich Brand is Professor of International Politics at Vienna University, Institute of Political Science. Previously, Dr. Brand worked as an assistant professor at Kassel University. He also taught at Rutgers University and the University of Applied Sciences, Bremen and was a visiting scholar with the Center for German and European Studies and the Faculty of Environmental Studies at York University, Toronto. His research focuses on state and regulation theory, global governance, international political economy and environmental politics, and NGOs and social movements. Together with Christoph Görg, Joachim Hirsch and Markus Wissen, he recently published *Conflicts in Environmental Regulation and the Internationalization of the State: Contested Terrains* (Routledge 2008). Dr. Brand received his PhD from the University of Frankfurt (Main).

Ken Conca (co-editor) is Professor of Government and Politics and Director of the Harrison Program on the Future Global Agenda at the University of Maryland. His research and teaching focus on global environmental politics, political economy, environmental policy, North–South issues, and peace and conflict studies. He is the author/editor of several books on global environmental politics, technology, and international political economy, including *Governing Water: Contentious Transnational Politics and Global Institution Building* (MIT Press, 2006); *Environmental Peacemaking* (Johns Hopkins University Press, 2003); *Confronting Consumption* (The MIT Press, 2002); *Green Planet Blues: Environmental Politics from Stockholm to Kyoto* (Westview Press, 1998); *Manufacturing Insecurity: The Rise and Fall of Brazil's Military-Industrial Complex* (1997); and *The State and Social Power in Global Environmental Politics* (Columbia University Press, 1993). Dr. Conca received his PhD from the University of California, Berkeley in 1992.

Matthias Finger (co-editor) is Chair and Professor of Management of Network Industries, as well as Dean of the School of Continuing Education, at the Swiss Federal Institute of Technology (EPFL) in Lausanne. He is interested in issues of liberalization, deregulation, globalization, and re-regulation, and has written extensively about the institutional aspects of global economic and environmental change. Among his publications are *The Earth Brokers. Power, Politics, and World Development* (with Pratap Chaterjee; Routledge, 1994); *Water Privatization: Transnational Corporations and the Re-Regulation of the Global Water Industry* (with Jeremy Allouche; SPON Press, 2001); and *Limits to Privatization: Report to the Club of Rome* (with Ernst U. von Weizsäcker and Oran Young; Earthscan, 2005). Previously, he was a professor at Syracuse University (1989–1991) and Columbia University (1992–1994). Dr. Finger has a PhD in Political Science and a PhD in Adult Education, both from the University of Geneva.

Christoph Görg is Professor of Environmental Governance at the University of Kassel, Department of Social Sciences. He is also Senior Researcher at the Helmholtz Center for Environmental Research (UFZ) in Leipzig, where he works in the areas of Governance and Institutions as well as

Nature Protection and Biodiversity. He has published widely on the critical theory of societal relationships with nature, global environmental and biodiversity politics, state transformation, and multi-level governance. His areas of interest also include the interface between science and policy and issues of inter- and transdisciplinarity. Together with Ulrich Brand, Joachim Hirsch and Markus Wissen, he recently published *Conflicts in Environmental Regulation and the Internationalization of the State: Contested Terrains* (Routledge, 2008).

Sanjeev Khagram is associate professor of Public Affairs at the University of Washington, where he directs the Marc Lindenberg Center for Humanitarian Action, International Development and Global Citizenship. Previously Dr. Khagram was on the faculty of Harvard University's Kennedy School of Government, where he also was affiliated with several interdisciplinary research centers. He is a scholar and researcher in the emerging field of transnational studies, and brings over 15 years of applied research experience on the role of non-governmental organizations (NGOs) in transnational dynamics, democratization, global governance, and international development. He was senior advisor for the World Commission on Dams. He is the author of *Dams and Development: Transnational Struggles for Water and Power* (Oxford University Press, 2004). Professor Khagram holds a BA in development studies/engineering, an MA in economics (food research), and a PhD in political science, all from Stanford University.

Gabriela Kütting is an associate professor in the Department of Political Science and a core faculty member of the Division of Global Affairs at Rutgers University, Newark. Previously, she was a tenured faculty member at the University of Aberdeen in Scotland. Her research interests lie in the field of global environmental politics and international/global political economy. She has published widely in the field of global environmental politics and is the author of two books: *Environment, Society and International Relations* (Routledge, 2000) and *Globalization and the Environment: Greening Global Political Economy* (SUNY, 2004).

Peter Newell is Professor of Development Studies at the University of East Anglia and James Martin Fellow at the Oxford University Centre for the Environment. Prior to this he has held posts as Principal Fellow in the Centre for the Study of Globalization and Regionalization, University of Warwick, Fellow at the Institute of Development Studies, University of Sussex, visiting researcher at FLACSO Argentina, and researcher and lobbyist for Climate Network Europe in Brussels. He is author of *Climate for Change: Non-State Actors and the Global Politics of the Greenhouse* (Cambridge University Press, 2000); co-author of *The Effectiveness of EU Environmental Policy* (MacMillan, 2000); and co-editor of *Development and the Challenge of Globalization* (ITDG, 2002), *The Business of*

Global Environmental Governance (MIT Press, 2005), and *Rights, Resources and the Politics of Accountability* (Zed Books, 2006).

Jacob Park (co-editor) is assistant professor of business strategy and sustainability at Green Mountain College in Vermont, where he specializes in teaching and research on the global environment and business strategy, corporate social responsibility, business ethics, and community-based entrepreneurship, with a special expertise/interest in Japan, China, and the Asia-Pacific region. His most recent book is *The Ecology of the New Economy: Sustainable Transformation of Global Information Technology, Communication, and Electronics Industries* (Greenleaf Publishing, 2002). Previously a senior fellow of the Environmental Leadership Program and lead author in the Scenarios Working Group of the Millennium Ecosystem Assessment, he currently serves on the International Planning Board of the Greening of Industry Network, the Steering Committee of the North America Green Purchasing Initiative, and the IUCN/World Conservation Union's Commission on Ecosystem Management.

Matthew Paterson is Professor of Politics at the University of Ottawa. His research focuses on the intersection of international political economy and global environmental politics. His books include *Automobile Politics: Ecology and Cultural Political Economy* (Cambridge, 2007); *Understanding Global Environmental Politics* (Palgrave, 2001); and *Global Warming and Global Politics* (Routledge, 1996). His current research includes a project on climate change politics and the "greening of the state."

Darrell Whitman is a licensed attorney, community activist, and educator. He has been an Instructor in Political Sociology and a Tutor in International Political Economy and Media Studies, worked professionally in practiced electoral, community, and environmental politics, and served as an advisor on global warming issues for the State of California's Resources Agency. Currently he is located at Keele University in the United Kingdom, where he is pursuing research into the politics of the Intergovernmental Panel on Climate Change and the role of finance in international political economy. Past and pending publications include: "Ghost Dance: The U.S. and Illusions of Power in the Twenty-first Century," *Alternatives: A Turkish Journal of International Relations* 3 (4), Winter 2004; "Good as Gold: Oil, Currency and Global Finance," in Bülent Gökay, ed. *Caspian Oil and the "New Great Game"* (Routledge, 2006); *Science, Politics, and Global Warming: The Political Discourse of the IPCC* (Praeger, forthcoming); and, with Bülent Gökay, *The Genie in the Bottle: Peak Oil, Modernity, and the Uncertain Future of the Global Carbon Economy* (Routledge, forthcoming).

1 The death of Rio environmentalism

*Jacob Park, Matthias Finger, and
Ken Conca*

What went wrong?

With the fading of post-Cold War optimism and the increasingly apparent inadequacy of responses to global environmental challenges, environmentalists around the world have begun to rethink the international strategies of the past few decades. Certainly, much has been accomplished to improve certain elements of international environmental governance. Multilateral agreements have proliferated; international institutions for trade and finance have begun to take more account of environmental considerations, either proactively or of necessity; many businesses around the world have begun to take the challenge of sustainability seriously. At the UN, Secretary-General Ban Ki-moon recently appointed former Norwegian Prime Minister Gro Harlem Brundtland, former South Korean Foreign Minister Han Seung-soo, and former Chilean President Ricardo Lagos as special climate change envoys, to help build the "institutional framework within which a global solution to this global problem can be reached" (UN 2007). In Europe and Asia, many new ideas about institutionalizing sustainability have emerged and are being discussed (Ott 2005, IGES 2005, ADB 2005). In the United States, many cities and states have sought to assume policy leadership, as a way to counteract the Bush administration's inaction and rollback on environmental matters.

Yet there is no denying that the scope and pace of change have been a source of major disappointment. The year 2007 marked the tenth anniversary of negotiations that produced the Kyoto Protocol on climate change. Progress toward global implementation of Kyoto, an agreement that falls woefully short of what is needed, can at best be described as uneven and sporadic. The same—or, in our view, much worse—could be said about progress in the case of faltered global initiatives on biodiversity, forests, the world's oceans, and the environment-development targets embedded in the UN's Millennium Development Goals. Ten years after the 1992 Earth Summit in Rio de Janeiro, a serious environmental agenda was almost entirely missing when governments met in Johannesburg for what was labeled the World Summit on Sustainable Development.

In the United States, disappointment with the flagging of initiatives for global environmental protection stirred up into a major controversy when a widely publicized essay on "The Death of Environmentalism" argued that "modern environmentalism is no longer capable of dealing with the world's most serious ecological crisis" of global warming (Shellenberger and Nordhaus 2004: 6; see also Shellenberger and Nordhaus 2007). The essay's foreword suggested that "It's time to ask: has the U.S. environmental community's work over the past 30 years laid the groundwork for the economic, cultural and political shifts that we know will be necessary to deal with the crisis?" (Teague 2004: 4).

Many American environmentalists rejected the core claims of the essay (see "Don't Fear the Reapers" 2005). Leaders of mainstream organizations such as the Sierra Club and the Natural Resources Defense Council offered rebuttals. Grassroots activists pointed to the failure of both the mainstream movement and those pronouncing its death to deal seriously with questions of race, class, and power in America. Several observers pointed to the fragmented character of American environmentalism, which makes it difficult to capture either success or failure through a single lens. Many noted that Shellenberger and Nordhaus, a pollster and a political strategist/public-relations expert, offered only incremental suggestions—that environmentalists work to recapture the Democratic Party, engage in values-based marketing initiatives, and promote alternative energy business development—raising questions about just how different their vision really was.

Few, however, disputed one of the central insights of the essay: that large, mainstream American environmental organizations were wedded to a set of strategies and tactics that increasingly misread the politics of the twenty-first century. As author Bill McKibben suggested, "The U.S. has wasted the 15 years since climate change emerged as a real problem. Its environmentalists have failed to make measurable progress on the greatest environmental challenge anyone's ever faced. So we better come up with something new." (McKibben 2005)

In the conversations that led us to produce this book, the editors and contributors have found themselves asking broadly similar questions about the state of global environmentalism. We use the phrase "global environmentalism" to refer not to a specific social movement or ideology, but rather to a broad historical trajectory of international initiatives that started with the 1972 UN Conference on the Human Environment in Stockholm, were strengthened institutionally with the 1987 World Commission on Environment and Development (Brundtland Commission), peaked with the 1992 Earth Summit in Rio de Janeiro, and, in our view, have been in decline ever since.

When governments converged on Rio de Janeiro for the 1992 UN Conference on Environment and Development (UNCED)—popularly dubbed the "Earth Summit"—the mood was one of cautious optimism about the challenge of sustainable development. Yet few can claim seriously that the period since the Rio meeting has been one of great accomplishment on global environmental governance, human development, or the chimerical notion of "sustainability." Governments of the North have shown little interest in investing in Agenda 21, the laundry list of responses crafted for endorsement at the Earth Summit. Fifteen years after its release, Agenda 21 has become the environmental equivalent of the League of Nations' resolutions against war—that is, high on political symbolism and low on policy impact. Governments of the South have shown little ability or inclination to stand in the way of the globalization of consumerism. International environmental diplomacy has stalled on issues ranging from climate change to the world's forests to toxic hazards. In many parts of the world, activism and social mobilization on environment-development themes have grown in recent years—but most of this growth has taken place outside the framework of officially sanctioned "NGO" activity envisioned by the UNCED process, not within it.

The current situation looks vastly different from that euphoric summer of 1992. When the world's governments came together at UNCED, they produced an official stance of cautious, pragmatically grounded optimism on the world's environmental and development problems. UNCED conjured a world in which governments were starting to come together to hammer out a cooperative path toward long-term sustainability. In this highly stylized vision, governments of the North and South shared a basic interest in responding to a set of problems linking environment and development goals. Allocating the costs of responding would not be easy, and countries would continue to defend their sovereignty against undue encroachment. But change was expected to follow from creating the proper institutional frameworks to overcome these barriers to collective action, making it possible to realize the larger, shared global interest in sustainability.

Assets in this effort included humankind's great capacity for technological and social innovation, the substantial gains in economic efficiency and quality of life to be had from doing things the sustainable way, and, above all, the growing recognition of the globally shared responsibility for the task. Enlisted in the campaign would also be a wide array of interested groups from civil society—everyone from farmers, youth groups, and civic associations to environmentalists, scientists, and transnational business elites. The premise was that these heterogeneous groups of actors, lumped under the general heading of "non-governmental organizations," would feed useful information and perspectives into the joint agenda of governments and, in doing so, become much more likely to accept the conclusions reached by governments about the proper path forward from Rio.

Some critics have described UNCED as an unmet vision—a basically sound blueprint for sustainability that has failed only because governments have failed to fund and implement it. The question of how to finance sustainable development proved to be one of the most contentious issues at the 1992 Earth Summit. A particularly heated debate centered on whether the industrialized countries should pay for the costs of policy measures undertaken by developing countries to tackle global environmental problems. This notion of "additionality"—financial commitments to sustainability that would be provided in addition to existing development assistance— became a rallying cry for the developing countries in the negotiations on Agenda 21 prior to the Earth Summit, and has been raised many times since. The euphoria following Rio soon dissipated as decision-makers came to terms with the difficulties of meeting the $300 billion price tag to implement Agenda 21. With the possible exception of the Montreal Protocol and the phase-out of ozone-depleting substances, one can see similar difficulties with implementing virtually all global environmental conventions. Desire for a sustainable future is rarely followed up with adequate institutional support and economic resources.

Others have argued that UNCED was not so much a failed vision as an improperly focused one—a problem not simply of implementation and follow-through but, more fundamentally, of agenda-setting and priorities. High-profile Northern concerns about climate stabilization, biodiversity preservation, and tropical forests became the focus of high-stakes intergovernmental bargaining in an effort to craft multilateral treaties. The day-to-day struggles of the world's poor for clean water, livable habitats, or healthy agro-ecosystems failed to muster political salience in the North, and as a result were consigned to the eco-political dumping ground of Agenda 21. They became problems for the next century, but not for the current political moment.

Still others have challenged the core premise of UNCED, rejecting its formulations of "sustainability" as a flawed, New Age, economistic vision. From this perspective, UNCED represented the institutionalization of incremental efficiency improvements or "ecological modernization," in which the idea of "development" remains capital- and, more recently, knowledge-intensive industrialization, rather than questioning industrialization itself. Such an approach might promise marginal efficiency gains, but falls far short of the more fundamental social, political, and economic changes needed to achieve true sustainability. In this view, UNCED turned out to be little more than a vehicle to legitimize further industrial growth by transforming environmental problems into developmental issues, which then could be tackled by means of more money, more technology, and more management. A key element of controlling this process was to lump together civil-society actors and powerful business organizations under the general heading of "non-governmental organizations."

Our purpose is not to formulate an institutional critique of global environmental governance or a deconstruction of the concept of sustainability. Indeed, such critical frameworks were available at the time of UNCED itself, for anyone willing to consider them. Perhaps the most compelling critique of UNCED is the spectacle that took place ten years after the Earth Summit, when the world's leaders gathered in Johannesburg for the World Summit on Sustainable Development in August 2002. The Johannesburg

Summit proved unable to offer a significant list of accomplishments since Rio, a coherent explanation of how to proceed, or even a clear description of the destination. Only ten years beyond Rio, the cracks in the official vision had grown into open fissures. As one director of a prominent environmental group active at the summit remarked, "Governments can't even agree to reaffirm the principles of the Rio Summit ten years ago. This summit could easily be remembered as Rio minus ten rather than Rio plus ten" (*London Times* 2002). If it is remembered at all, the Johannesburg Summit is likely to stand as a perverse watershed in the history of global environmental governance: something that can only be described as the death of Rio environmentalism.

The inadequacy of current approaches to global environmental governance raises two important questions. First, how and why have serious approaches to global sustainability come to be so politically marginalized? How is it possible—15 years after UNCED, 20 years after the Brundtland Commission, and more than 30 years after the Stockholm UN Conference on the Human Environment—that the great global challenge of securing the ecological future of the planet and its peoples has reached a point of such political and social insignificance? Much of the problem lies, unsurprisingly, in opposition from powerful interests. But the problem has significantly been worsened by an inadequate grasp of the linked challenges of sustainability, globalization, and governance. The most damaging myths of Rio, in our judgment, were those that misrepresented, or simply ignored, this crucial triangular relationship. One central goal of this volume, therefore, is to begin to draw a clearer picture of this relationship and its implications.

Second, and ultimately more important, where do we go from here? If the path from Stockholm to Rio to Johannesburg cannot provide the basis for a serious approach, what are the alternatives? In particular, what institutional mechanisms and governing arrangements are consistent with a serious approach to sustainability in a globalizing world political economy? Here we are less interested in the narrower (albeit important) question of United Nations institutional reform, or the call for a "world environment organization." Instead, we are interested in more basic questions: What are the core functions of environmental governance? Who are the agents best suited to perform them? At what levels of social aggregation—ranging from the most local to the genuinely global—are these functions most effectively performed?

How did we get here?

The clarion call for the can-do optimism of enlightened self-interest that pervaded what we will term the "Rio model" was *Our Common Future*, the 1987 report of the World Commission on Sustainable Development (WCED 1987). Chaired by Prime Minister Gro Harlem Brundtland of Norway, the WCED sketched a vision of sustainability as economic development; a world in which Southern governments implemented policy reforms with the help of Northern funding and technology transfer; and international cooperation around a shared global vision of the future which would break the logjam of perceived conflicts among national interests. Unfortunately, these premises can only be described today as wildly optimistic, particularly when it comes to the role of the state in promoting sustainable development.

In our assessment, the deep, underlying problems embedded in the Rio model, and the most fundamental failings of the path from Stockholm in 1972 to Johannesburg in 2002, have been threefold. First is a profound underestimation of the underlying dynamics of industrial development, technological change, and economic globalization, and the almost total failure to grapple with the questions of governing functions and governing agents in the world's increasingly globalizing political economy. Second is an inadequate understanding of global environment-development problems, in which the main task is limited to managing transboundary environmental problems, while stabilizing national trajectories of growth-as-development. Third is an excessively state-centered vision of the political blueprint for change, in which deeply contested social conflicts over environmental protection and serious problems with both the authority and capability of states were largely denied or papered over. The net effect of these flawed ways of understanding the problem and its politics has been to steer us away from serious discussions of the links between sustainability, globalization, and governance.

In order to state our arguments clearly, it is important to examine each of these three flawed premises in more detail. The first incorrect premise of the UNCED/Rio process was to underestimate the dynamics of industrial society and miss the significance of globalization, particularly its economic dimensions. The Rio process underestimated—indeed, ignored—the dynamic trajectory of industrial civilization in the second half of the twentieth century and failed to account for the underlying, reinforcing dynamics of economic growth and technological diffusion that have come to define industrial development on an increasingly global scale. Chapter 2 by Ulrich Brand and Christoph Görg, "Sustainability and globalization: a theoretical perspective," explores in more depth this problematic relationship between globalization and sustainability using a regulatory and critical-state theoretical framework. Matthias Finger's chapter, "Which governance for sustainable development? An organizational and institutional perspective," examines this decoupling by analyzing the dynamics of globalization and sustainability as governance dilemmas from an institutional and organizational perspective.

Centered in the comfortable traditions of interstate diplomacy, and strongly influenced by an underlying neo-liberal agenda of furthering economic growth, the Rio process offered no answers to core questions about the functions and agents of governance in a globalizing political economy. Deregulated, growth-liberating economies were expected to be able to solve many of the problems. Where they did not, the implicit belief was that the harmful side effects of progress could be contained by political will, with nation-states agreeing among themselves to limit these impacts voluntarily. Most of the emphasis was placed on economic incentives to do good things, rather than any notion of serious regulatory mechanisms at a global scale to prevent the doing of bad things. Matthew Paterson's chapter, "Sustainable consumption? Legitimation, regulation, and environmental governance," illustrates this problem in his examination of the contemporary discourse surrounding "sustainable consumption." Paterson discusses the intellectual and political origins of sustainable consumption and shows how this concept acts as a general legitimizing strategy of economic globalization in relation to the environmental crisis. Henri Acselrad's chapter, "Between market and justice: the socio-ecological challenge," argues that sustainable development has been framed as a "technifying" of environmental discourse, in which the global environmental crisis is presented as manageable through the adoption of technical innovations and existing economic growth paradigms.

It is important to stress that the most important elements of this trajectory—the globalization of production systems, the rising power of transnational corporate interests, the diffusion of consumerist tastes and lifestyles, and the weakening of national regulatory systems—do not represent "post-UNCED" restructuring in the world system. Rather, they are longer-term trajectories that were in fact visible from the vantage point of the late 1970s, and that had clearly become apparent by the time of the 1987 Brundtland report. That they have spawned political controversies about "globalization" since the mid-1990s does not mean that they are new, but simply that they are getting increasingly difficult to ignore or obfuscate. In his chapter, "The marketization of global environmental governance: manifestations and implications," Peter Newell discusses the important link between this global economic trajectory on the one hand and the increasing difficulty of devising an effective solution to international environmental dilemmas on the other hand. He argues that an important reason why the contemporary institutions of global governance are not working well in terms of sustainability lies in the practice of global environmental politics being subjected to market disciplines and market-based solutions. This visible global trend of "marketizing" environmental policy and dilemmas explains in part the near hegemonic acceptance of market-based solutions, trade rules and property rights before assessing the implications for environmental policy effectiveness.

The second flawed premise of the UNCED process and the Rio model stems from its failure to adequately conceptualize the scope and scale of global environmental problems. UNCED was organized around a very limited conception of the transnational character of environmental problems, neatly parsing international environmental challenges into two categories. Those with physically apparent border-crossing dimensions (essentially, transboundary pollutant flows and shared international commons) are understood as appropriate subjects of interstate treaty making. In contrast, the physically localized problems that dominate Agenda 21—involving soils, watersheds, coastlines, wetlands, forests, agro-ecological systems, and urban settlements—are understood to be the primary responsibility of national governments, with the "international" dimension limited to the financial and techno-managerial support of a sympathetic and supportive global community. Case in point: the Brundtland report could call for interstate cooperation in shared river basins, but ignored almost completely the larger problems surrounding freshwater ecosystems around the world.

The problem with this understanding is that it fails to come to grips with the socio-economically transnationalized character of environmental problems, as opposed to their more obvious physically transnationalized character. It privileges the first class of problems, almost exclusively, as the focal point of interstate environmental diplomacy. But what if it is the second class of issues that constitutes the far greater challenge of global environmental governance? What if the heart of our global environmental problem is not the failure to control pollution-across-borders or dumping into the global commons, but rather the failure to respond to the inherent, system-wide pressures and cumulative effects on the world's myriad forests, deserts, grasslands, meadows, soils, wetlands, lakes, rivers, and watersheds? We may think of these systems as physically localized and thus, in the UNCED framework, as domestic matters. But they are hardly "local" in a world marked by massive, rapid, and growing flows of people, goods, money, ideas, images, and technology across increasingly porous borders. These flows produce a dense, socially constructed web that can transmit the causes and effects of seemingly localized environmental problems from one place to another just as surely as (and perhaps a good deal quicker and further than) a river or a gust of wind might carry them (Conca 2006). Gabriela Kutting's chapter, "A global political economy of textiles: from the global to the local and back again", illustrates the problem of organizing ideas and regulatory frameworks around this very limited conception of international environmental governance. Using the global political economy of textiles as an illustration, Kutting examines the complex interplay of power, equity, environmental, social, and economic issues that weave together to form the reality of sustainability challenges on the global level.

The third flawed premise stemming from the UNCED/Rio process is an excessively optimistic miscasting of the character of the state's eco-political authority. The Brundtland report includes an appendix setting out 23 core principles for environmental protection and sustainable development. After an initial principle defining the individual's right to a sound environment, the remaining 22 principles each begin with the words "States shall ... ." Following the logic of "states shall ... ," there has been an enormous vesting of intellectual energy and political capital in efforts to build issue-specific interstate agreements—despite precious little evidence of their effectiveness and despite the increasingly fictional world of sovereign diplomacy presumed by such efforts. The problem with the notion that "states shall ..." is that states typically cannot, even if they would, which they often will not. The conflicts that swirl around the effort to control people and nature make it impossible to quickly cobble together international institutions based on authoritative states whose governing acts are clothed in broadly based legitimacy. Frequently, the state lacks the uncontested authority to control local access to or uses of nature, and efforts to exert such control become part of larger struggles to legitimize authority or consolidate material power.

As environmental problems have been redefined into a particular kind of socio-economic problem, to be solved with further growth within traditional political mechanisms of decision and distribution, serious questions about governance, growth, and the state have been evaluated. Complex problems such as intra- and inter-generational equity are pushed to the side, while victory is proclaimed on less significant or urgent dilemmas. This problem is complicated by the inability of the paradigm to admit failure or setback. Nothing in the UNCED process was allowed to fail, so there has never been a clear idea of what would constitute success. Darrell Whitman's chapter, "'Stakeholders' and the politics of environmental policymaking," examines the increasingly popular concept of "stakeholder participation" as the lens through which to examine the scope and limits of state authority. While the demands for more participation in environmental policy have increased as part of the growing call for greater democratic input and accountability, Whitman argues that there has been little discussion within the current stakeholder discourse about who properly constitutes a stakeholder and how a "stakeholder" should participate in public policy making.

Where do we go from here?

We offer our criticisms of the Rio model not simply for the purposes of critique. Finding more ecologically effective and socially just ways to deal with global environmental challenges must be a forward-looking task, and not simply an exercise in criticizing past or ongoing failures. Nor is it our intent to paint everything following from the Earth Summit with a single broad brush. Many of the initiatives around the Rio process can be read as efforts to make the environment safe for global capitalism; but there have also been many genuine efforts of many people and organizations to use the Rio framework to chart a course toward sustainability (as seen in the myriad "Agenda 21" initiatives in communities around the world). More to the point, even if Rio environmentalism were simply a new mode of social regulation to support global business practices with some green window dressing, it has hardly succeeded in doing so. The problems remain as apparent as ever, even if the mobilized political energy to confront them has dissipated.

Rather, our purpose is to focus particular attention on Rio's flawed and outmoded *governance* model. While the challenge of global sustainability can hardly be reduced to the question of governance, the fact remains that

Rio's flawed and outmoded understanding of the functions, levels, and agents of environmental governance fits quite poorly both the scope of global environmental challenges and the new economic terrain of global neoliberalism.

If the path from Stockholm to Johannesburg defined by the UN and other virtuous global governance actors cannot provide the basis for a serious approach, what can? In particular, what institutional mechanisms and governing arrangements are consistent with the challenges of sustainability in a globalizing world political economy? One important yet still underdeveloped theme is related to civil society and political participation. Instead of presuming that the state is the authoritative unit of distributive justice and political voice, much more serious forms of civil society engagement, political participation, and articulation of what people really want and need are urgently required. Rather than marginalizing civil society's voice via perfunctory "stakeholder consultations," the idea of far more active, indeed activist, forms of participation will have to be taken seriously. This raises questions about the entire policy cycle (from formulation to implementation and evaluation), about the multiple levels at which participation must take place (local, regional, national, supra-national, global), and about the constituted groups of actors beyond conventional entities such as political parties or "NGOs."

Along with governance, a second and arguably more problematic forward-looking theme is related to institutional arrangements. The UNCED process and the Rio model were particularly weak on this, as it was believed that one could shift problems to a higher (regional/global) level, while applying a traditional nation-state approach. Instead of limiting ourselves to sovereign interstate diplomacy and ad hoc arrangements on specific problems such as the ozone layer, climate change, or persistent organic pollutants, serious multi-level and cross-cutting institutional arrangements for sustainability must be developed. As suggested previously, this means asking some fundamental questions: What are the core functions of environmental governance? Who are the agents best suited to perform them? At what levels of social aggregation—ranging from the most local to the genuinely global—are these functions most effectively performed?

Sanjeev Khagram's and Saleem Ali's chapter, "Transnational transformations: from government-centric interstate regimes to cross-sectoral multilevel networks of global governance," offers some preliminary ideas on civil society, political participation, and new multi-level institutional arrangements through their analysis of the emergence of global policy networks. Through an empirical analysis of four global policy networks (the Global Reporting Initiative, the Global Compact, the Mining, Minerals, and Sustainable Development Initiative, and the World Commission on Dams), Khagram and Ali suggest that these networks have the potential to achieve important global governance goals as long as there is a concerted effort to allow for constructive contestation by NGO groups and an inclusiveness of decision-making of the respective communities of interest.

Using rivers, watersheds, and freshwater ecosystems as illustrative examples, Ken Conca's chapter, "Rethinking authority, territory, and knowledge: transnational socio-ecological controversies and global environmental governance," also engages the question of transnational institution building. Conca argues that the study and practice of international environmental institutions have been grounded primarily in cooperation theory and have focused primarily on the creation of formal interstate regimes for the problems of the global commons and pollution across borders. This approach has made little progress, either in theory or practice, for a wide array of contentious environmental issues related to critical ecosystems impacted by processes of economic globalization. Conca contrasts the limited success of the traditional international tools of science and diplomacy to create robust governance regimes around water. He also contrasts these failures with processes of transnational institution building that emerge from social controversies surrounding water, including the construction of large dams and water marketization controversies. He notes that one effect of these controversies has been to deepen the institutionalization of practices that take a fundamentally different approach to authority, knowledge, and territoriality than the more conventional interstate-regime approach. A critical challenge for the future, thus, will be to find effective ways to acknowledge and manage social conflict rather than simply render it invisible, and to nurture a wide array of innovative institutional forms of governance that may emerge from it.

During the (northern latitudes) summer of 2007, as we were putting the finishing touches to the manuscript for this book, a burst of optimism on the prospects for serious action on climate change swept through elite global media outlets. A combination of factors seemed to be driving greater attention to the issue: the reports of the Intergovernmental Panel on Climate Change (IPCC) and the Stern review commissioned by the British government; the attention surrounding Al Gore's prize-winning film, *An Inconvenient Truth*; the actions of many local communities, businesses, universities, and others frustrated with stagnation and evasion in national policies; the vulnerabilities exposed by the accumulation of such "natural" disasters as hurricane Katrina in 2006, the Indian Ocean tsunami of 2004, and the Paris heat wave of 2003; and the insistence of some governments, particularly host Germany, that the topic be discussed at the 2007 meeting of the G-8. According to IPCC chair Rajendra Pachauri, "The fact that people are paying attention to this assessment clearly gives us some satisfaction. *With the knowledge that has been provided, there should be some impetus and momentum for action*" (Reuters, May 14, 2007; emphasis added).

Attention to the sobering findings of the fourth IPCC assessment is of course welcome. It may be that a tipping point has been reached in global political discourse on climate change. Pachauri may even be correct that knowledge will provide the "impetus and momentum for action." Our reading of the lessons of the rise and fall of Rio environmentalism suggest that approaching the world's environmental challenge as a question of technical knowledge, to be filtered through existing institutional government arrangements, is very much part of the problem.

References

Asian Development Bank (ADB) (2005) *Making Profits, Protecting Our Planet: Corporate Responsibility for Environmental Performance in Asia and the Pacific*, Manila, Philippines: ADB.

Conca, Ken (2006) *Governing Water: Contentious Transnational Politics and Global Institution Building*, Cambridge, MA: MIT Press.

"Don't Fear the Reapers" (2005) *Grist magazine special series on the Death of Environmentalism.* Available www.grist.org/news/maindish/2005/01/13/doe-intro/ (accessed February 10, 2005).

Institute for Global Environmental Strategies (IGES) (2005) *Sustainable Asia and Beyond: In Pursuit of Innovative Policies*, Kanagawa, Japan: IGES.

McKibben, Bill (2005) "Changing the Climate Change Debate," *Grist magazine*, January 25, 2005. Available www.grist.org/comments/dispatches/2005/01/25/mckibben/ (accessed February 10, 2005).

Ott, Herman (2005) "The European Union: A Strategic Actor for Sustainable Global Governance," in Andreas Rechkemmer, ed., *UNEO: Towards an International Environment Organization*, Baden-Baden: Nomos.

Shellenberger, Mark and Nordhaus, Ted (2004) *The Death of Environmentalism: Global Warming Politics in a Post-Environmental World.* Available www.thebreak through.org/images/Death_of_Environmentalism.pdf (accessed February 10, 2007).

—— (2007) *Break Through: From the Death of Environmentalism to the Politics of Possibility*, New York: Houghton Mifflin.

Reuters (2007) *U.N. Climate Expert Hopeful on Environment Policies*, Geneva, May 14.

2002 "Summit disarray as EU officials walk out," *London Times*, August 31.

Teague, Peter (2004) "Foreword," in Shellenberger and Nordaus, *The Death of Environmentalism.* Available www.thebreakthrough.org/images/Death_of_Environ mentalism.pdf (accessed February 10, 2007).

UN Department of Public Information (2007) *Secretary-General Appoints Three Special Envoys on Climate Change*, Available www.un.org/News/Press/docs//2007/ sga1061.doc.htm (accessed May 10, 2007).

World Commission on Environment and Development (WCED) (1987) *Our Common Future*, New York: Oxford University Press.

2 Sustainability and globalization

A theoretical perspective

Ulrich Brand and Christoph Görg

A broad range of environmental measures, from the local and regional up to the global level, cannot deceive about the ever deepening crisis of global environmental change. To understand these contradictory processes a critical analysis—which assesses the relevance of environmental policy in light of the broader societal context in which such attempts are situated—is helpful. From its very beginning, the enthusiastic "Spirit of Rio" of the early 1990s was overshadowed by two developments relatively independent of one another, which already gave rise to pessimism. On one hand, neoliberal politics, which, following the debt crisis, was expressed and enforced in North–South relationships in neoliberal structural adjustment programs and also gained importance in Northern countries and international political institutions. On the other hand, a "New World Order" was called for by then-President George Bush in reaction to the first Iraq war in 1991.

Ten years later, at the World Summit on Sustainable Development (WSSD) in Johannesburg in 2002, the major frame of the debate had become that of globalization. Within this frame, optimistic and critical perspectives were reproduced. Despite the fact that the originally celebrated institutions of sustainable development had not reached their aims, voices could be heard ever more frequently that linked Johannesburg with far-reaching expectations regarding the renewal of the deadlocked environmental negotiations and the reduction of global inequalities. Statements such as that of then-UN General Secretary Kofi Annan set the motto: "Making globalization work for sustainable development and to jump start implementation efforts" (Annan 2001). Others followed him in this by recommending, of all things, transnational corporations and the central institutions of neoliberal globalization such as the World Trade Organization (WTO), World Bank and International Monetary Fund (IMF) as the most important allies in the struggle against global environmental changes and world poverty (IIED 2001). The emphasis was and is put on partnership, the changes of recent developments and the creation of win–win situations. It is obvious that none of the different players is interested in a more profound analysis of the causes of the deficits of the Rio process, particularly one that would have included the structural causes.

Critics, however, argued that exactly this analysis was needed as a precondition of shifting politics and that the Rio process was superceded by neoliberal globalization and blocked by rivalries and antagonistic interests. Neither the environmental aspect nor the emphasis on social development in the South could be worked out as expected. In both directions a deepening aggravation of the problems had occurred. In recent years it has become evident that the social and ecological problems connected with globalisation—despite all the institutional reforms and international agreements—were not resolved (cf. the Millennium Ecosystem Assessment 2005, which links prominently environmental and developmental/poverty aspects). The consequences of this judgment, however, are rather contested. Moreover, the attacks in New York and Washington, the beginning of the "war on terrorism," and the wars in Afghanistan and Iraq made clear that the emerging new world order was and is shaped by violent action and counteraction. In the background, the intensifying crisis of neoliberal globalization and the crisis of legitimacy of neoliberal politics became more and more obvious. Finally, the established institutions of sustainable development—particularly the Framework Convention on Climate Change and the Convention on Biological Diversity—themselves experienced a transformation process over the course of the 1990s. Dominant political and economic players were increasingly able to enforce their own interests and, thus, the model of sustainable development was concretized primarily in the form of the economization of nature (cf. Betsill 2005; Conca and Dabelko 2004; Brunnengräber 2006; Brand *et al.* 2008).

Nevertheless, the processes that are only imprecisely described by "globalization" or "environmental and development policy" do not take place without contradictions. The critique of dominant trends clearly has been increasing for a number of years. The words "Seattle" and "Genoa" express more than simply momentary occurrences of protest, and the World Social Forum is more than an isolated five-day event. Rather, these are the crystallization points of an increasing critique that articulates itself in very different areas and in various ways across countries (della Porta 2007; Patomäki and Teivainen 2004; Fisher and Ponniah 2003; on transnational environmental movements, see Ford 2003). In these confrontations, concepts play an important role because they offer orientation, they characterize certain political suggestions as legitimate or absurd, and they lay the foundations for new viewpoints of real relationships and intended transformation towards a more sustainable society.

It is precisely for this reason that there is a grave danger here, particularly from a critical-emancipative perspective. If those voices should gain the upper hand that place their bets on new "partnerships" with the players and institutions that carry the main responsibility for neoliberal globalization, then the critique of neoliberalism, which has been articulated more strongly recently, could be weakened by the debate on sustainability. To the extent to which cooperation, "mutual interests" and win–win situations are insisted upon, more fundamental critique appears to be disruptive. Even the protest "on the streets" will then only be understood as a place for the expression of dissatisfaction that, at best, serves to "put pressure on" experts and governments. More radical critiques of the ruling relationships must be suspect to the extent that they are intended to win over the addressees of the critique to cooperation. In addition, radical critique is increasingly rejected with the argument that there are no alternatives. A more far-reaching questioning of political forms and content, questions concerning power and rule, democracy and justice—which are among the basic issues of the more recent movement of globalization critics—are in danger, from this perspective, of being ignored or even losing their legitimacy.

From these processes a theoretical and a political problem emerge. Strategies of environmental policy and ways of linking it with other issue areas such as development are always situated in a broader societal context in a global dimension. Not only is *explicit* environmental policy connected with other politics having more and *implicit* impact on the human environment (Conca 1993; Lipschutz 2004; Paterson 2006). More than this, any attempts to shape the relationships with nature are themselves reshaped and redirected in their own logic. That exactly is the case with the concept of "sustainable development" at the beginning of the twenty-first century.

Thus, we need a broader theoretical framework to understand the reshaping of environmental and developmental politics in the light of an encompassing restructuring of global societies. Moreover, this theoretical framework should also be able to deal with political counter-strategies against neoliberal hegemony. In this chapter we will argue against the background of the concept *societal relationships with nature* and *regulation approach*. Starting with a short outline we will link these theoretical approaches with an investigation of the current post-Fordist restructuring processes and the meaning of sustainable development in these complex processes. We argue that from this perspective we can see that the existing institutions and discourses are dealing with the environmental crisis in a highly selective way. This selectivity leads to a major bias in environmental affairs, and to concerns that the crisis should not become a major problem for the existing social structures, modes of accumulation and regulation, and hegemonic norms of production and consumption. In this sense, the dominant understanding of "sustainable" development is one grammar of an "ecological" capitalism, as we want to show in the following, referring to the example of biodiversity politics. At the end of the chapter we sketch out some aspects of possible emancipatory actors and action.

A theoretical framework: societal relationships with nature ...

In recent years it has become obvious that the real challenge for a critical approach to environmental politics is to overcome the false alternative between a naturalistic environmentalism and a constructivist post-modernism

(Cronon 1995; Braun and Castree 1998; Biro 2005). The former refers to an ontologically given nature, while ignoring that nature is always economically, culturally, and scientifically produced; the latter ignores that, while being produced or constructed, nature always represents some biophysical conditions that we cannot ignore completely. Thus, the real challenge is to investigate the relationships between a cultural or discursive construction of nature (including science) and the material-substantial processes on which society depends.

The concept of *societal relationships with nature* tries to address these challenges. The concept comes from the Marxist tradition and is at the core of the social theory and historical diagnosis of the "dialectic of enlightenment" in the critical theory of Horkheimer and Adorno (cf. Horkheimer and Adorno 1982; Görg 2003a; on Critical Theory in environmental politics see also Biro 2005). According to that concept, neither can society be discussed independently of nature, since the social process is constitutively imparted through nature, nor does the process of history aim towards an ever more comprehensive control of nature. Certainly, the process of modernism is based on the growth of the domination of nature, but this domination does not lead to more control; rather, it rebounds in the destruction of nature and in ever greater dependence on the results and secondary effects of the domination of nature (Beck 1992). Thus, society basically cannot free itself of its dependencies in relation to nature because the social process always contains material-substantial elements and this process is therefore dependent on metabolism with nature. The mutual conveyance of nature and society is central, however, not only for the one side, namely society, but vice versa—it also affects the side of nature. At the beginning of the twenty-first century, nature untouched by human activity virtually no longer exists. Marx and Engels were completely aware of this tendency to transform nature from the state in which it was found (Marx and Engels 1974: 44). But in spite of this transformation, the material-substantial conditions of human existence retain their own meaning, which can be respected or ignored by human activity—with potentially destructive results for society in the form of ecological risks. Following Adorno's critical theory this meaning can be designated the *non-identity of nature* (Görg 2003b).

The starting point for a critical theory of relationships with nature was provided by the processes of a practical—that is, economic/technical and cultural/discursive—construction of nature, and not by the supposedly unchangeable laws of nature to which humanity or society must adapt. Today, scientific constructions, closely linked to the technical and economic strategies of their application, have come into the foreground, which have found their expression in the diagnosis of the "knowledge society." It should be remembered, however, that there are also other practical constructions of nature not to be forgotten in analyzing the dominant one. In contrast, there is an unavoidable pluralism of societal relationships with nature that, particularly under capitalist conditions, is characterized by relationships of dominance. Thus, even in the age of globalization, cultural interpretations and, linked to them, forms of knowledge and practices, can be found that cultivate a completely different treatment of nature. These forms of knowledge and their agencies have even been given a greater value by the ecological crisis, for one can discover in certain practices dealing with the tropical rainforest or in certain forms of agricultural production elements of a more respectful handling of natural resources. This poses the question of whether these practices are today merely marginal, whether they have a chance of influencing the shaping of global relationships with nature, or whether they can even preserve their own forms. The dynamic elements of this process are determined by actors with quite different strategies and power resources. And the example of biological diversity also makes clear that, after all, the dominant strategies for the appropriation of nature are increasingly aimed at its commercialization, that is, at a purely economic appraisal of nature (Görg and Brand 2006).

Here, the tendency towards the domination of nature is reproduced in a new and even stronger form, even after the experience of the ecological crisis. The domination of nature is not defined as every form of the appropriation of nature without differentiation (for then the development of society without the domination of nature would be inconceivable) but one that completely subjects nature to its objectives and ignores every non-identity of nature. This is without doubt the case in the tendencies towards the commercialization of biological diversity, for nature is reduced here to its usability and elements that are incompatible with this are ignored. It is now recognized that the increase of the domination of nature has led to a dominion of secondary effects (Beck 1992). Societies are confronted more and more with the consequences of the unhindered domination of nature, which causes additional costs and a great deal of trouble. The idea of the complete control of nature has therefore largely been abandoned and the scarcely controllable risks involved in the appropriation of nature taken into account. The utilization of nature is therefore increasingly accompanied by attempts to mitigate its destructive effects prophylactically or to eliminate them reactively—more precisely: to engage in the protection of nature and the environment. But the question is whether this goes beyond the attempt at an accompanying cushioning of the domination of nature because of the uncontrollable consequences, or in other words, whether we are dealing with a reflexive form of the domination of nature. This question can be empirically tested in the fate of strategies that follow a different, less destructive form of the appropriation of nature—a handling of nature that attempts to take account of its non-identity (see, with a pessimistic answer, Brand and Görg 2003 and Görg 2003a).

This approach differs from the questions often analyzed as to the general chances of the protection of the environment and nature. Of course, it also deals with whether and to what extent aspects of the protection of nature can hold their own against commercialization strategies. But especially in the field of biological diversity the problem cannot be grasped with a confrontation of economic and ecological dimensions, of maintenance and utilization strategies, for here maintenance and utilization, ecology and economy, are indissolubly intertwined. On one side there is a growing economic interest in biodiversity, leading to its privatization. At the same time, "humanity" cannot possibly renounce completely the utilization of "biodiversity" as a whole. Since biological diversity also includes the diversity of the animals and plants used in agriculture, it is of central importance to ensuring human nutrition and food security. Thus, the maintenance of nature cannot be played off abstractly against its utilization. The strategy of a pure protection of nature can be a solution for, at most, parts of biodiversity, for example the tropical rainforest or the coral reefs. Even in the tropical rainforest, however, nature supplies a habitat for many people and for greatly differing forms of human use. Thus, even there the strategy of protection clashes with interests in the utilization of biodiversity—and even the setting up of a nature reserve is basically only a change in the form of social construction of nature, namely utilization for ecotourism or as "natural capital." It is basically always a question of the different forms of the socialization of nature, of different cultures and practices in the handling of biodiversity. In this constellation the tendency toward their greater commercialization determines the direction of the organization of the relationships with nature. In the process, other forms of organization are marginalized and tend to be dissolved, and nature is more and more reduced to its economic value, that is, subsumed under the practices of marketing. In the strategies of the reflexive domination of nature, moreover, even attempts at maintenance are functionalized for strategies of valorization. For with regard to the subject of the conflicts, biodiversity or genetic resources, it is not only a question of quite new forms of their scientific description, but of a new constitution of the subject itself and of new processes for its practical appropriation. Even the political structures and terrains are in a state of upheaval. The valorization of genetic resources is an integral part of a new phase of capitalist development and of what we call *post-Fordist relationships with nature* (see below). Only if the novelty of this phase and its central elements are adequately taken into account, can the conflicts over the organization of relationships with nature be grasped adequately. And only then can the chances of alternatives in the organization of relationships with nature be estimated.

... and the regulation approach

To understand this new historical constellation an analysis of capitalist development is necessary that can justify two conditions sometimes in tension with each other. On one side, the overwhelming dynamics of capitalist development have to keep in mind; on the other side, the historical ruptures and the counteraction of social protests and social movements should not be neglected. The regulation approach, or at least those versions of it that are still based on Marx (cf. Jessop, 1990), continues to assume the existence of an imperative of accumulation, a compulsion to expand and to subsume spheres of life under the capital relation which lies in the structures of capitalist societalization, although the internal logic of socio-cultural processes in themselves is not lost because of this subsuming.

Another assumption is that there is a fundamental contradiction between the rationality of individual activities (whether in the following of accumu-lation strategies or in any attempt to steer this process politically), on the one hand, and the logic of the course of social reproduction, on the other. The latter, in principle, produces non-intended results (crises, etc.) and the rationality of the former can only be determined ex-post. But this does not mean that the multitude of social relations is irrelevant (for then there would be no contradiction). The regulation approach, in addition to the production and class relations taken into account by Marx, takes into con-sideration much broader social relationships, such as gender relations of cultural self-identification. The contradiction manifests itself, then, in the social forms (the value- and the state-form) becoming independent of the actors, even though these independent forms cannot be reproduced without the activity of the actors. This contradictory process thus can only stabilize itself if it is able to develop institutional forms of regulation that are also a more or less coherent mode of regulation. The existence of such a mode of regulation does not eliminate the contradictory character of the process, but enables its stabilization despite, and because of, these contradictions (Lipietz 1985: 109). Settings incorporate and reproduce precisely this con-tradictory character. In their function as an element of a mode of regulation they express contradictory social relations—and the question of the destructive consequences for humanity and nature is decided not least by these concrete institutions and their interplay, which are the products of social conflicts.

One central aspect of the regulation approach is the difference between *political regulation* or directed control on the one hand and *societal regulation* on the other.[1] While directed control is essential for the treatment of environ-mental problems, it is only one element of the (societal) regulation of socie-tal relations with nature. That is to say, societal regulation also includes—in addition to directed control—the contingent stabilization of social relations, which can be the result both of antagonistic power-based strategies and of the interplay of different systemic processes.

A comprehensive examination of this regulation must therefore give greater prominence not only to questions of domination but also to the fact that for the stabilization of social development it is not necessarily essential to provide a "solution"—of whatever nature—to problems; the contra-dictions of social development simply have to be institutionally secured (and not necessarily removed). This perspective is of utmost importance in order to understand the actual relationship between globalization and the ecolo-gical crisis, because it challenges the treatment of globalization as a purely autonomous market process undermining the steering capability of nation-states and political institutions as a whole—without making the reverse failure of taking environmental policy and the creation of international and national institutions as problem-solving instruments without looking for their over-determined shaping by neoliberal globalization. National and international institutions do matter in the shaping of globalization—but at the same time the societal regulation of capitalist globalization is a contingent stabilization based on power relations and the structural forms of capitalist reproduction.

As an institutional theory, the regulation approach deals with the basic political-economic issue of the embedding of market processes in the supporting political, economic and cultural framework. Moreover, as a historically oriented approach, it turns this issue into an examination of the historical phases of capitalism (cf. Boyer 1990; Esser et al. 1994; Alnasseri *et al.* 2001; Albritton *et al.* 2001). Furthermore, the political form of the national state and the encompassing role of political institutions need theoretical reflection. The power relations and the fundamental class relations of a society are condensed in the apparatuses of the state, especially the national state (Poulantzas 1980). Its actual or potential regulating functions are thus superimposed by its character of domination, that is, by its function within the framework of the fundamental social antagonisms. At the same time, capitalism developed from the beginning as a world system, although this did not exclude—and still does not exclude—competition between different states and groups of states and the expansive trend of this system of competing individual states (Hirsch 1997).

The societal regulation of social relations is therefore a much more comprehensive process than that of explicit (political) re-regulation, at least as the latter is usually understood. By concentrating on intentional activity by political actors such as governments and also on international political instruments, the much wider social context in which market processes always take place is ignored. The result is too little attention to the more comprehensive process of post-Fordist restructuring. The fact that processes of "primitive accumulation" continue to occur today also risks being ignored (Alnasseri 2004; similarly Harvey 2005), when attention is focussed strictly on intentional and explicitly political actions. Moreover, this social "dis-embedding" of economic processes at the local and national level—the commodification of social relations that previously functioned according to other cultural patterns—leads to resistance and social conflicts. Integration into the capitalist world market continues to be a contested and violent process.

Elements of post-Fordist relationships with nature

Against this background, the global ecological crisis must be regarded primarily as an institutional crisis of the appropriation of nature by society.

Questions of environmental policy were and are a part of the crisis of Fordism, but they are not its cause. The connection between the crisis of Fordism and the crisis of societal relationships with nature is, rather, to a considerable degree both politically and culturally mediated. Socio-ecological problems were first placed on the agenda in certain countries and internationally in the 1970s by new social movements and epistemic communities. Although the material aspects of the ecological crisis—the consumption of materials and energy and the resulting pollution, as well as the risks involved in certain key technologies—are induced by the Fordist growth constellation and its consumption patterns, they have not necessarily led to the crisis being regarded *as* an environmental crisis. As well as taking the political and socio-cultural mediation processes into account, this approach also leads to the examination of ruptures and continuities in the post-Fordist development model, the bare outlines of which are at best beginning to emerge (and the success of which, as a "stable formation," is not at all certain).

Today the changing relationships between economic and political elements in the process of globalization are crucial to understand the regulation impact of environmental institutions. In many contributions, the process of economic globalization is considered to be at the center of present developments, but that does not mean that there is a general consensus, at least not when it is a question of developing concrete problem-solving strategies and steps towards their implementation. Rather, a similar deficit can be observed as in other aspects of sustainability policy. This process, its causes and the powers that drive it forward, as well as the role of existing institutions, are not analyzed in more depth and, above all, are not questioned.

In these discussions the connection between the ecological problems and the restructuring of society is being lost sight of, a connection which is to be understood as the transition from Fordism to post-Fordism and which has considerably changed both inner-societal and international structural patterns. As it was argued previously, the ecological crisis was, symbolically and materially, closely connected with the crisis of Fordism. On the material side, the Fordist-fossilized welfare model of the Northern industrial societies was decisively responsible for the enormous expansion of the consumption of resources and the increasing strain on the natural environment from pollutants (Altvater 1993; Graz *et al.* 2007). On the other, symbolic side, social movements and intellectuals discussed the ecological crisis as a crisis of society, that is, they attempted to name the social causes of the crisis of society's relationships with nature. But in the 1980s, this constellation came increasingly under the influence of the neoliberal restructuring of society. The central strategy for the establishment of post-Fordist capitalism was the neoliberal orientation of society to the imperatives of efficiency and international competitiveness. Even government policy was increasingly aligned towards this end (Hirsch 1997). Our central argument is that since the 1990s the development of new technologies, particularly information and communication technologies and, more recently, biotechnology and genetic technology, has contributed to the emergence of changed "post-Fordist relationships with nature" (Görg and Brand 2006).

With the transition to post-Fordism a change takes place both in the way in which central societal institutions function and in the utilization of natural resources, the latter in a rather contradictory way. With the growing strength of the imperative of international competitiveness, formulated by powerful interests, the way of dealing with nature as a resource, or its valorization, is increasingly subjected to the profitability calculus of capital (this is particularly important in the Southern countries in the context of foreign debt and debt service obligations). Due to new technological methods and new production structures this utilization takes on a new quality. Especially, the new biotechnology and genetic technology partially necessitate this different utilization and make parts of non-human, but also of human, nature "strategic resources" (Ceceña and Barreda 1995).

At the international level a cooperation–competition paradox emerges as a central condition of international environmental policy. Only one side of this is normally mentioned in both the social scientific and the public discussions: a growing pressure for the cooperative treatment of transnational ecological problems. This pressure does not come about naturally as a direct result of the ecological problem but always indirectly through its public symbolification by social actors (NGOs, scientists, the so-called "epistemic communities," etc.). The political pressure for cooperation has led in recent years to a large number of international environmental agreements (Axelrod *et al.* 2005; Lipschutz 2004). However, these agreements and regimes do not at all eliminate the competition between states and between different economic sectors and regions. Rather, this competition to a great extent characterizes the existing agreements—the more so the more the individual agreements touch upon complex cross-sectional problems, which usually brings to the fore the relationships of tension between different international agreements (Brand *et al.* 2008). In general, it can be said that in both national and international measures for dealing with ecological problems, completely different and partly contradictory interests are articulated which "carry" the competition between various national and international interest groups into the wording of the agreements and the further process of negotiation.

Two elements are of particular importance here. First, there is a new, post-Fordist drawing of the line between politics and economics. This development is often misunderstood in the social sciences as the erosion of the nation-state. In fact the nation-state is partially losing its ability to control and its sovereignty over a certain territory. But it is not simply disappearing; it is transforming itself in the direction of a *national competition state* that is more strongly subjected to the global conditions of competition. At the same time, however, an *internationalization of the state* is taking place (Hirsch 2005; Görg and Brand 2006). The changes in politics in the course of the transformation of the state are extensive. They are little suited, however, to awaken hopes of an excessive influence by "civil society." Politics in international regimes and institutions continues essentially to be politics between states. This does not happen by accident and is not temporary. Rather, the internationalized state is also primarily an instrument of rule, in which global interests and relationships of power are "condensed" (according to a formulation by Nicos Poulantzas in 1980; cf. also Hirsch *et al.* 2001). Stephen Gill (2003) has described the dominant orientation of international politics as "global constitutionalism." To an increasing degree, the international level is also concerned with securing the civil legal system and property rights. This is also, and particularly, true of international environmental policy.

Second, it can be stated that post-Fordist capitalism has up to a point adjusted itself to ecological problems. This does not take place in the sense of a successful treatment of the material dimensions of the ecological crisis. Nevertheless, a largely accepted pattern of dealing with the crisis has emerged. Above all strategies of ecological modernization, which either help to reduce operational costs or open up a new market for new technologies (cf. Jänicke and Jacob 2004; Hajer 1995; Toke 2001), have a prospect of success. However, as we have argued, the room for maneuver for such strategies is defined by other processes, not least the increasing competition for capital and production locations, and is subjected to the neoliberal strategy of economic liberalization. In addition, at the interstate level all measures and their chances of success are subordinated to the priority of a global power policy of central states. And in recent times, ecological and social questions are increasingly subordinated to the discussion on production location and security, which only represents a badly disguised vehicle for global strategies of dominance (Ceceña 2006).

Sustainable development and the path towards an "ecological" capitalism

These developments do not leave the concept of "sustainable development" untouched. Against the background of neoliberal globalization, the "New World Order" and the changing forms of the appropriation of nature, it must also be remembered that the direction of further development will be decided by social conflicts at different levels. Here the concept of sustainable development plays an important role. In a certain way it represents a compromise formula in which very different and partly contradictory interests reappear. Even though it has repeatedly been emphasized that the exact content of this concept remains unclear or vague (O'Connor 1995; Redclift 1989), it is precisely the vagueness of the concept that is its strength. The growing environmental crisis on both the material level and the political-discursive level made it necessary to find a formula that could be used to organize socio-ecological compromises between actors with diverging and partly antagonistic interests. We can call it a discourse: there is a dispute as to what "sustainable development" means and that meaning "takes place within boundaries" (Dryzek 1999: 36; cf. also Bridge and McManus 2000; Bruyninckx 2006; Sachs 1999; Fischer 2003) that are, at least, not opposed to existing power relations.

Therefore, it is only consistent that at the center of this model is the idea of cooperation. Competitive, conflictive, or perhaps contradictory relationships are ignored or at least represented as surmountable. For if the problem of competition were taken seriously, then both the economic sphere, which has not been questioned in dominant discussions, and the global relationships of power would have to be taken issue with more strongly than has been the case until now. In "the North" at least, the quest for development in the global South was increasingly ignored or transformed: from the demand for fairer conditions in North–South relationships to the necessity of enabling "sustainable development" for all countries.[2] Moreover, an "ecological bias" can be observed in which the development problem, in the form in which it was still contained in the international compromise of the Brundtland Commission report, is not taken into account. This abbreviation of the original objective is connected with a strong focus on the national level (Jörissen *et al.* 2000: 11), which could be called a "national bias." Many approaches, such as the study "Sustainable Netherlands" (ISOE 1994) take the "national environmental space"—that is, the environment used by a national state—as their starting-point, without reflecting on this methodological nationalism critically. This focus is connected with a preference for a networking of procedures and dialogues and cooperation by the different players, which not only does not allow us to expect an intervention in economic interests but limits the possibilities of critique altogether (see, for the German case, K.-W. Brand and Jochum 2000: 185–191). We can therefore speak of an "affirmative bias" in which critical questions with regard to the conditions for the realization of sustainable development are pushed into the background in favor of more pragmatic concepts that are above all kindly disposed towards the established interests.

As a result, three important dimensions, in which originally a critical potential did in fact exist, have been pushed aside by the discussions of recent years: the problematizing of the North–South relationship, a fundamental reorientation of international politics and the reflection on the relationship between the capitalist economy and its material foundations.

With regard to North–South relations, the connection between environmental problems and global relationships of power is often ignored; instead, a pragmatic mode of regulation is favored. Moreover, the insight is ignored that under the guise of international environmental policy often quite different processes are advanced (see below the example of capitalist valorization of genetic resources in connection with the Convention on Biological Diversity (CBD)). Both problems are reflected in the question of the relationship between international environmental agreements and other international agreements and institutions. To put it sharply, we would argue that the most important agreement of the 1990s, which transforms societal relationships with nature profoundly, is neither the CBD nor the Framework Convention on Climate Change (FCCC), but the World Trade Organization (WTO). This is connected with the observation that, in particular, the non-observance of environmental or social issues has extensive consequences in the most important international institutions. The "liberalization of world trade" has not only direct ecological and social consequences, for example in the increasing flows of goods or the intervention in national environmental, social, or health policy. In addition, in the field of environmental policy it is usually a question of the establishment of new technologies and the political and legal conditions for this. The best-known examples here are genetic technology in the treatment of biological diversity or genetic resources, and the economic instruments for climate protection (such as emission trading).

The case of biodiversity politics

As a result of the forgoing explanations we would state that the environmental and development policy institutions in the pure sense are no longer simply reservoirs for progressive interests. These agreements, thus, often serve goals quite different from those that their name suggests. The consequences shall be briefly illuminated using the example of biological diversity (for more details cf. Görg and Brand 2000; Brand and Görg 2003; Brand *et al.* 2008). While in the public discussion the opinion dominates that it is only a question of environmental measures intended to stop or slow down the loss of biological diversity, the state measures and the international agreements fulfill different functions. Beside the fact that the CBD aims not only at the conservation of biodiversity but also at the sustainable use of its components—in particular genetic resources—and the fair sharing of benefits, it actually provides much broader input for the global regulation of nature. From a regulationist perspective, on the whole the CBD's provisions serve the institutional regulation of the treatment of genetic resources, from issues of biological safety when handling genetically modified organisms to the establishment of global markets including a regime for the distribution of property rights. The primary issue is that of the regulation of the rights of access and the more or less exclusive rights of utilization of genetic resources.

It can be seen particularly clearly in the field of international biodiversity policy that attempts are being made to secure, institutionally and politically, the appropriation of the "green gold of genes" for the agrarian and pharmaceutical industries. In North–South relations the central issue is that of legal and planning security for the dominant players, especially of access that is secured and effective (meaning, among other things, inexpensive). Quasi-state politics has—in close cooperation with the nation-state level—functions such as the setting of rules for competition and economic transactions, the guaranteeing of the flow of resources or the security of property and money. Questions concerning intellectual property are therefore closely linked to the new forms of utilization and valorization of biological diversity and genetic resources. The intention is to set down who profits from the advantages that result from the utilization of genetic resources.

There is a certain paradox in the fact that the most modern players (research institutions and, above all, transnational high-tech enterprises) are dependent upon access to these resources and thus in a certain way to "marginalized" population groups in the South, for such resources are to be found above all in Southern countries and there often in the areas populated by "marginalized" groups. In addition, in the appropriation of genetic resources the "traditional" knowledge of how to use these resources plays an important role, since it often serves as a "filter" in the search for economically valuable substances. Due to this economic interest in genetic resources and in the knowledge connected with them, however, both are regarded increasingly from a commercial angle. The question of the non-commodification of nature and "traditional" knowledge is accordingly seldom asked at the international level.

The recognition of national sovereignty (in the sense of judicial regulatory competency) as resulting from the CBD is, at a time of the supposed loss of competence of nation-states, a necessary condition for the valorization of biodiversity. At the same time it must be taken into account that the CBD represents a terrain of conflict on which different players struggle for the establishment of their interests. Thus, other interests have also been included in the CBD, particularly those of local communities and indigenous peoples. In the prominent Article 8(j) it is laid down that their knowledge and practices are to be respected, protected and preserved and that they must share in the developments. However, their interests have found expression in a way that weakens the players. First, the regulations of Article 8(j) are characterized by an instrumental understanding of the rights of local players: these are only to be respected in as far as they serve the preservation of biological diversity. Furthermore, they are to be subordinated to national sovereignty. The concrete translation is the concern of the national implementation of the CBD.

Thus, the commercialization of biodiversity as an element of globalization, that is, the shaping towards post-Fordist societal relationships with nature, is not only an economic process induced by market forces, but is politically established. This means that ecological aspects become a factor of "locational competition"—a strategic element of trade and competition policy. Questions of the use of genetic resources, of access to them and tenure over them, and the resulting consequences and strains, are intermixed here with questions of profit and the distribution of the benefits out of their use—above all, but not only, in the North–South relationship. But if agreements between states gain greater relevance, the national state does not lose it central importance. On the contrary, it increases.

Beside economic interests in a narrow sense and their political embeddedness, the framing of problems and possible political action is important.[3] To give an example: It suggests that global environmental policy would best be fulfilled by centralized institutions with decision-making and power resources and could thus only be pursued "from above" (Biermann and Bauer 2005). This understanding is, however, inadequate, because it implies a technocratic managerial optimism or *"managerism"* (Redclift 1994), which assumes that problems are basically soluble with the right management and in "top-down" processes. This is somewhat naïve because it neglects societal power relations—which are inscribed in the institutions—and tends to exclude weaker actors who have less means to articulate themselves and who are less represented. Especially in biodiversity politics, top-down approaches are problematic with regard to the treatment of the so-called global commons or public goods. It is argued that the protection of these common goods is a "global problem of humanity" and that everybody should really have an interest in finding its solution (e.g. in Reinicke 1998). What is left out is the fact that their character *as* global commons always represents a discursive and often highly controversial construction. In fact, a form of global management emerges here that is permeated by interests relating to power and rule, which Michael Goldman (1998) has described as global resource management. With the assumption that the local overuse of common goods is the decisive problem to be corrected by a global management, it is ignored that it is in fact a question of specific conflicts over use in which the conflicts between the global and the local levels and between North and South overlap.

> By shifting the commons inquiry from local to global, pastures are no longer simply defined as sites of conflict between or amongst pastoralist and farmers, but are rationalized as small fragments of terrestrial biomass whose misuse negatively affects not just local or regional populations, but us all. In other words: local commons-use patterns in the South are also a problem for the North.
>
> (Goldman 1998: 35)

With global resource management a new type of authority and power is emerging, since global institutions are to administer the resources and sources of conflict defined as global. The domestic and regional institutions, it is argued, are badly equipped for this. The greatest problem for the global resource managers logically lies in the fact that the global institutions do not have enough power. Against the background of capitalist restructuring and its new forms for the appropriation of nature, Goldman (1998: 23) comes to his judgment of the Rio conference: it was the greatest "commons" show of all times,

> to restructure the commons (e.g. privatize, "develop," "make more efficient," valorize, "get the price right") to accommodate crisis-ridden

capitalisms. The effect has not been to stop destructive practices but to normalize and institutionalize them, putting commoners (the local population; the authors) throughout the world at even greater risk.

This undermines the knowledge of the local population as well as their opportunity to take part at all in the debates on how common goods are to be defined in the first place. Particularly in the NGO sphere, the environment for many long ago became green business, in which international organizations such as The Nature Conservancy or Conservation International, with their strong orientation towards preservation, pay little attention to the concerns of the local population and a great deal to benevolent financing by transnational enterprises (cf. Görg and Brand 2003; more generally, Chatterjee and Finger 1994; Princen and Finger 1994). The NGOs contribute quite consciously to the fact that firms and research institutes can conduct their bioprospecting projects in protected areas better than in those in which the local population might put up resistance against the appropriation of their resources and their knowledge (cf., on Mexico and Central America, Delgado-Ramos 2004).

New dynamics: critique of globalization

Despite all these tendencies, it must be stated that there are contradictions in the system of international politics. This means that an eye must be kept on the different terrains, with their own specific conflicts: the CBD is not the WTO and is not fully dominated by it. Above all, the contradictions between different forums often offer the opportunity to articulate weaker interests successfully. This can be demonstrated, for example, in the international discussions on the protection of traditional knowledge, which arose not least out of the considerable tensions between the CBD, the Seeds Treaty of the FAO (accepted in November 2001) and the TRIPS Agreements of the WTO, but which affects also other forums such as the World Intellectual Property Organization (Brand *et al.* 2008). In these discussions, weaker actors such as indigenous peoples or, more generally, translocal actor networks (Jasanoff 2004), were able to articulate and encourage their interests using international treaties to strengthen their position against their national governments. Within this framework it is not only a question of legal regulations but also of changed power relations and of other orientations far beyond those of environmental or development policy in the strict sense.

The actual hope of a trend towards "sustainable development" which would make serious fundamental changes to the pattern of societal development, that is, its power structures, modes of production and consumption, and so on, comes from quite another corner. Relatively independently of the debate on sustainability, the practical and theoretical critique of neoliberal-imperial capitalism has strengthened in recent years. Words such as "Seattle" and "Genoa" stand for a variety of protests against the negative results of the dominant power-driven and exclusive forms of globalization (della Porta 2007; Brand and Wissen 2005). This led to a politicization of the concept of globalization: the process thus named, its catastrophic effects on large numbers of people, and the interests involved are no longer understood as "risks" that must be accepted or as coincidental symptoms that must be removed, but increasingly as immanent parts of societal changes and as the result of social struggles.

Particularly at the local and national level, the dominant trends of "sustainable development" outlined here do not at all remain uncontested. The World Social Forums that have taken place since 2001 are impressive evidence of the fact that critique and alternatives are being formulated and advanced precisely at the local and national level. This heterogeneous movement is politicizing the increasing contradictions (the existence of which, in themselves, mean nothing). The critique of globalization that has been becoming ever more obvious since Seattle is also a rejection of the idea that "world problems" can be solved from above, by experts and cooperatively. The politics of the "global round table," which was first widely propagated by UNCED in 1992, and the accompanying loss of legitimacy by confrontational approaches to politics, is being fundamentally questioned by the global justice movement—which always means: by many different movements and organizations at the national and local level.

The task, therefore, is to give the crisis of relationships with nature a more important place once again in the critique of the dominant strategies of global restructuring. In this field, important advances were made in the last few years, with the World Social Forum an impressive indicator. Catastrophism is not very appropriate for this task. It always serves the purpose of strengthening inert forces and deprives critique of its legitimacy with the reproof that action must be taken immediately.

The greatest danger, in contrast, probably arises from the metaphor of sustainable globalization. Not from the concept itself, of course, but from the understanding it transmits. Also "civil society's" understanding of politics in the Rio process was for a long time based on the assumption that, with cooperation, alternative expert opinions, and the appeal to enlightened self-interest in economics and politics, this model could be put into practice. The 1990s and even more the developments since 2001 have shown particularly clearly that the political concepts connected with this assumption have not proved to be successful. Often enough they tended to serve the legitimation of the "greater" decisions of governments, businesses, and media. These actors could pick out those aspects of the critique that suited them and thus legitimize themselves in this way.

Neoliberal-imperial globalization has established itself—not cooperatively, but primarily in a "top-down" manner. To believe today that this unequally more powerful process could be stopped by cooperation, experts, and an appeal to reason is at best naïve. One of the most important contributions of the current movement of globalization critics is to not be taken in by this belief. "Sustainable globalization" could become the glue holding the fragments of neoliberalism and new forms of imperialism together.

Instead of this, it would be important in the public discussions to question the belief in the technocratic panacea and the "management" of problems. Self-determination, human dignity, and the satisfaction of elementary needs will not be achieved by ideas based on efficiency and managerism. On the contrary, critical practices must be strengthened. Whether and how these relate to the formula of "sustainable development" appears secondary. More important is how concrete issues are taken up, how social interests are treated, and whether critique of the ruling relationships—a comprehensive critique of rule—is included. Despite and because of pragmatic managerism, the belief in the non-changeability of societal relationships, of the lack of an alternative to capitalist globalization, must be undermined. And it is here that the movements of recent years have shown the most success. The objective of a truly sustainable development must be not a "sustainable globalization" but the sustainable pushing back of its driving forces. In these conflicts, alternatives, suggestions for reform and concepts for a different society, which can perhaps then be called "sustainable," are already being developed today.

Translated into English by Irene Wilson.

Notes

1 This distinction is based on regulation theory, the German version of which provides the framework for this chapter and which has influenced the perspective developed in it (cf. Esser *et al.* 1994). For the German term *Regulierung*, we use *political regulation* or *directed control*, and *Regulation* is translated as *societal regulation*.
2 Dryzek (1999: 42) points out that business associations such as the World Business Council on Sustainable Development or the Global Climate Coalition have strong influences (cf. Walk and Brunnengräber 2000 for international climate politics). See, for an opposing way of operationalization from the perspective of the global South, Barkin 1998.
3 This means also that specific questions are left out. In the field of international biodiversity politics, three major and highly controversial issues are hardly dealt with because dominant actors are not interested in them: the question of technology transfer; gender relations, despite their enormous relevance (cf. for example Howard 2003; FAO Focus 2006); and the growing militarization of the appropriation of biodiversity linked to the ongoing practices of biopiracy (Burrows 2005; Ceceña 2006).

References

Albritton, Robert, Itoh, Makoto, Westra, Richard, and Zuege, Alain (2001) *Phases of Capitalist Development: Booms, Crises and Globalization*, Houndmills: Palgrave.
Alnasseri, Sabah (2004) *Periphere Regulation, Regulationstheoretische Konzepte zur Analyse von Entwicklungsstrategien im Arabischen Raum*, Münster: Westfälisches Dampfboot.

Alnasseri, Sabah, Brand, Ulrich, Sablowski, Thomas, and Winter, Jens (2001) "Space, Regulation and the Periodisation of Capitalism," in R. Albritton, M. Itoh, R. Westra and A. Zuege (eds.), *Phases of Capitalist Development. Booms, Crises and Globalization*, Houndmills: Palgrave.

Altvater, E. (1993) *The Future of the Market*, London: Verso.

Annan, K. (2001) *Implementing Agenda 21: Report from the Secretary General to the ECOSOC*. Available www.johannesburgsummit.org (June 2002).

Axelrod, Regina S., Downie, David Leonard, and Vig, Norman (eds.) (2005) *The Global Environment: Institutions, Law, and Policy*, Washington: Congressional Quarterly Press.

Beck, U. (1992) *Risk Society: Towards a New Modernity*, London: Sage.

Betsill, Michele M. (2005) "*Global Climate Policy: Making Progress or Spinning Wheels*," in Regina S. Axelrod et al. (eds.) *The Global Environment: Institutions, Law, and Policy*, Washington: Congressional Quarterly Press.

Biermann, Frank and Bauer, Steffen (eds.) (2005) *A World Environment Organization: Solution Or Threat For Effective International Environmental Governance?* Aldershot: Ashgate.

Biro, A. (2005) *Denaturalizing Ecological Politics*, Toronto: University of Toronto Press.

Boyer, Robert (1990) *The Regulation School: A Critical Introduction*, New York: Oxford.

Brand, K.-W. and Jochum, G. (2000) *Der deutsche Diskurs zu nachhaltiger Entwicklung*, Text of the Munich Project Group for Social Research 1.

Brand, U. and Görg, C. (2003) "The State and the Regulation of Biodiversity. International Biopolitics and the Case of Mexico," *Geoforum* 34: 221–233.

Brand, Ulrich and Wissen, Markus (2005) "Neoliberal Globalization and the Internationalization of Protest: A European Perspective," *Antipode* 37,1: 9–17.

Brand, Ulrich, Görg, Christoph, Hirsch, Joachim, and Wissen, Markus (forthcoming 2008) *Contested Terrains. Conflicts about Genetic Resources and the Internationalisation of the State*: London: Routledge.

Braun, B. and N. Castree (eds.) (1998) *Remaking Reality: Nature at the Millenium*, New York: Routledge.

Bridge, G. and McManus, P. (2000) "Sticks and Stones: Environmental narratives and discursive regulation in the forestry and mining sectors," *Antipode* 32,1: 10–47.

Brunnengräber, Achim (2006) "The political economy of the Kyoto protocol," in Leo Panitch and Colin Leys (eds.) *Socialist Register 2007: Coming to Terms with Nature*, London: The Merlin Press.

Bruyninckx, Hans (2006) "Sustainable development: the institutionalization of a contested policy concept," in Michelle M. Betsill *et al.* (eds.) *International Environmental Politics*, Houndmills: Palgrave.

Burrows, B. (ed.) (2005) *The Catch, Perspectives in Benefit Sharing*, Edmonds: The Edmonds Institute. www.edmonds-institute.org/thecatch.pdf

Ceceña, Ana Esther (ed.) (2006) *Los desafíos de las emancipaciones en un contexto militarizado*, Buenos Aires: CLACSO.

Ceceña, A.E. and Barreda, A. (eds.) (1995) *Producción Estratégica y Hegemonía Mundial*, Mexico City: Siglo XXI.

Chatterjee, P. and Finger, M. (1994) *The Earth Brokers: Power, Politics and World Development*, London: Routledge.

Conca, Ken (1993) "Environmental Change and the Deep Structure of World Politics," in Ronnie D. Lipschutz and Ken Conca (eds.) *The State and Social Power in Global Environmental Politics*, New York: Columbia University Press.

Conca, Ken and Dabelko, Geoffrey D. (eds.) (2004) *Green Planet Blues: Environmental Politics from Stockholm to Johannesburg*, Boulder, CO: Westview Press.

Cronon, W. (ed.) (1995) *Uncommon Ground: Rethinking the Human Place in Nature*, New York: W.W. Norton.

Delgado-Ramos, Gian Carlo (2004) *Biodiversidad, desarrollo sustentable y militarización: Esquemas de saqueo en Mesoamérica*, Mexico City: Plaza y Valdéz, UNAM.

della Porta, Donatella (ed.) (2007) *The Global Justice Movement. Cross-National and Transnational Perspectives*, Boulder, CO: Paradigm.

Dryzek, J.S. (1999) "Transnational Democracy," *The Journal of Political Philosophy*, 7,1: 30–51.

Esser, J., Görg, C., and Hirsch, J. (eds.) (1994) *Politik, Institutionen und Staat: Zur Kritik der Regulationstheorie*, Hamburg: VSA.

FAO Focus (2006) *Women: users, preservers and managers of agro-biodiversity*. Available www.fao.org, FOCUS, E, Women, Biodiv-e.htm

Fischer, Frank (2003) *Citizens, Experts, and the Environment. The Politics of Local Knowledge*, Durham, NC: Duke University Press.

Fisher, William F. and Ponniah, Thomas (eds.) (2003) *Another World is Possible*, London: Zed Books.

Ford, Lucy H. (2003) "Challenging Global Environmental Governance: Social Movement Agency and Global Civil Society," *Global Environmental Politics* 3,2: 120–134.

Gill, S. (2003) *Power and Resistance in the New World Order*, Houndmills: Palgrave.

Goldman, M. (1998) "Inventing the Commons," in M. Goldman (ed.) *Privatizing Nature*, New Brunswick, NJ: Rutgers University Press.

—— (2005) *Imperial Nature. The World Bank and Struggles for Social Justice in the Age of Globalization*, New Haven, CT: Yale University Press.

Görg, C. (2003a) *Regulation der Naturverhältnisse. Zu einer kritischen Theorie der ökologischen Krise*, Münster: Westfälisches Dampfboot.

—— (2003b) "Nichtidentität und Kritik Zum Problem der Gestaltung der Naturverhältnisse," in G. Böhme and A. Manzei (eds.) *Kritische Theorie der Natur und der Technik*, München: Wilhelm Fink, 113–133.

Görg, C. and Brand, U. (2000) "Global environmental politics and competition between nation-states: On the regulation of biological diversity," *Review of International Political Economy* 7,3: 371–398.

—— (2003) "Postfordist Societal Relationsships with Nature: NGOs and the State in Biodiversity Politics," *Rethinking Marxism* 15,2: 263–288.

—— (2006) "Global Regulation of Genetic Resources and the Internationalization of the State," *Global Environmental Politics* 6,4: 101–123.

Graz, Jean-Christophe, Damian, Michel, and Abbas, Mehdi (2007) "Towards an Evolutionary Environmental Regulation: Sustainable Development 20 Years Later," paper for the workshop "Future Routes for Regulation Theory," Université de Lausanne, March 22–23, 2007.

Hajer, M. (1995) *The Politics of Environmental Discourse: Ecological Modernization and the Policy Process*, Oxford: Clarendon Press.

Harvey, David (2005) *The New Imperialism*, Oxford: Oxford University Press.

Hirsch, J. (1997) "Globalization of capital, nation-states and democracy," *Studies in Political Economy* 54: 39–58.

—— (2005) *Materialistische Staatstheorie: Transformationsprozesse des kapitalistischen Staatensystems*, Hamburg: VSA.

Hirsch, J., Jessop, B., and Poulantzas, N. (2001) *Die Zukunft des Staates*, Hamburg: VSA.

Horkheimer, M. and Adorno, T.W. (1982) *Dialectic of Enlightenment*, New York: Continuum.
Howard, Patricia L. (ed.) (2003) *Women and Plants. Gender Relations in Biodiversity Management and Conservation*, London: Zed Books.
International Institute for Environment and Development (IIED) (2001) *The Future is Now*, For the UN World Summit on Sustainable Development, vol.1, April, London: IIED.
ISOE (ed.) (1994) *Sustainable Netherlands: Aktionsplan für eine nachhaltige Entwicklung der Niederlande, herausgegeben vom Institut für sozial-ökologische Forschung*, Frankfurt: IKO.
Jänicke, Martin and Jacob, Klaus (2004) "Lead Markets for Environmental Innovations: A New Role for the Nation State," *Global Environmental Politics* 4,1: 29–46.
Jasanoff, S. (2004) "Heaven and Earth: The Politics of Environmental Images," in S. Jasanoff and M.L. Martello (eds.) *Earthly Politics: Local and Global in Environmental Governance*, Cambridge, MA: MIT Press, 27–79.
Jessop, B. (1990) "Regulation Theories in Retrospect and Prospect," *Economy and Society* 18,2: 153–216.
Lipietz, A. (1985) "Akkumulation, Krisen und Auswege aus der Krise: Einige methodische Überlegungen zum Begriff 'Regulation'," *Prokla* 58: 109–137.
Lipschutz, Ronnie D. (2004) *Global Environmental Politics*, Washington: Congressional Quarterly Press.
Millennium Ecosystem Assessment (2005) *Ecosystems and Human Well-being: Biodiversity Synthesis*, Washington DC: World Resource Institute.
Marx, Karl and Engels, Friedrich (1974) *The German Ideology*, London: Lawrence & Wishart.
O'Connor, M.T. (ed.) (1995) "Is Capitalism Sustainable? Political Economy and the Politics of Ecology," New York: Guilford Press.
Paterson, Matthew (2006) "Theoretical perspectives on international environmental politics," in Michele M. Betsill *et al.* (eds.) *International Environmental Politics*, Houndmills: Palgrave.
Patomäki, Heikki and Teivainen, Teivo (2004) *A Possible World: Democratic Transformation of Global Institutions*, London: Zed Books.
Poulantzas, N. (1980) *State, Power, Socialism*, London: Verso.
Princen, T. and Finger, M. (eds.) (1994) *Environmental NGOs in World Politics. Linking the Local with the Global*, London: Routledge.
Redclift, Michael (1989) *Sustainable Development: Exploring the Contradictions*, London: Routledge.
—— (1994) "Development and the Environment: Managing the Contradictions?" in L. Sklair (ed.) *Capitalism and Development*, London: Routledge, 123–139.
Reinicke, Wolfgang H. (1998) *Global Public Policy. Governing without Government?* Washington DC: Brookings Institution Press.
Sachs, Wolfgang (1999) *Planet Dialectics: Explorations in Environment and Development*, London: Zed Books.
Toke, Dave (2001) "Ecological Modernisation: A Reformist Review," *New Political Economy* 6,2: 279–281.
Walk, Heike and Brunnengräber, Achim (2000) *Die Globalisierungswächter. NGO und ihre transnationalen Netze im Konfliktfeld Klima*, Münster: Westfälisches Dampfboot.

3 Which governance for sustainable development?

An organizational and institutional perspective

Matthias Finger

This chapter takes its point of departure in the observation that the mainstream literature on global environmental politics does not problematize institutions, neither when it comes to diagnosing the causes of the crisis, nor when it comes to addressing it (e.g., most recently, Speth and Haas 2006). More precisely, this literature does not problematize the state as an institution. Indeed, causes of the current global environmental crisis are said to be bad (or failed) policies, inefficient or even destructive technologies, lack of political will, ideas (or ideologies) that are detrimental to the environment (e.g., capitalism), the behavior of particularly evil actors (from transnational corporations to CEOs), culture (e.g., consumerism, individualism), misguided individuals, and more. Similarly, the solution to the global environmental crisis is said to ultimately come from better policies, new and different technologies, more political will, other ideas and ideologies (e.g., green thinking, anti-capitalism, etc.), the elimination of evil actors, or a change in culture, individual behavior, or consciousness.

Institutions are simply seen as being neutral instruments in the hands of policies, politicians, ideologies, people, organizations, or even technologies. Rarely are institutions considered to be a problem, let alone *the* problem when it comes to diagnosing or addressing the global environmental crisis. For example, and in particular, the nation-state is still perceived as being simply a tool in the hands of politicians and citizens, but not an institution (or a set of institutions) in its own right. Sometimes it is said that the nation-state is abused (i.e., lobbied by the dark forces), but this view still sees the state as an instrument, and not as an institution with a logic of its own.

This chapter questions the very idea that institutions in general and nation-states in particular are neutral instruments in light of the global environmental crisis. Rather, it looks at institutions (and institutional arrangements) as being the result of a historical (co-)evolution, in which technology is the other element of the equation. In this sense, institutions may be problematized as not being appropriate for achieving certain societal objectives such as sustainability. Worse, certain institutions can actively contribute in themselves to unsustainability, regardless of whether they are controlled by good or bad people, regardless of whether they serve good or bad policies, and regardless of the type of actors that lobby them.

This chapter is structured as follows: in a first section I will present the conceptual building blocks of my approach. In a second section, I will then briefly recall the destructive, and increasingly institutionalized, dynamics of industrial development, only to show, in a third section, how the nation-state has played a pivotal role in the institutionalization of these destructive dynamics. Section four will discuss the still state-centric international system, which is currently emerging and which in my view accompanies, rather than addresses, these destructive industrial dynamics. In conclusion, I will discuss alternative institutional approaches that may be more in line with sustainable development.

Conceptual foundations

Actors be they individuals or organizations always act under rules, which are sometimes also called "institutions." These rules—which can be formal or informal—set the incentives for the actors' behavior. As such, institutions (rules) are *never* neutral. Williamson (1996) distinguishes four levels of such institutional rules, depending on the timeframe it takes to change them (i.e., the degree of "institutionalization"), namely resource allocation and employment rules (ongoing), governance rules (1–10 years), basic institutional rules (10–100 years), and cultural rules (100–1000 years). In other words, no matter how well intentioned the actors (individuals and organizations), their behavior is always framed by more or less institutionalized rules. Changing these rules is generally beyond the power of single actors, as it requires both a long-term perspective and coordination with other actors. Actors always aspire to increase their "degree of freedom," that is, to somewhat influence to their advantage the rules (institutions) that constrain their behavior. In doing so, they try to increase the "degree of uncertainty," which is identical to their "discretionary power" (Crozier, 1963).

Nation-states are a quite particular form of institution, for three different reasons. First, nation-states have managed to attribute to themselves the monopoly of legitimate violence, which makes their rules more easily enforceable than any other rules. Second, and building on this monopoly of legitimate violence, an entire legal apparatus and profession has been built around nation-states, which institutionalizes state-backed rules more deeply than any other rules (Weber, 1925). Finally, and precisely because of this process of institutionalization, nation-states' rules have not only developed a life of their own, but actively contributed to "disembedding" modern society from their (bio-physical and cultural) environments, as well as to perpetuating such "disembeddedness" (Polanyi, 1944; Giddens, 1990). Indeed, when it comes to modern society's relationships with its environment, most rules shaping the relevant actors' (unsustainable) behavior are influenced, if not directly determined, by the nation-state. Of course, new supra-national institutions have been emerging since, but they remain heavily shaped by nation-states to this day. Moreover, when focusing on an international level, nation-states can also be actors.

In this section, I intend to outline briefly the conceptual framework that underlies my approach. Its purpose is to show that there is indeed a body of literature that can be brought to bear on the institutional analysis of the global environmental crisis. In this sense, I will present the key relevant elements of organization theory, new institutional economics, and (economic) governance theory.

Organization theory

Historically, organization theory (just like new institutional economics later on) has not been interested in questions of governance and even less so in questions of global and environmental governance. Rather, organization theorists have focused on how individuals and groups behave within organizations (historically the army, later the industrial factory, notably the car factory), or at best try to shape organizations. Nevertheless, I believe that many of the insights of organization theorists are highly relevant even when extrapolated beyond organizations and applied, by analogy, to the behavior of organizations within larger institutional systems.

The basic building blocks of organizational theory are actors and rules that shape actor behavior (e.g., Crozier 1963; Etzioni, 1964). Actors can be individuals, teams, or organizations themselves. Such actors are characterized by their *strategic* behavior, as well as by the fact that they pursue specific *goals*. To recall, organizations are structures (i.e., institutionalized rules) that have been deliberately set up so as to enable them (and the actors that compose them) to achieve specific goals. Quite logically, then, the behavior of these actors is significantly influenced by the formal and informal rules (whose aim it should be to make sure that the organization and the actors composing it achieve the set goal). It is no contradiction that organizations can be simultaneously actors (when behaving strategically vis-à-vis other actors/organizations) and institutions (when shaping the behavior of the actors that compose it). Similarly, nation-states can be simultaneously actors (when behaving strategically vis-à-vis other nation-states or supra-national actors/organizations) and institutions (when shaping the behavior of the actors that compose it).

However, there is never a perfect match between the set goal(s) of the organization and the goals of the actors that compose the organization. This is even more so as—over time and because of organizational growth—organizational goals change (goal displacement), multiply (goal multiplication), or become confused (goal confusion). Consequently, actors always strategize in order to shape (use, change, or avoid) the organizational rules under which they (must) behave. Crozier's major contribution to organization theory has been to show that actors' strategies ultimately aim at increasing their own *discretionary power* (which is a form of freedom). Discretionary power, in turn, may translate into economic or political advantages, but does not necessarily have to.

Building on Max Weber's theory of bureaucracy, Crozier's second major contribution to organization theory pertains to the process of *institutionalization*. Indeed, says Crozier, over time (and because of size and strategic behavior) rules become institutionalized, not the least because it is in the strategic interest of some of the actors to institutionalize the rules (at least the ones that are to their advantage, i.e., the ones that cement their discretionary power). Nevertheless, and paradoxically, even these actors who actually are losing out because of the rules in place actively contribute to cementing the existing rules; this is because the more precise the rules, the better they can strategize against them (fuzzy rules playing mainly into the hands of the ones who are already in power).

Over time, therefore, flexibility is lost, and change can only come from outside any given organization. The older (and therefore the more institutionalized) but also the more conflictual an organization is, the more unlikely it is to change, and the more likely change will take the form of outside pressure. If environmental pressure is sufficiently strong, organizations may adapt but they may also be unable to adapt and subsequently disappear. Over time, organizations become conservative, unable to change, and simply perpetuate the (increasingly multiple, incoherent, and irrelevant) goals for which they have been set up to begin with. In other words, the older, the bigger, and the more rigid an organization, the more likely change will be disruptive, as conflicts will become destructive (Coser, 1956, 1967). While this argument of institutionalization and inability to change other than by disruptions is generally valid for all organizations, it is particularly valid for so-called "disembedded social systems," of which the modern nation-state is a perfect illustration. In disembedded systems, according to Giddens (1990: 21ss), social relations are "lifted out" from local contexts of interaction; this has occurred in human history thanks to the creation of so-called symbolic tokens (e.g., money) and expert systems. Both operate on the basis of trust, and the nation-state has over time replaced the church as the guarantor of such trust.

In short, anthropologically informed organization theory helps us to understand the dynamics of organizations, in particular the process of institutionalization and subsequent barriers to change and adaptation other than by disruptions. We have also argued that the modern nation-state can be conceptualized as being a particularly institutionalized form of organization.

New institutional economics

New institutional economics (NIE) adds to the preceding considerations, focusing in particular on the (transactional) relationships between the actors. As such, NIE builds on a combination of *principal-agent theory*

(Laffont and Martimort, 2002) and *decision theory* (e.g., Simon, 1945) and focuses on the ways and means by which actors coordinate their actions in order to either achieve their personal strategies or to collectively achieve goals that they cannot reach by themselves. NIE, however, looks at these transactional relationships only in (economic) efficiency terms.

NIE thus assesses different modes of organization (different ways of coordinating among actors) in economic terms. In particular, it distinguishes between three modes of organization (ways to coordinate, also called forms of governance; see below)—namely, *markets* (competition), *hierarchies* (integration), and *hybrids* (networking)—and seeks to establish which mode is most cost-efficient (e.g., Williamson, 1996) in which contractual (but not environmental) situation. In order to do that, NIE further builds on transaction cost economics (e.g., Jensen, 2000), which in turn originates in the question of whether "to make or to buy." Transaction cost theory thus distinguishes between different types of "contracts," which in turn are influenced by the frequency of the transaction, the degree of uncertainty involved (e.g., incomplete contracts), and the level of asset specificity (i.e., the amount of upfront investments that are required for a transaction even to take place). Over time, simple transaction cost theory has evolved to include ever more organizational dimensions (see above), in particular opportunism (e.g., strategic behavior of the actors) leading to so-called "hold-up" (i.e., the appropriation of economic rent) as well as bounded rationality (Simon, 1945; Williamson, 1973).

If organizational theory is helpful when it comes to explaining strategic behavior of actors in a given institutional environment, as well as the process of institutionalization of nation-states, NIE helps one to understand that such behavior and corresponding (coordinating) actions (within any given institutional arrangement) do have an economic cost. Different institutional arrangements (ways of coordinating) are thus differently efficient in achieving identical goals. As a matter of fact, NIE focuses exclusively on the cost efficiency of different types of contractual relationships (e.g., competition, integration, and networking) under specific conditions (e.g., uncertainty, asset specificity, frequency). This is because (institutional) economists believe that institutions are competing against each other (i.e., operating in a market) and that the most efficient institution will ultimately prevail. Although these assumptions are highly questionable, this does not put into question the main insights of NIE, which can therefore be applied to matters of governance more generally.

Governance theory

Governance theory first stems from the observation that nation-states increasingly have to collaborate with non-state actors so as to achieve their goals. This is especially true at the global level, where nation-states increasingly have to share power with transnational corporations and non-governmental organizations. Thus, the concept of governance is also linked to the idea that the nation-state level is no longer necessarily the most appropriate level to solve collective problems. The concept of governance is approached in the international relations literature from a variety of perspectives, some of which are quite normative (e.g., the legitimacy of governance, the question of participation in governance, and more). However, in the context of political science and international relations, governance is above all a pragmatic concept, defining less state-centric ways to solve collective problems (Young, 1994). States, in the age of globalization, increasingly have to work in networks.

And this is precisely where a relationship can be established between political science and new institutional economics. Indeed, one can apply the question of the optimal modes of coordination among actors—namely hierarchies (e.g., government ordering), markets (e.g., competition), and hybrids (networks, i.e., neither markets nor hierarchies)—to all forms of institutional arrangements, and not only to institutional arrangements competing in a market. As a matter of fact, different types of institutional arrangements—hierarchies, markets, and hybrids—not only have different degrees of efficiency; they can also be more or less performing in social, environmental, and even technical terms, something which Williamson (1996) implicitly admits in his opus *Mechanisms of Governance*.

To recall, at the nation-state level, hierarchies or government ordering historically appeared to be the preferred way of organizing the coordination among actors. While in liberal countries markets were considered to be the most appropriate coordination mechanisms for economic activities, even markets remained hierarchically subordinated to government ordering (e.g., regulation). This situation substantially changes with globalization, which changed the rules under which nation-states behave. International relations theorists have highlighted the fact that, with globalization, nation-states increasingly have to coordinate with non-state actors (in particular, business and civil-society actors) so as to achieve their goals (e.g., Rosenau and Czempiel, 2000), even at the subnational and national levels. Such coordination typically takes the form of networks or hybrids, and involves, one way or another, nation-states (e.g., Kooiman, 2002).

NIE tells us that such coordination—that is, different forms of governance—can be more or less efficient (to achieve a given goal) or effective (to achieve different goals). In all of this, organization theory applies and, furthermore, tells us that each way of coordinating (governance mechanism, institutional arrangement) incentivizes actors differently, thus leading to different strategic behaviors, which in turn will lead to coordination problems and coordination costs. Their strategic behavior is shaped not only by the behavior of the other actors—some of which can be nation-states, and others, non-state actors—but also by the formal and informal rules that regulate all actors' behavior, as well as by their internal rules. To recall, the ultimate goal of each of the actors is to increase their respective discretionary power (which can translate into economic benefits or other advantages), thus the relative inefficiency and ineffectiveness of coordination.

Such is the conceptual framework that underlies my analysis of current (unsustainable) global environmental governance. This framework is contingent inasmuch as it implies that there is significant path-dependency, meaning that, once institutionalized, actors' behavior, as well as governance mechanisms and institutional arrangements, are hard to change unless there exists substantial pressure from environmental factors (e.g., competition, crises) or if actors are sufficiently strategic and organized to be able to change the rules.

The (destructive) dynamics of industrial development

In this section, I will discuss the dynamics of industrial development. This discussion should contribute to understanding the fact that industrial development is profoundly intertwined with the institutional development of the relevant actors of such industrial development, in particular the nation-state. More precisely, industrial development—the root cause of today's ecological problems of global and systemic proportions—is a dynamic process fueled by a combination of (militaristic) values, cheap non-renewable energy, a certain type of (cheap fuel-consuming) technology, and modern institutions, among which the institution of the nation-state plays the most prominent role. Let me also mention here that recent developments in information and communication technologies (ICTs), often considered to be the equivalent of a new industrial revolution, do not replace industrial development but simply exacerbate it.

Industrial development is basically the product of the Industrial Revolution of the nineteenth century (e.g., Landes, 1969). Its main characteristic is the systematic use of fossil (non-renewable) fuels (first coal and now oil) for the purpose of military, technological, economic, and political conquest and expansion (e.g., Cottrell, 1955). Not surprisingly, therefore, economic growth has become, since the Industrial Revolution, almost totally correlated with fossil fuel consumption (Hall, 2004). Modern public institutions, in particular the nation-state, have been instrumental in spreading this Industrial Revolution in particular and industrial development in general both geographically and societally (i.e., to all aspects of social life) (Clarke, 1971; McNeill, 1963). Indeed, the nation-state, as we will see in the next section, has first served as an actor of territorial conquest and has later evolved into a mechanism for organizing the ever expanding market (McNeill, 1982). As of today, industrial development has reached every single corner and aspect of the world (e.g., Commoner, 1966).

Large-scale environmental degradation of a systemic nature—which has come to be called "global change" and which encompasses profound alterations of the Earth's life support systems (e.g., soil pollution, erosion, and degradation, water pollution, air pollution, climate change, natural resources depletion, and biodiversity loss)—is inseparably tied to industrial development (Clark and Munn, 1986). I am of course not talking here of sporadic pollution such as toxic waste, which can be controlled or at least reduced by further scientific and technological progress. Rather, I am referring to the systemic degradation of the biosphere due to resources consumption and depletion (input problems), as well as to the alterations of the planet's "life support systems"[1] (output problems), both of which are either necessary conditions for or unavoidable consequences of industrial development. In other words, anthropogenic transformations of the Earth's life support system go hand in hand with industrial development. Put another way, since and thanks to the Industrial Revolution, mankind has become a geological force (Georgescu-Roegen, 1971). Again, one must mention here the *institutionalization* of this evolution, in particular in the form of actors and rules that promote, perpetuate, and sustain industrial development. From an institutional and organizational perspective, the nation-state, as I will show below, plays a key role here, to the point that it has become, over time, an integrated part and driving force of industrial development.

However, this Industrial Revolution is not an accident of history. Rather, it is the logical next step following previous developmental steps of the West (Nef, 1954). The most significant of these steps are, in reverse order, the French Revolution of the eighteenth century, leading to the creation of the modern nation-state (see next section); the Scientific Revolution of the Renaissance; and the technical revolutions of the Middle Ages, leading to geographical expansion and subsequent colonization. Some authors go back even further, as they see the Industrial Revolution and expansion rooted in Judeo-Christianism (e.g., Noble, 1998; White, 1967). In this sense, the Industrial Revolution is simply the (intermediate) result of a systematic application of science and technology to the types of societal problems that resulted from Western expansion (trade and commerce with the colonies, as well as the need for mobility), population growth, and urbanization. In other words, the steam engine—which is the first concrete manifestation of the Industrial Revolution—helps solve problems of production (e.g., mass production), transport, and mobility.

Furthermore, the Industrial Revolution and industrial development more generally embody a very particular kind of problem solving, namely a militarist one (Grinevald, 1975). Be it the technical improvements of the Middle Ages (driven by military objectives), the scientific progress of the Renaissance (again having military problems as a background, e.g., ballistics), discovery and colonization (by its very nature a military exercise), the emergence of the modern nation-state (another development mainly motivated by military considerations), or the Industrial Revolution itself (driven significantly by the need for more power in warfare), the military is an ever present feature of Western industrial development (e.g., Clarke, 1971). In ethno-psychoanalytical terms, one may see the military as the very cultural archetype of Western civilization (Richter, 1997). Of course, this militaristic nature of the West did not stop with the Industrial Revolution. Rather, Western civilization progressed alongside and thanks to some other significant "military drivers" such as the First, Second, and Cold Wars.

From a philosophical point of view, these ultimately destructive military-industrial dynamics cannot be separated from capitalist principles and their institutionalization (e.g., Foster, 2002). But my main point and focus here is precisely on the *institutionalization of permanent warfare* (even in times of peace), which is the main characteristic and driver of Western (industrial) civilization since its very inception, and at least since the Roman Empire. That is to say, the driver of industrial development, as well as of the conquest of peoples and nature, has been, at least since the French Revolution, the modern nation-state.

Emergence, institutionalization, and adaptation of the nation-state

In this section I want to crystallize the fact that the nation-state is not a neutral institution, but rather an interested institutional actor. More precisely, the nation-state has been a, if not *the*, tool of Western expansion, conquest, and development, which embodied, as seen previously, an essentially militaristic perspective and motivation. Furthermore, and since the Industrial Revolution, the nation-state also plays an active role in pushing industrialization further on the one hand and in institutionalizing this process of industrialization on the other hand. The discussion then turns to how the nation-state has triggered a process of globalization, by which the state is subsequently "overtaken," so to speak, yet without becoming obsolete. Indeed, as we will see, the nation-state learns to adapt to such globalization, and, by doing so, evolves into a useful tool for further (and this time, global) industrial development. Let me also state that, from an organizational and institutional perspective, the nation-state constitutes a particular way of "coordinating" and controlling the actors (individuals and organizations) living within a given territory. The nation-state is unique insofar as it uses legitimate violence as *the* means of "coordination," and as such has had and still has a significant competitive advantage over other actors.

Conjoined twins: the nation-state and industrial development

Let me recall that the nation-state is indeed a significant—if not the most significant—step in the process of industrial development. Indeed, after the Scientific Revolution of the Renaissance and within the broader context of Western expansion and colonization, the nation-state emerged as the most appropriate unit for organizing the extraction of the necessary resources for warfare, including capital, and thus the most appropriate unit for organizing such warfare (Finer, 1997; Tilly, 1990). Furthermore, the nation-state is also the most appropriate unit for legitimizing such warfare, by involving citizens rather than relying on mercenaries (Giddens, 1985).

The mobilization of the citizens and resources necessary for waging war required quite substantial organization. Such organization was done by the nation-state and, more precisely, by its administration. Max Weber (1925) described this process of "bureaucratization" in detail and highlighted in particular how the bureaucracy became the most efficient model of organizing complex activities in a hierarchical mode (e.g., government ordering in new institutional economic terms). He also described, in organizational terms, the very process of institutionalization (e.g., bureaucratization), which by way of cementing rules ultimately leaves little leeway for alternatives (see above). In short, bureaucracy as the institutionalized version of the nation-state is able to mobilize natural and financial resources, as well as peoples, not only for waging war but also for promoting the development of the nation-state itself. Given that the nation-state is in essence about war, conquest, and control, its administration is the institutionalization of precisely that.

As such, the nation-state is still a rather "pre-industrial model" of territorial defense and conquest. However, within the context of industrialization of the late nineteenth century, the nation-state came to apply its capacity to mobilize peoples and resources to the pursuit and active promotion of industrial development (Cerny, 1990). Indeed, within this new context of industrial development, the nation-state now developed—in addition to warfare and territorial conquest, which are not abandoned—its own infrastructures by means of electrification, roads, railway tracks, and other means, so as to enable and actively promote industrial development. Corresponding administrative entities—often public enterprises—were set up, so as to institutionalize by now combined military-industrial development, that is, the so-called "national economy." In other words, and in parallel to being a "war machine," the modern nation-state also became a "development machine," approaching development as if it were just another form of (economic) warfare. Natural and financial resources as well as peoples were still being mobilized by the nation-state, but now for purposes of combined military-industrial development.

Until the end of the Second World War, industrial development was primarily organized and actively pushed forward by individual nation-states, generally with a military aim in the back of their mind. In other words, at least until the end of the war, and probably until the end of the Cold War in the late 1980s, the modern nation-state was in essence an institutional embodiment of combined industrial development and warfare (Meinecke, 1957). Or, more clearly, the nation-state is not the neutral collective problem-solving tool that theoreticians (in particular, lawyers, political scientists, and political economists) would like it to be. Rather, it has become, thanks to its institutionalization and institutionalized growth, an increasingly powerful vehicle for apparently unlimited military-industrial development. Because of the institutionalization of this combined militaristic and developmental logic, the nation-state will always approach the problems with which it is confronted as a threat to be combated by warlike means, as a developmental opportunity, or as a combination of both, something which was well understood by Galbraith in his concept of the "military-industrial complex" (Galbraith, 1970). This was also the understanding of the early Frankfurt School of Critical Theory, which insisted on the profound ambiguity of the modern nation-state as both a modernizing and fundamentally destructive actor (e.g., Horkheimer and Adorno, 1944).

After the Second World War, thanks to the economic boom, and especially after the end of the Cold War, this situation changed somewhat. As a result of state-centric and military-driven industrial development, the economy integrated at a higher level. Similarly, the consequences of the wars (especially the Second World War), the threats of a third world war, and the consequences of industrial development (including environmental degradation), increasingly required a supra-national approach, with corresponding supra-national (yet still "inter-state," i.e., international) institutions. However, the nation-state did not disappear, but rather adapted to this new situation.

From the nation-state to international institutions

As said above, the Second World War triggered a certain awareness of a need to contain the militaristic ambitions of nation-states. The idea became to seek "peace through development," and this is precisely the underlying philosophical idea of the then-created United Nations. The main purpose of this section, therefore, is to show how, after the Second World War, reinforced and accelerated industrial development among cooperating nation-states (of the traditional kind) came to be considered *the* answer to some of the problems of the nation-state. And this cooperation became institutionalized in turn. However, I will also show how this institutionalization triggered a dynamic of its own, during which the nation-state was somehow "overtaken" not only by new, state-created, international actors, but also by multi- or supra-national actors, who are now actively making use of the nation-state for their own purposes. This was particularly the case after the end of the Cold War, which opened the door for even more accelerated industrial development, called globalization, and which gave rise to the so-called transnational corporations (TNCs). These TNCs, over time, became more powerful than states themselves and increasingly succeeded in instrumentalizing nation-states for their own purely financial development purposes (e.g., Ietto-Gillies, 2005).

To recall, the Second World War gave rise to a new type, or rather to three new types, of international institution, namely the United Nations (UN), the Bretton Woods institutions, and the General Agreement on Tariffs and Trade (GATT). All three emerged at the same time, but with different functions. The UN was given the mission of peace, development, and human rights. The human rights function has never really been embraced, and peace was quite rapidly said to be achieved through the active promotion of (industrial) development. In essence, this means that the UN and its numerous specialized agencies saw their role as promoting development, no longer at a national but now at a global level.

The Bretton Woods institutions are made up of four different organizations, the two most important of which are the World Bank (WB) and the International Monetary Fund (IMF). Both fulfill a so-called support function for the UN, as they actively contribute to the financing of such development. If the UN organizations today mainly serve a think-tank and technical expertise function, the Bretton Woods organizations financially support development. Over time, and especially because of their governance and their respective finance mechanisms, the Bretton Woods organizations have increased their power at the expense of the UN and have subsequently adjusted even their legitimization. This is especially the case of the World Bank, which has redefined itself more and more as a development-promoting organization in itself, rather than as a support function for the UN as a whole.

As for GATT, which in 1994 became institutionalized in the form of the World Trade Organization (WTO), the function is slightly different, although philosophically entirely aligned with the idea of "peace through development." The role of GATT and later the WTO is to open markets for further industrial development, with the underlying assumption that trade not only leads to development (which leads to peace) but also weakens nation-states, with interlinked national economies making war among states less likely.

Before discussing how all this plays out in the environmental arena, it is necessary to mention the fact that accelerated industrial development from the Second World War through the 1970s led to substantial growth in industrial organizations. Not only have markets grown and become increasingly global, to a large extent because of cheap oil, but also industrial organizations have become increasingly powerful non-state actors. From national origins, they have first become international, then multinational, and now transnational corporations (TNCs) (UN, 1994). It should be stressed, however, that these large corporations are never separate from the nation-state: they may be the (privatized) results of state-owned enterprises, or remain state-owned enterprises, or they may simply have very close ties with particular governments. In other words, none of today's TNCs are separate from the nation-state, as they generally owe their existence and well-being to the nation-state, be it through ownership, subsidies, or other advantages granted by the nation-states to them. The only thing that has changed since the age of globalization (i.e., since the 1980s) is that nation-states have now also become dependent on TNCs, and no longer only the other way round.

Since the late 1970s one can observe a similar evolution of yet another type of non-state actor, namely so-called non-governmental organizations

(NGOs) (Princen and Finger, 1994). From a purely institutional perspective, this evolution has led to the fact that so-called non-state actors have become equally powerful, if not more powerful, than some nation-states (Strange, 1996). This phenomenon has, of course, significantly accelerated with the end of the Cold War in the late 1980s, which not only contributed to weakening the nation-state further, but also led to further liberalization, often accompanied by privatization, thus creating new (formerly) state-owned global economic players (von Weizsäcker, Young, and Finger 2005). Needless to say, these so-called civil society organizations are in turn heavily dependent upon nation-states, be it through funding or because they are ultimately recognized and accredited by nation-states.

As a matter of fact, and especially as a result of globalization, we now have, from an institutional point of view, a situation with multiple actors (nation-states, some of which are still powerful, TNCs, NGOs, and international organizations), multiple and often conflicting objectives, multiple levels (global, regional, national, and sub-national) and, as a result of all of this, much greater need to coordinate among these actors. In other words, the outlined intellectual perspective of the first section, whereby all of these actors struggle for power and must seek new ways of coordinating their activities, now applies at a global level as well. It is therefore no longer clear what the outcomes of such a multi-actor, multi-level, and highly dynamic institutional system are and will be in the long run; nor is it clear whether the coordination among all these actors is ultimately efficient and effective. However, it is clear that nation-states remain relevant and powerful actors even in the age of global governance, given that TNCs, NGOs, and international organizations are dependent upon them. To recall, all three emerging global institutional arrangements—the UN, the Bretton Woods organizations, and the WTO—remain state-centric institutions. But before making this case in the next section, I turn to the question of what the nation-state, which originally triggered this evolution, is becoming in this new global system.

The changing nature of the nation-state in the new international system

Obviously, the nation-state is now only one among these globally relevant actors. Also, with the exception of a few states—in particular the United States, China, and the European Union, if it manages to structure itself as a "supra-national nation-state"—most are no longer relevant global actors. In this section, I would like to show how nation-states adapt to this process and what one can expect from such "adapted" nation-states.

As said, a nation-state is both an actor and an institution. As an institution it is characterized by some key features, namely the fact that it is built on an underlying philosophical assumption of "development as permanent military conquest," an assumption which can also be found in the international organizations. But the nation-state is itself composed of actors and organizations, which, as such, can and do adapt to change. On a purely material level, such adaptation of nation-states takes the form of deregulation, privatization, and public sector restructuring (Finger and Allouche, 2002). Indeed, a nation-state put into a global context comes under both financial and legitimation pressures (Finger 2002). It must adapt so as to remain perceived as a relevant actor by its citizens. Therefore, it privatizes, either to generate income or to get rid of unprofitable activities; it deregulates, to stimulate markets and satisfy citizen-consumers; it restructures its public services, to become more service-oriented and to have lower operating costs; and it develops regulations that are favorable for and even actively promote further industrial development. Most nation-states have undergone such a restructuring process since the 1990s, often to a greater extent in the poorer or "developing" countries, because of World Bank and TNC pressures.

There is no question that the nation-state, like most other organizations and institutions, will be capable of adapting to globalization, and therefore will continue to exist. The question, rather, is a philosophical one: what will such adapted nation-states look like and how will they behave? Already we can see how nation-states transform from "developmental" states, whose aim is to develop in the spirit of permanent military-style conquest, to so-called "regulatory" states (Majone, 1996), whose aim is basically to control operations within their territories. Philosophically, this means that the nation-state is giving up its developmental mission, yet retains its militaristic nature. In other words, it reverts to its so-called "core business" of law and order, as advocated by the World Bank since 1997 (World Bank, 1997). Not surprisingly, we have seen over the past 15 years the emergence and growth of national regulatory activities of an unprecedented nature. In other words, the nation-state subcontracts the lucrative parts of its operational activities to the private sector and the non-lucrative parts to the non-profit sector, while outsourcing essentially all of its former developmental activities (including postal services, health services, educational services, and others). It limits itself to regulating the operations done by others, hoping to keep control by way of regulation. As such, it is increasingly becoming dependent upon the very actors (organizations) it is supposed to regulate, that is, the TNCs.

The emerging international system

In this section, I will discuss the institutionalization of globalization, arguing that the new global or, rather, *international institutions* that have emerged since the Second World War perpetuate (and not alter) the functions formerly performed by the nation-state when it comes to promoting industrial development. The result, therefore, is basically the same: the pursuit of industrial development at a higher level, militaristic problem solving, and now (market) regulation as well. In other words, the new global organizations have simply institutionalized industrial development at a higher level. I then discuss how environmental issues are being approached within this new global institutional context. In particular, I will highlight how the environment is being adapted to the needs of the new global institutions, and not the other way around, with the consequence that environmental problems are being redefined either as development problems, problems of military-style crisis management, or problems of state-centric regulation.

The nature and objectives of the new inter-national institutions

The new global institutions described above remain state-like or state-centric institutions. It is not surprising, then, that they continue to display state-like approaches to collective problem solving. Previously, I characterized the behavior of the state as "militaristic-developmental" and argued that, in the age of globalization, the state adapts by dropping its developmental ambitions and focusing primarily on law-and-order regulation promoting development. Quite logically, we can now find these same approaches on a supra-national level. Previously, I had highlighted the three types of institutions that have emerged after the Second World War, namely the UN, the Bretton Woods organizations, and the WTO.[2] Indeed, collective problem solving at the supra-national level is being crystallized, since the 1980s, around these three types of institutions. Rather than displaying alternative approaches to collective problem solving at the global level, both TNCs and global NGOs are clustered around these three institutions, as will be shown below.

Each of these three institutionalized governance clusters has a different way of looking at the global reality and global problems and, therefore, a unique approach to them. The approach of each of them to collective global problem solving can be explained by a combination of its history and original mandate (which evolved over time), its own governance structure, and, especially, its financing mechanisms and financial situation. Let me briefly present here the three unique approaches to collective global problem solving that emerge from these three clusters of organizations:

- The *United Nation's* original mandate was, as said above, peace, human rights, and development. In order to do that, the UN set up a series of specialized agencies in different topical areas, some more geared at policy advice, others more operational. Since the end of the Cold War, the UN is faced with ever more severe financial problems forcing it to gradually drop its developmental function, at least at the operational level. Given the context of the Cold War, the UN had never been very active on the human rights side, and is therefore mainly left today with a peacekeeping mission. However, given the UN's financial problems, peacekeeping is only possible in periods of crisis, that is, when money can be leveraged. Thus, the UN's approach to global collective problem solving more and more clearly emerges as one of ad hoc crisis management with humanitarian arguments as the core justification of often military-style intervention. The developmental dimension is now almost entirely left out or limited to post-crisis (infrastructure) reconstruction efforts. In short, the UN institutions essentially focus on military-type crisis management (Dijkzeul and Beigbeder, 2003).

- The *Bretton Woods institutions'* original mandate was to assist the developmental agenda of the UN by providing and guaranteeing loans to countries that engaged in infrastructure projects. One must also recall that the World Bank, probably the most influential of the Bretton Woods institutions, is a commercial organization, which makes profits by making loans. In addition, the Bretton Woods organizations have a different governance structure from the rest of the UN, giving power to the donors and not to the recipients of the loans. Thus, the Bretton Woods organizations can be managed much more efficiently and much more strategically. Not surprisingly, then, the Bretton Woods organizations and the World Bank in particular have managed to take considerable advantage of the decline of the UN, and have subsequently taken over the development discourse, if not the development agenda. They have done so by promoting private-sector participation in infrastructure development and by advocating public-sector reform involving substantial restructuring and privatization and, more recently, a regulatory state serving mainly to protect investors in industrial development projects (Kessides, 2004). In short, the Bretton Woods institutions now focus mainly on infrastructure development led by the private sector, with the state as a regulator and guarantor of investments and investors.

- The original mandate of the *WTO* was to open national markets to trade, with the underlying agenda, as suggested above, that trade leads to development and development leads to peace. The WTO has been more or less successful in doing so, depending on whose judgment one listens to. The result of the WTO's actions is indeed that markets have been opened, significantly boosting global trade and especially the growth of TNCs. This has proceeded to the point that the pressure from the TNCs for further market opening has substantially declined. The WTO is therefore challenged today—by both TNCs and consumers—to evolve from a "market opener" into a global "market regulator," an activity for which it has no explicit mandate. In this context, one must also mention the European Commission, which is faced with the same challenge, yet at a regional level, and with an explicit mandate to perform market-regulatory functions. In both cases, the institutions are evolving from a policy function to a more judicial function and approach, thus assuming ever more, on a regional or global level, the law-and-order role that nation-states had formerly played on the national level (Abbott and Snidal, 2001).

These three approaches to global collective problem solving evolve in parallel and in strategic relationship with one another, as seen for example in the case of the UN and the World Bank. While each of these three types of institutions produces a somewhat coherent approach, the overall approach to global governance is at best fragmented, contradictory, and biased by the strategic interests of the actors involved. Nevertheless, one must see that all three types of institutions are responses to the fact that industrial development, originally triggered and actively promoted by the nation-state, has now taken on a supra-national life of its own; each of these three types of organization is now trying both to respond to and to take advantage of this fact. In doing so, all three institutionalized global governance mechanisms actively contribute to cementing and further institutionalizing industrial development. Most likely, these global institutions will not solve the problems caused by industrial development, but rather channel them in a way that they can be approached either in terms of (global market) regulation (WTO, EU), crisis management (UN), or further industrial development opportunities (Bretton Woods). Let us now see how this approach to global governance plays out in the case of environmental problems.

Current approaches to (global) environmental problems

In this section, I will apply the preceding analysis to global environmental issues and problems. More precisely, I want to show how each type of global institution approaches environmental issues and problems, given its perspectives and strategic interests, and what one can expect from each such approach.

Let me first turn to the UN organizations, characterized as they are by a lack of funds and therefore a lack of relevance on the ground. Mainly because of their lack of funds, they have basically given up their developmental function. Only in the case of major crises are the UN organizations, including the general secretariat, capable of mobilizing funds, and then only for crisis management. The UN's new focus is therefore increasingly on "security," generally combining or rather confusing human and military security. The environment constitutes for the UN another such security threat, offering a justification for UN intervention or an opportunity to prove its usefulness. Such environmental security threats may include earthquakes, floods, or famines (due to environmental causes). In all of these cases, and especially when accompanied by a major human disaster, the UN can offer its new humanitarian security approach. It then tries to coordinate rapid intervention among its agencies and furthermore involves numerous local and global NGOs to assist it on the ground. Needless to say, this ex-post crisis management approach to environment security threats is quite the opposite of a precautionary, long-term, and future-oriented way of dealing with environmental issues and problems. However, *environmental crisis management*—as a response to the environment seen as

a threat to human security—has become and increasingly will b
can expect from the UN institutions when it comes to environr
all other) matters.

The second institutionalized approach to global problem s
lesces around the Bretton Woods institutions—in particular, t.
Bank—and involves most of today's relevant business actors. This includes
not only the major TNCs that are in direct contact with the World Bank,
but also global business organizations such as the World Business Council
for Sustainable Development (WBCSD), the International Chamber of
Commerce (ICC), and the World Business Forum (WBF), not to mention
the major donor countries of the United States, France, Germany, and
Japan. Even some of the UN organizations (e.g., the UN Environment
Programme and the UN Development Programme) try to integrate this
institutional arrangement—for example, around what came to be known as
the Global Environment Facility (GEF). The main characteristic of these
organizations is that they have money and clearly formulated strategic
interests. Not surprisingly, the Bretton Woods institutions have assumed the
UN's original development agenda and translated it into their own commercial logic. The gradual adoption and integration of the Rio process into
World Bank-led "sustainable development" may serve as a case in point. As
a result, environmental issues and problems have been redefined into further
opportunities of industrial development, investment, and overall economic
and financial growth. As part of their new "sustainable development"
agenda, the Bretton Woods organizations now actively support investments
into sustainable development, thus using environmental problem solving as
one more argument for further technological and economic development.

The environment, here, becomes not only an additional investment
opportunity, but also an opportunity for Northern TNCs and governments
to offset some of their environmental wrongdoings by means of investments
in the South (e.g., pollution credits). Finally, entirely new markets and even
industries are being created as a result of this market approach to solving
environmental problems (for example, the pollution-rights trading industry
and the certification industry). This market approach, which basically *turns
environmental problems into an additional opportunity for further and even
accelerated industrial development*, is being accompanied, actively supported, and legitimized by global environment and development NGOs,
such as the World Conservation Union (IUCN), the World Wide Fund for
Nature (WWF), or the Nature Conservancy. One can expect that this type
of institutionalized approach to environmental issues and problems will
further expand both conceptually and in practice. It has all of the major
actors behind it, including the nation-states whose logic this approach mat-
ches perfectly, and it actively legitimizes pursuit of the logic of industrial
development. Again, it goes without saying that this institutionalized
approach in no way solves or even addresses the underlying environmental
problems caused by industrial development. Rather, it probably sustains and

exacerbates these problems. In institutional terms, this approach is probably the most innovative: if the UN-led approach (above) and the WTO-led approach (below) are still mainly state-centric, that is, following government ordering (hierarchy, integration), the World Bank-led approach is essentially hybrid in nature, combining public, private, and Third Sector actors into quite innovative governance networks. From a new institutional economics point of view, such hybrids, in the age of globalization, are probably much more effective in promoting industrial development than government ordering (which was probably the more effective way of promoting industrial development immediately after the Industrial Revolution). The question remains, however, as to whether such hybrids would also be effective governance mechanisms to address the consequences of industrial development.

The third institutional approach coalesces around the World Trade Organization and related organizations. Grounded in the GATT, the role of the WTO has been to open up markets for competition, a process that has accelerated substantially because of the end of the Cold War. Increasingly, therefore, there is a call—by both critics of further liberalization and TNCs that have basically already achieved their goals—to re-regulate such deregulated global markets. In this effort, and because it lacks an explicit mandate in this matter, the WTO has to turn to other organizations, and thus also evolves, in new institutional economics terms, from government ordering (hierarchy, integration) to hybrids (networks). Here I refer in particular to those UN agencies that are also focusing on regulation, such as the World Intellectual Property Organization (WIPO) or the International Organization for Standardization (ISO), but also to multinational certifying business actors (for example, the inspection, certification, and verification company SGS). Again, the environment appears to be a major opportunity for such re-regulation, which otherwise is hard to justify on neo-liberal ideological grounds (Finger and Tamiotti, 1999). As such, *the environment becomes an opportunity to set globally valid trading standards*, often through private mechanisms, namely certificates (for example, ISO 14000 or FSC). The underlying objective of such environmental re-regulation is only accessorily environmental protection. Rather, the often unacknowledged objective is to cement the market power of those TNCs that have already been able to take advantage of global market opening, so as to prevent other firms, especially from developing countries, from entering these global markets, and of course to increase the power of the WTO and related organizations. Many NGOs are also able to take advantage of this evolution towards (privately led) global regulatory environmentalism, such as WWF. In other words, this third institutionalized approach to the environment fits perfectly into the previously identified trend of a regulatory state and new global regulatory institutions, as regulation is a means for nation-states and state-like institutions to adapt to globalization by keeping some power (e.g., enforcement of regulations) (for the case of Europe, see Ott, 2005). Needless to say, however, such (environmental and other) regulations do not have environmental protection as their main objective, but rather are the expression of lobbying efforts by actors who can derive competitive advantages from such regulation.

In this section I have presented the three currently dominant approaches to global collective problem solving, focusing in particular on what these approaches mean when it comes to environmental issues and problems. I have also discussed what one can expect from these approaches taken separately. Obviously, the three approaches obey and proceed from three totally different institutional logics—*environmental security* and corresponding crisis management, development opportunities and corresponding rhetoric of "*sustainable development*," and market regulation and corresponding environmental regulations. Thus, the environment is now simultaneously a *security threat*, a *development opportunity*, and a *case for re-regulation*. Following my organizational and institutional framework, the environment has now become an opportunity for UN organizations to justify their existence; for the World Bank and related organizations to further promote industrial development; and for national, regional, and global regulators and firms to establish their (market and political) power. In other words, there is today no coherent institutional approach to addressing global environmental problems, which stem from the pursuit of industrial development. Rather, all three approaches are complementary in that they all create new opportunities for further industrial development. The environmental regulation approach is complementary inasmuch as it offers market-regulatory solutions to those environmental problems that clearly result from a too-free market (e.g., CO_2 emissions). The environmental security approach is complementary inasmuch as it helps to give the illusion that, through crisis management, the worst effects of global environmental degradation can be mitigated.

Having identified these three now globally institutionalized approaches to environmental issues and problems, one can see the type of actions to which they are likely to lead. Indeed, these institutions are likely to promote and fund either purely technical and technocratic approaches to environmental issues and problems (e.g., regulatory approach, crisis management approach) or financial and economic approaches. This also means that environmental issues and problems that cannot be addressed by either of these approaches will fall in between the cracks and simply not be addressed. This is, as I have argued, the case for global environmental problems of a systemic nature, namely those that stem directly from the pursuit of industrial development such as resources depletion, global warming, the destruction of local livelihoods, biodiversity degradation, and more. Similarly, environmental issues and problems that do not have the nation-state as the relevant institutional entity will also fall into the cracks. These are typically problems that are either not limited to national boundaries (e.g., consumption, loss of cultural diversity) or which are so-called "global common problems" (e.g., ocean fisheries, Antarctica). As a matter of fact, most of today's global environmental problems of systemic proportion precisely fall in between these institutional cracks and will therefore not be addressed.

Which governance for sustainable development?

In institutional terms, one can clearly see an evolution from (state-centric) integrated and hierarchical approaches to hybrid approaches, parallel to globalization. However, at least at the global level, these hybrid forms of governance are shaped by the main global actors—namely, nation-states, TNCs, and inter-national organizations—whose strategic interests coalesce around the pursuit of further industrial development. This in turn raises the question of whether and how the global environmental crisis can indeed be addressed by such hybrid forms of global governance at all.

Indeed, the currently dominant institutional approaches to environmental (and all other forms of) global governance are clearly inadequate and unsustainable. First, they are inadequate and unsustainable on their own, as neither a security-oriented nor developmental nor regulatory approach by itself will contribute to solving environmental problems. Second, they are also unsustainable in combination, as the regulatory and security approaches are merely a legitimization for further industrial development, rather than an alternative to it. In other words, the currently institutionalized approaches to global environmental problem solving will not contribute to addressing the ever more pressing issues of the degradation of life support systems.

This chapter has identified the underlying institutional arrangements that command, among others, the ways by which the global environmental problems are, and will continue to be, "addressed." It has shown that there are three such co-existing and complementary institutional arrangements, each rooted in the militaristic-developmental nature of the nation-state, which aims above all at conquest, expansion, and control. Therefore, not surprisingly, all three institutional arrangements will be inadequate to understand, let alone address, the dynamics of industrial development. Worse, they actually contribute to legitimizing and furthering such unsustainable industrial development. In short, this new global institutional framework builds on the nation-state logic of militaristic industrial development, yet now instrumentalizes the nation-state by means of more hybrid forms of governance. In other words, and in the age of globalization, the nation-state and still quite state-centric yet more hybrid supra-national institutions are no alternative to this institutionalized logic, but rather a supporting and accompanying factor. It is unfortunate that most of the discussions about global environmental governance and institutions, including the various proposals to create a World Environmental Organization (Oberthür and Gehring, 2004), have never really problematized the organizational and institutional dimensions of such governance (Haas, 2004, Najam, Christopoulou, and Moomaw, 2004).

And even those who have argued against such an organization have done so from a political rather than institutional perspective (Najam, 2003).

The main purpose of this chapter was to highlight the *non-neutrality of the currently dominant actors and institutions* when it comes to addressing the global environmental crisis, in particular the non-neutrality of the nation-state and the newly emerging hybrid, yet still quite state-centric, global governance institutions. Elsewhere, we have used the concept of "institutional pollution" (Finger and Finger, 2003) to highlight the fact that institutions can be as destructive and detrimental to the planet as is industrial development and pollution itself. Although the purpose of this chapter was not to outline or even design alternative institutions, I hope I have contributed to becoming more realistic as to what can be expected from both the nation-state and the global governance institutions in the current and accelerating global environmental crisis. Obviously, such institutions and actors capable of addressing the global environmental crisis would have to be sought and designed below and beyond nation-states (Bookchin, 1982; Escobar, 1998). But this could only be done after becoming disillusioned with the nation-states' and inter-national institutions' roles in addressing the global environmental crisis.

Notes

1 See www.eolss.net
2 Technically speaking, as mentioned before the Bretton Woods organizations and the WTO are part of the United Nations. However, I will treat them separately here, given that, as I have argued, they pursue quite distinct objectives.

References

Abbott, K.W. and Snidal, D. (2001) "International Standards and International Governance," *Journal of European Public Policy* 8,3: 345–370.
Bookchin, M. (1982) *Ecology of Freedom: The Emergence and Dissolution of Hierarchy*, New York: Cheshire Books.
Cerny, P. (1990) *The Changing Architecture of Politics*, London: Sage.
Clark, W. and Munn, R.E. (eds.) (1986) *Sustainable Development of the Biosphere*, Laxenburg: International Institute for Applied Systems Analysis.
Clarke, R. (1971) *La Course à la Mort ou la Technocratie de la Guerre*, Paris: Seuil.
Commoner, B. (1966) *Science and Survival*, New York: Viking.
Coser, L. (1956) *The Functions of Social Conflict*, New York: The Free Press.
—— (1967) *Continuities in the Study of Social Conflict*, New York: The Free Press.
Cottrell, W. (1955) *Energy and Society: The Relation between Energy, Social Change, and Economic Development*, New York: McGraw-Hill.
Crozier, M. (1963) *Le Phénomène Bureaucratique*, Paris: Seuil.
Dijkzeul, D. and Beigbeder Y. (eds.) (2003) *Rethinking International Organizations: Pathology and Promise*, New York: Berghahn Books.
Escobar, A. (1998) "Whose Knowledge, whose Nature? Biodiversity, Conservation, and the Political Ecology of Social Movements," *Journal of Political Ecology* 5: 53–82.

Etzioni, A. (1964) *Modern Organizations*, Englewood-Cliffs: Prentice-Hall.

Finer, S.E. (1997) *The History of Government, Vols. I–III*, Cambridge: Cambridge University Press.

Finger, A. and Finger, M. (2003) "State versus Participation: Natural Resources Management in Europe," *International Institute for Environment and Development (IIED) / Institute for Development Studies (IDS) Institutionalising Participation Series*; French edition published 2004.

Finger, M. (2002) "The Instrumentalization of the State by Transnational Corporations: The Case of Public Services," in D. Fuchs and F. Kratochwil (eds.) *Transformative Change and Global Order*, London: LIT.

Finger, M. & J. Allouche (2002) *Water Privatisation: Transnational Corporations and the Re-Regulation of the Water Industry*, London: SPON Press.

Finger, M. and Tamiotti, L. (1999) "New Global Regulatory Mechanisms and the Environment: the Emerging Linkage Between the WTO and the ISO," *IDS (Institute for Development Studies) Bulletin* 3,3: 8–15.

Foster, J.B. (2002) *Ecology against Capitalism*, Washington: Monthly Review Press.

Galbraith, J.K. (1970) *How to Control the Military*, New York: NCLC.

Georgescu-Roegen, N. (1971) *The Entropy Law and the Economic Process*, Cambridge, MA: Harvard University Press.

Giddens, A (1985) *The Nation-state and Violence*, London: Polity Press.

—— (1990) *The Consequences of Modernity*, Stanford, CA: Stanford University Press.

Grinevald, J. (1975) "Science et Développement: Esquisse d'une approche socio-épistémologique," *Cahiers de l'IUED* 1: 31–97, Paris: PUF

Haas, P. (2004) "Addressing the Global Governance Deficit," *Global Environmental Politics* 4,4: 1–15.

Hall, C. (2004) "The Myth of Sustainable Development: Personal Reflections on Energy, its Relation to Neo-Classical Economics, and Stanley Jevons," *Journal of Energy Resources Technology* 126: 86–98.

Horkheimer, M. and Adorno, T. (1944) *Dialektik der Aufklärung*, New York: Social Studies Association.

Ietto-Gillies, G. (2005) *Transnational Corporations and International Production: Concepts, Theories, and Effects*, London: Edward Elgar.

Kessides, I. (2004) *Reforming Infrastructure: Privatization, Regulation, and Competition*, Oxford: Oxford University Press.

Kooiman, J. (2002) *Governing as Governance*, London: Sage.

Jensen, M.C. (2000) *A Theory of the Firm: Governance, Residual Claims, and Organizational Forms*, Cambridge, MA: Harvard University Press.

Laffont, J.-J. and Martimort, D. (2002) *The Theory of Incentives: The Principal-Agent Model*, Princeton, NJ: Princeton University Press.

Landes, D. (1969) *The Unbound Prometheus: Technological Change and Industrial Development in Western Europe from 1750 to the Present*, Cambridge: Cambridge University Press.

Majone, G. (ed.) (1996) *Regulating Europe*, London: Routledge.

McNeill, W. (1963) *The Rise of the West*, Chicago, IL: University of Chicago Press.

—— (1982) *The Pursuit of Power. Technology, Armed Force, and Society since 1000 AD*, Chicago, IL: University of Chicag Press.

Meinecke, F. (1957) *Die Idee der Staatsräson*, Munich: Oldenbourg Verlag.

Najam, A. (2003) "The Case against a New International Environmental Organization," *Global Governance* 9,3: 367–384.

Najam, A., Christopoulou, I., and Moomaw, W. (2004) "The Emergent 'System' of Global Environmental Governance," *Global Environmental Politics* 4,4: 23–35.

Noble, D. (1998) *The Religion of Technology. The Divinity of Man and the Spirit of Invention*, New York: Alfred Knopf.

Oberthür, S. and Gehring, T. (2004) "Reforming International Environmental Governance: An Institutionalist Critique of a Proposal for a World Environmental Organization," *International Environmental Agreements: Politics, Law, and Economics* 4: 359–381.

Ott, H. (2005) "The European Union: A Strategic Actor for Sustainable Global Governance," in A. Rechkemmer (ed.) *Towards an International Environmental Organization*, Baden-Baden: Nomos.

Polanyi, K. (1944) *The Great Transformation*, Boston, MA: Beacon Press.

Princen, T. and Finger, M. (1994) *Environmental NGOs in World Politics: Linking the Global and the Local*, London: Routledge.

Richter, H.-E. (1997) *Der Gotteskomplex*, Munich: Econ Verlag.

Rosenau, J. and Czempiel, E.-O. (eds.) (2000) *Governance without Government: Order and Change in World Politics*, Cambridge: Cambridge University Press.

Simon, H. (1945) *Administrative Behavior: a study of decision-making processes in administrative organizations*, New York: Simon and Schuster.

Speth, J.G. and Haas, P. (2006) *Global Environmental Governance*, London: Island Press.

Strange, S. (1996) *The Retreat of the State. The Diffusion of Power in the World Economy*, Cambridge: Cambridge University Press.

Tilly, C. (1990) *Coercion, Capital, and European States AD 990–1992*, London: Blackwell.

United Nations (UN) (1994) *Transnational Corporations: A Selected Bibliography*, New York: United Nations.

von Weizsäcker, E., Young, O., and Finger, M. (eds.) (2005) *The Limits to Privatization*, Report to the Club of Rome, London: Earthscan.

Weber, M. (1925) *Wirtschaft und Gesellschaft*, Tübingen: JCB Mohr.

White, L. (1967) "The Historical Roots of Our Ecological Crisis," *Science* 155: 1203–1207.

Williamson, O. (1973) "Markets and Hierarchies: Some Elementary Considerations," *American Economic Review* 63: 316–325.

—— (1996) *The Mechanisms of Governance*, Oxford: Oxford University Press.

World Bank (1997) *World Development Report 1997: The State in a Changing World*, Oxford: Oxford University Press.

Young, O. (1994) *International Governance. Protecting the Environment in a Stateless Society*, Ithaca, NY: Cornell University Press.

4 A global political economy of textiles

From the global to the local and back again

Gabriela Kütting

This chapter is concerned with an area of development-environment linkages that has not seen a process of institutionalization, whether in connection with the Rio–Johannesburg concern for sustainable development or otherwise. International institutions—including treaty-based accords, regulatory regimes, soft-law arrangements, and the programmatic activities of intergovernmental organizations—are undeniably important, and the study of actors and institutions are where the heart of political analysis lies. There is, nevertheless, a wide variety of environment-development challenges that do not neatly fit either the pattern of existing institutions or the tendency of most environment-development scholarship to focus its analysis on institutional case studies. This happens particularly with regard to global–local linkages; disconnected power relations of distant locales, whose political and economic regimes intermesh mostly in uneven ways, make it impossible to devise institutional frameworks that can address this layer of dislocated power spheres, and address the serious side effects of political and economic arrangements.

In this chapter, I will look at a case—textiles—that illustrates clearly why a focus away from institutions makes an important contribution to the study of international relations (IR) more generally. The global political economy of textiles is a classic example of the complex nature of power, equity, and environmental, social, politica,l and economic issues that interweave to form social reality at global and local levels. The case also suggests that local frameworks of governance can have a significant global impact and may provide alternatives to a global institutional framework of regulation and governance.

In exploring these global–local interactions, the equity dimension of North–South relations is at the forefront of this chapter. The connection between equity and the environmental dimensions of international relations is rarely made in conventional scholarship on these topics; the environment in IR or in global political economy studies is generally treated from a strictly scientific perspective or as a purely regulatory, or institutional, matter. Although there is a growing substantive literature on the rise of transnational actors and the changing architecture of the international system, this work has focused primarily on the changing nature of institutions in international relations rather than the equity dimension of North–South issues. There is also a body of research concerned with environmental justice (Martinez-Alier, 2002; Agyeman *et al.*, 2003), but the concept has not been fully translated into Global Environmental Politics literature and has only rarely been addressed from a global political economy perspective (notably by, for example, the editors of this book). This chapter makes a first attempt at bringing these dimensions out more forcefully through exploring the global–local linkages and socio-ecological ramifications of textile production and consumption. As this is a very wide and complex field, I will focus on cotton garments and not synthetic fibers.

The equity dimension is the best analytical tool for bringing local–global linkages into the debate. Social and environmental justice and equity are not part of the neoliberal institutional framework that has dominated the study of international institutional development. The neoliberal approach is concerned mainly with the political dynamics of forming and sustaining institutions and, therefore, tends to disregard cases where institutions have not been formed.

A useful alternative for bringing global–local linkages into the debate is to use a commodity-chain approach. One advantage of the commodity-chain approach is that it highlights power relations within the garment sector, by disaggregating the sector into the various nodes of production and consumption that constitute it. Another advantage is that it highlights environmental problems and social relations that run up and down the chain as well as those that are specific to particular nodes. This brings local–global linkages, and the possibilities for and limits of action on different social scales, into sharper focus. This will be achieved by giving a historical overview in order to contextualize the global dimension of today's situation, followed by a discussion of both the production and consumption cycles.

Historical overview

The history of cotton and textiles is inextricably linked to the history of modern capitalism. Clothing and garments are signs of civilization and all societies have been engaged in some form of garment production, be it weaving or the preparation of bear hides. In some cases, these endeavors may be called industries, while in others they may have taken place at the household level. A dramatic rise in the production and consumption of garments took place after 1750 with the emergence of a modern fashion industry in the industrialized countries. Between 1760 and 1850, the amount of unprocessed cotton transformed in the British textile economy increased from £2 to £366 million (Braudel, 1993: 382). The scope of this fashion and consumer society has increased steadily since that time, dramatically picking up in speed in the 1970s. However, this is not a uniform global phenomenon. In many non-western societies, fashions are longer lasting and the turnover rates of garments are much slower as a consequence. Despite such variations, textile production transformed the economic landscapes in both developing and industrialized countries and encapsulated all the socio-economic changes of the past few centuries in a nutshell: colonialism, technological innovation, scientism, capital accumulation, and the rise of environmental degradation. This section will give a brief overview of colonial practices in order to provide a basis for comparison with contemporary global practices and their claim for uniqueness.

The historical relationship between core and periphery in the global political economy of cotton is illustrated well by Isaacman and Roberts in the case of Africa:

> European efforts to promote African cotton production have a long history. It is a history that is intimately connected to the development and maturation of the world economy in the same period. Indeed, European interest in African cotton waxed and waned in direct relationship to the complex set of factors integral to the making of the world economy in the nineteenth and twentieth centuries, to the changing place of European nation states in that system, and to the changing political economies of European nation states. The cotton textile industry was a central consumer production sector in all of the European nations that scrambled to control African territories in the late nineteenth century. Not surprisingly, cotton held a primary place in European colonial agricultural policies throughout Africa ... European efforts to promote cotton production in Africa were linked to the development of industrial capitalism and to imperfections in the world supply of raw materials.
>
> (1995: 1)

Colonial attempts to establish an African supply network of cotton were only partially successful and other world regions became more prominent cotton producers, notably the United States (after it had recovered from the boll weevil plague) and Asia. After 1945, colonial officials realized that for cotton production to be successful in Africa, prices had to be competitive for farmers and cotton needed to fetch a price as good as or better than that of other crops (Isaacman and Roberts, 1995: 11). In response to this wisdom and the numerous food crises, Africa tended to produce largely for regional consumption up to the mid-1990s. The United States and many Asian countries, including China, India, and Pakistan, became the largest postwar cotton producers.

The historical context of cotton production shows that with the rise of colonialism and the ensuing social relations, technological innovation, and increases in world trade were evermore directed at ensuring the maximum supply and efficiency at minimum price for the colonizing countries. Thus cotton and colonialism are intrinsically linked in the experience of many developing countries. The use of African land for European cotton mill supplies was not an unproblematic one, however, as experiences of unrest and food shortages due to the displacement of food production show. Although African farmers were bound into global production and power structures, their ways of resistance to the cotton regime were manifold and influenced colonial cotton policy—for example, through reluctant, unmotivated labor and the secret use of land for groundnut production. The modern situation of cotton as a cash crop to pay off debt can in many ways be compared to the colonial situation in terms of global production and power structures. Thus, the fact that cotton has emerged as a major cash crop in West Africa is both an undeniable consequence of the colonial experience and tends to perpetuate colonial-era power relations between the region and outside forces.

From an environmental perspective, the consequences of the colonial period are not documented. However, the existence of food shortages shows that there was a land-use conflict. Today, the global nature of the food economy makes land-use conflicts less central to food shortages, but this does not mean that pressures on the land are less likely to happen. In fact, the biggest environmental challenge in cotton agriculture is the use of intensive farming methods and the excessive use of fertilisers, insecticides, and pesticides. Although these problems are global in the sense that they affect all cotton-growing regions, the nature of the resulting environmental problems makes it difficult or impossible to regulate these problems at the regional or global level. Because the specific manifestations of these problems are felt locally, they are typically perceived to be problems to be addressed at the grass-roots level. This means that their regulation is meant to take place at the local level, for example through farmer union education campaigns, although the same problems are reproduced all over the world.

In addition, environmental problems are intrinsically related to issues such as access to livelihood resources and the distribution of both economic and ecological costs and benefits. These dimensions rarely find their way into institutional frameworks, as they are issues of political ecology and unequal power relations that are not traditionally at the forefront of the concerns of the actors with power to shape international regulatory regimes. Thus, it is the nature of the global economy rather than simply the nature of the environmental problems involved with cotton agriculture that demonstrate most clearly the full scope of the sustainability challenges associated with the production and consumption of cotton. Moreover, although this global dimension has existed since colonial times, different ownership patterns and the emergence of a global institutionalized economic framework have led to significant differences between the colonial and contemporary organization of the political economy of cotton. These dimensions will be explored in more detail in the next two sections, on production and on consumption.

The cycle of production

Today, cotton is grown in over 80 countries under a variety of social and geographical conditions (UNCTAD, 1996). The five largest cotton producers are China, the United States, India, Pakistan, and Kazakhstan while the biggest per-capita garment consumers are located in the United States, Switzerland, and Germany. Although the United States is the world's second largest cotton producer, the majority of cotton growers are located in developing countries. Ownership patterns vary from large corporate plantations to small-scale farming. The textile industry is one of the most important industries globally with 15 million jobs depending on it both in developed and developing countries, as well as a further 8 million in the clothing sector (Dicken, 1992: 234). The cotton sector of the textile industry still constitutes about 50 percent of world textile needs although synthetics are catching up rapidly (Pesticides Trust, 1990). This trend is fashion-dependent and cyclical. The textile industry is also one of the world's most environmentally degrading industries. Nearly a quarter of the world's pesticides and insecticides are used in cotton farming and the range of chemicals used to treat and dye fabrics is legendary. Thus, both production and processing stages in the global cotton commodity chain have profound consequences for water, air, soil, and human health. These problems are addressed through pesticide regulation such as the Protocol on persistent organic pollutants rather than through international regulation for particular crops or production processes.

The last few decades have seen drastic changes in production methods and trade in this sector and the rise of developing countries as major producers. However, world trade is still dominated by developed states' output (Dicken, 1992: 239). Cotton crops are bought by cotton commodity traders who operate in a largely oligarchic market (Clairmonte and Cavanagh, 1981; Dicken, 1992). These commodity traders sell the raw material to the textile industry, which processes it into yarn and then cloth. A variety of large and small companies operate in the textile sector. A large, concentrated market exists at the next stage of the textile commodity chain, when the textiles are processed into garments (about 50 percent of textiles become garments) (Dicken, 1992: 234). Concentration is also high at the end of the chain: The largest share of the cotton crop ends up in the developed world's malls and High Streets, which are dominated by relatively few large retailers in most countries.

Policies of the World Bank and International Monetary Fund (IMF) encourage the growing of cash crops for world markets in order to alleviate the problems of the debt crisis in developing countries. At the same time, however, there is resistance to opening up developed-country markets for textiles. As Banuri argues:

> Because of shifting comparative advantage, there has been a rapid expansion of the textile industry in the South, especially among cotton growing countries. Textile production has traditionally been the first industrial sector of many developing countries and has paved the way for broad scale industrialization and economic expansion.

[A] stylized fact of the market for cotton and cotton products is the existence of special trade barriers against southern industrial products. Textiles are a labor-intensive industry and provide a comparative advantage to southern producers. However, the shift of the industry to the South has been slowed down, and the interests of traditional northern manufacturers protected under various unilateral, bilateral and multilateral agreements.

(1998: 7)

I will further emphasize this point by outlining the existing political framework for the trade-related aspects of the global cotton chain. This global production process was, until recently, regulated by the Multi-Fiber Agreement (MFA), a system of quotas adopted in 1974 that was phased out at the end of 2004. Textile trade has now been incorporated into the framework of the General Agreement on Tariffs and Trade (GATT) and the World trade Organization (WTO). However, this type of international regulation is solely concerned with barriers to trade, tariffs, and quotas and their abolition. There are a multitude of studies of the MFA and power relations in the textile trade (Schott, 1998; Yang, 1994; Hale, 2002). It is particularly noteworthy that the textile industry has until recently been excluded from the trade liberalization moves of the postwar period and is one of the most heavily regulated trade areas which imposes hefty trade restrictions on developing countries. The studies on trade regulation through the MFA provide insightful analyses of the trade aspect of the textile industry and on the discourse of free trade in general, but they ignore the environmental as well as the social aspects relating to the global political textile economy. The same problem can be identified in the commodity trade field relating to, in this case, cotton. The world cotton market is distorted by cotton subsidies despite a commitment to free trade though the multilateral development agencies (Kütting, 2003).

Harrison (2001) summarizes the situation by showing that the IMF and the World Bank effectively make economic policy in Africa in general, thus also influencing cash-crop policy decisions. However, textile issues are of minor relevance to many least developed countries, such as in West Africa, as the textile industry plays no important role in these countries' export figures despite many tariff exemptions (Mshomba, 2000). This is of course not so in the case of cash crops.

In the absence of international regulation, attempts to mobilize against the problems in the cotton chain have largely been initiated by civil society. These efforts have thus far largely focused on introducing codes of conduct for social rather than environmental standards. The large retailers have been singled out for engagement by the social movements in, for example, Great Britain, although social movements have taken a more confrontational approach in the United States with the anti-sweatshop campaigns against, for example, the Gap and Nike. It remains unclear how interested the clothing multinationals are in introducing environmental standards or codes of conduct in the garment sector and how effective an approach based on voluntary codes of conduct can be. However, the focus of the new social movements on clothing multinationals shows quite clearly that there are strong linkages between the local and the global and that some locals have more influence over the global than others. It also shows that the focus of societally based regulatory efforts is on production and that the role of consumption in this economic activity and its attendant socio-ecological effects tends to be marginalized.

The social side of production

The social and working conditions of textile and garment manufacturing in developing countries, particularly in the economic exporting zones (EEZ) in Southeast Asia, have often been described as one of the most visible signs of globalization. In the past 20 years, profound changes have taken place in the geographical location of garment production as an aspect of the post-Fordist mode of production, which has led to the outsourcing of production to low-wage countries, particularly in South East Asia and Latin America. Industrialized states are still garment producers; however, their efforts are concentrated in niche markets or at the upper end of the garment market. For example, designer products, high quality merchandise, and specialist products are still produced in industrialized countries. However, the lower end of the market, and many high-fashion items depending on just-in-time manufacturing, have indeed been relocated to developing countries, where scandalous working conditions have often grabbed the headline news (Green and Jones, 1998).

There are several noteworthy social aspects to this kind of production practice. First, there are the actual working conditions. Workers often earn a minimum wage that is not a living wage. As production takes place in countries for which low wage rates are the main advantage in the global market, this competitive advantage has to be exploited to the fullest extent possible. If the wage structure gets revised, other countries may offer cheaper labor and the employment opportunity may go another way (Green and Jones, 1998). This is common practice and therefore the interplay between state, company, and worker is a difficult and fraught one. The developing state has to argue that low-wage labor is better than no work at all for its citizens and, furthermore, that the prevailing local wage is usually no higher than the one offered by the international textile company. Thus the criticism leveled against multinational corporations (MNCs) that they exploit low wage countries is a concern not shared by developing countries. Rather, they see this as their competitive advantage. The worker cannot survive on the wages offered but without these jobs, the situation would be even worse. The winner all round is the company, which gets its products manufactured with the cheapest labor cost. In the contemporary world of substantial capital mobility, it can play off one state against the next in getting the best deal. However, some writers argue that there is no empirical evidence for the lowering of labor standards and that conditions for workers have actually improved under globalization (Drezner, 2001: 66). This may be true in some sectors but certainly the existence of below living wage standards has been used to advantage in the global economy at the expense of jobs that were paying living wages or were subject to labor standards.

A second point of grievance is the conditions under which textile production takes place. The term sweatshop, conjuring up conditions from another era, is used to describe what is going on in garment factories, particularly in South East Asia and Latin America but often also in industrialized states such as the United States or the United Kingdom. In particular, forced overtime, no breaks, child labor, and inhumane work environments with no windows and no circulation are the main issues. These conditions have been documented elsewhere in much detail (Ross, 1997).

The response to these catastrophic conditions in the apparel sector has of course been collective organization through unionization. However, many factories have banned unions in order to keep up Victorian conditions. Here the fear goes in two directions. On the one hand, owners fear the demands of a collectivized work force and the cut in profits that will result from a work force with enhanced labor rights. On the other hand, a collectivized work force cannot remain competitive at the international level; in such a fast-moving environment, a loss of profitability and price competitiveness will more than likely lead to the closure of the factory and thus to the loss of the jobs involved.

This point is not just an idle threat of factory owners. Production mostly takes place in economic export processing zones that are exempt from international import and export restrictions. These zones are incentive areas for attracting foreign investment and thus highly competitive. In fact, in the garment industry, production facilities used by the large multinationals usually change every three months or so, always in search of the cheapest labor force.

The international and global aspects of the organization of garment production show quite clearly that international solutions are required for the problems listed above. National legislation is not an answer, as the political economy of textiles is currently structured in such a way as to play off the needs for foreign investment by the various developing countries involved in garment production. Therefore, there is a race to the bottom in terms of wages, workers' rights, and environment regulations, improvements in which interfere with price competitiveness.

This problem has been recognized more by industrialized states than developing ones. In the true spirit of "it is better to be exploited than not to be exploited at all," the exploitation of work forces is not a primary concern of developing countries' governments, as they know that an unemployed work force would be even worse. The resistance at Seattle in 1999 during the infamous WTO ministerial round by developing countries to global labor and environmental standards has to be seen in this light. Global standards would take away their competitive advantage of offering the cheapest (and by implication most exploited) labor.

So, ironically, there is a tacit alliance between clothing manufacturers exploiting the competition for garment production facilities and developing countries suffering from the abuse of the situation but still being dependent on this type of investment. This makes the tackling of these problems particularly difficult and it also raises questions of agency and legitimacy. Since many developing countries are clearly against global standards, who will then speak out for the plight of the exploited labor force? Further, those actors who have taken on this cause, such as non-governmental organizations (NGOs) and even some consumers, work very hard to improve the situation through tactics such as the awakening of corporate responsibility. Actors such as the Clean Clothes Campaign, World Economy, Ecology and Development (WEED), and anti-sweatshop campaigns in the United States have put the issue on the agenda through campaigns, investigative research, and policy-directed action. However, there is reluctance in certain quarters of the labor force in developing countries to accept a campaign for change as it is felt that this would erode the cheap-labor advantage in the global economy and thus be counter-productive. This, in turn, leads to questions about the legitimacy of representation on this issue.

The environment, production and institutional frameworks

Continuing the contextualization of the political economy of textiles, this section looks at the international/global political economy of textiles in relation to the environment, including a discussion of international efforts to regulate environmental problems relating to textile production.

In terms of cotton agriculture, the intensification of agricultural production methods has resulted in a worldwide increase in pesticide use. The adverse effects of pesticides on humans and the environment are several: Excessive or inappropriate use leads to pesticide poisoning with severe health effects such as allergies, liver and kidney damage, cancer, or male sterility (Sanbon and Cole, 2004; Keifer, 1997). Local pesticide residues affect air and water quality. Due to their mobility in air and water, pesticides also affect ecosystems and people far removed from the site of application. The presence of pesticides in breastfeeding mothers' milk is a case in point. As Murray summarizes with reference to Central America:

> Pesticides contributed mightily to the increase in wealth and productivity in Central America, but so too did they contribute to the increase in misery in the region. Hidden within the ecological transformations that allowed cotton farming to thrive was an ecological crisis that played a

significant role in the demise of the cotton sector. Degraded land and water, escalating pest problems, resurgence of malaria and other diseases, all combined with high rates of pesticide poisoning to seriously affect the well-being of rural society in the cotton-growing region.

(1994: 54)

About 11 percent of global pesticide sales and 24 percent of insecticides can be attributed to cotton production (Myers and Stolton, 1999). The World Bank (Eisa *et al.* 1994) cites price factors and lack of local knowledge or the misinformation of farmers as the main factors leading to excessive or inappropriate pesticide use. Murray and Taylor (2000), for example, show quite conclusively that campaigns for the safe use of pesticides (paid for and run by the pesticide industries) are clearly constructed around the idea that persistent and high-level pesticide use are necessary and desirable, thus shaping the problem in a particularly limiting framework. Although there are multilateral agreements phasing out particular pollutants, the general use of pesticides is regulated at the local level, if at all.

The processing of cotton into garments is also riddled with environmental problems. The cotton is treated with various chemicals to facilitate the processing stage and the bleaching and dyeing of the cloth or garment also leads to exposure (routine in the textile dyeing industry) to carcinogenic substances by both product and worker (Michaelowa and Michaelowa, 1996: 52).

Another environmental problem associated with textile/cotton production, both in agriculture and industry, is water pollution. Cotton is a particularly water-intensive crop, meaning that plantations may require higher rates of irrigation than water available in the region. Further down in the production chain, during the processing and dyeing stage, water will be discharged into rivers or streams and thus also affect drinking water and freshwater ecosystems. In many ways, the environmental problems associated with garments are worst at the individual household level; the production process may be only a relatively small part of the full environmental burden. As Fletcher *et al.* argue:

The use stage [of textiles] has major environmental impacts. A lifecycle study by the American Fiber Manufacturers Association of a synthetic fiber blouse showed that as much as 88 percent of atmospheric emissions, 86 percent of energy and 68 percent of solid waste attributable to the total textile lifecycle are massed during washing and drying. These results, however, should be placed in context. Only garments were studied and results could be significantly affected by a change in laundering habits. If the garment is washed at cold temperatures and dried on a line, total energy consumption is reduced by 78 percent and the bulk of the environmental impacts would be in production rather than in use.

(Fletcher *et al.*, 1999: 46)

This point again raises issues about the analytical distinction between production and consumption in the global political economy and the need for the inclusion of consumption as a field of study. It also shows that some activities cannot be regulated, as they are social practices not easily accessible to regulation. For example, people's laundry habits cannot be subjected to legal patterns regardless of their environmental impact. They can only be influenced through wastewater charges, energy taxes, technology standards, and the like. Although the boundary between public and private will vary over time and across different societies, the commodity chain perspective and a consumption-centered focus highlight that many important sources of environmental burden lie beyond the easy reach of production-centered regulations.

The global cotton/textile chain in general has not been controlled or regulated at the international or global level. However, some national or regional regulations have an effect on the global textile chain. For example, Banuri reports that the German government has outlawed garments containing azo dyes (1998: III/5). This means that a flouting of this legislation may lead to shipments being burnt at the manufacturer's expense. Other European states have followed suit with similar legislation. Since European consumers make up a significant share of global textile consumption, such regional legislation obviously has an impact on production patterns elsewhere. Although these measures have had limited success, the German ban on azo dyes still has implications for the nature of the textile trade and the working of the international political economy because of the market clout of such a measure when applied to a major national market. Therefore, this strategy has at least some success and makes a case for unilateral action.

There are no specific attempts to regulate pesticide use in the garment sector at the international level. In the food sector, the Food and Agricultural Organization (FAO) and the World Health Organization (WHO) have established the Codex Alimentarius Commission, which has commented on and recommended "safe" pesticide levels since 1966. However, the Codex's primary goal is to harmonize legislation between different states rather than to introduce global health and safety or environmental regulations. In addition, it deals only with food-related agricultural problems. There are other problems relating to this organization, including its rather cozy industry–government relations, which cannot be discussed here (Sklair, 2002: 144). A major problem with this organization and other FAO and OECD working groups on pesticides is that the chemical industry is heavily represented in these working groups and has a strong influence in shaping pesticide control policy. This approach, therefore, provides a limited scope for the introduction of environmental concerns into an economic framework.

Pesticides are an issue in Agenda 21 of the 1992 UN Conference on Environment and Development. Agenda 21 called for the reduction of pesticide use and for integrated pest management (chapter 21, point 45). However, the term "integrated pest management" can be interpreted as ranging from conventional pest management to ecological farming methods. Although Agenda 21 does not specifically mention pesticides in textile production, it refers to agricultural production in general rather than a narrower focus on food.

Another approach to controlling the environmental consequences of the global textile trade has been through eco-labeling. This policy has been particularly popular in Europe. It implies that a product undergoes certain tests stipulated by the national regulatory authority or another named institution; if the product fulfils these conditions, it will be awarded the specific eco-label. The best-known eco-label is the Blue Angel, which originated in Germany in 1977 and has since spread widely in Europe. Eco-labeling has been criticized as a strictly voluntary approach and because the criteria used for awarding the label have been controversial. In the textile sector, eco-labeling has been limited to certifying azo-dye-free products or products that do not contain certain named chemicals (but are not chemical-free). Therefore, this approach is limited and has not had a major impact on the global textile chain. Even supra-national voluntary codes have been of limited effect unless consumers take up their message in a big way. This has not been the case with eco-labeled textiles, which are not widely available, have received relatively little media attention, and are not used as a competitive tool by most textile manufacturers.

An analysis of these existing forms of regulation or the lack of them suggests that in some areas of the textile chain a global regulatory "regime" is not necessarily essential and would not effectively deal with the problems associated. The case of azo dyes shows that regional regulatory efforts or unilateral action by major markets can have an impact on the global textile chain. However, in the case of pesticide pollution, such a scheme would not work. In this case a state-based regulatory approach does not seem very promising, due to the globally dispersed nature of production and use. Therefore, different problems in the cotton/textiles/garment chain require different solutions.

The cycle of consumption

Consumption is a culturally as well as economically informed activity and the socio-cultural side has been under-represented in political economy accounts. Featherstone (1991) distinguishes among three main perspectives on consumer culture. First, consumer culture has developed alongside the expansion of capitalist commodity production, which has provided the opportunity for accumulating vast amounts of consumer goods and has made this hoarding desirable. Second, consumption is used as a way of asserting social bonds or distinctions, or affirming or transcending one's class status. Third, the emotional pleasures of consumption and the concept of aestheticism associated with it have a powerful hold on industrial society, or even on what can loosely be termed human nature. The latter two points can also be seen in conjunction with the ever-rising importance of symbols in the legitimation of society. When these three perspectives are applied to the consumption of textiles, or specifically garments in the fashion industry, it can be observed how the concept of consumption has changed over time. The fashion revolution starting in the 1960s has affected both producers and consumers by fundamentally changing consumers' attitudes towards the volume and type of clothes they wear throughout the year and by exponentially increasing the demand for natural and synthetic fibers. The annual average new garment consumption in Europe is around 10 kg per capita.

Discussions on the environmental consequences of textile production rarely focus on consumption. There are debates on the comparative sustainability of natural versus synthetic fibers, the viability of organic cotton, or the possibility of hemp as a major fabric, but the volume and nature of consumption is not a part of this discourse. In addition, the practice of second-hand clothing markets and the impact of the "dumping" of second-hand clothing on local markets in developing countries will be discussed in detail here, highlighting how consumptive practices go hand in hand with production patterns in determining the social and environmental consequences of the textile chain.

The concept of consumption has changed over time. As recently as the 1950s, consumers in Northern industrialized states usually possessed only one good suit or dress, which was supposed to last for many years and was not subjected to the fierce fashion dictates known in the 1990s and early twenty-first century. One reason for increasing consumption is the steadily declining price of clothing, which obviously provides the opportunity for consuming more. Second, clothes are not just something we put on to keep warm or to express our feelings for a certain social occasion; they make a statement about our values and our class status or the class status to which we aspire. Clothes have become not only image statements but primary indicators of a person's personality. Third, the ever-changing fashions require that our wardrobes be updated continuously to fit in with the aesthetic requirements of the professional or social fields in which we interact.

Naomi Klein takes this argument even further in her book about branding:

> The scaling-up of the logo's role has been so dramatic that it has become a change in substance. Over the past decade and a half, logos have grown so dominant that they have essentially transformed the clothing on which they appear into empty carriers for the brands they represent. The metaphorical alligator, in other words, has risen up and swallowed the literal shirt.
>
> ... Advertising and sponsorship have always been about using imagery to equate products with positive cultural or social experiences. What makes nineties-style branding different is that it increasingly seeks to take these associations out of the representational realm and make them a lived reality.
>
> (Klein, 2000: 28–29)

Thus fashion, and clothing as a substantial part of it, has a profound impact on the consumption patterns of the consuming elites. This fashion revolution, starting in the 1960s, has affected both producers and consumers by fundamentally changing consumers' attitudes towards the volume and type of clothes they wear throughout the year and by exponentially increasing the demand for natural and synthetic fibers. Fashion is described as a post-Fordist industry (Miles, 1998: 94) that is highly flexible and responsive to consumer demand. Thus, fashion is seen as consumer- rather than producer-driven, supposedly giving the consumer more input into a previously producer-dominated product chain. This is not always the case, however. Although certain logos fall from grace rather suddenly and are thus dependent on the consumer's whims, the political economy of fashion in many ways effectively steers demand and determines consumption patterns through advertising, use of media, and personality cults around movie stars or other fashion icons. This leads to questions about power relations in the fashion industry. First, power in the fashion industry is concentrated in the hands of relatively few large retailers who have effectively ousted or radically reduced the market share of smaller manufacturers (Miles, 1998: 95). Second, as Miles argues,

> In effect, the fashion industry is not as flexible as it might seem on the surface. It would be naïve to contest the idea that changes have taken place in the economy. Common sense tells us that there are more products on the market. But there could equally be an argument for suggesting that such choice is largely illusory. There may well be hundreds of different versions of the classic pair of jeans but essentially each of those jeans offers the consumer the same thing. The choice that is available is not only unnecessary but barely constitutes a choice in the first place because it so often amounts to little more than a very slight variation on a mass produced theme. In effect, consumer choice in the realm of fashion is inherently artificial.
>
> (1998: 95)

Third, and intrinsically related to the previous point, choice for the consumer is inherently limited to choice within a particular fashion paradigm, that is what products are considered to be in vogue in any particular season. A consumer will find it impossible to purchase a garment that does not conform to the standards of what is considered fashionable during that season. Therefore consumers may have increased choice and influence on the production process but this choice only exists within certain clearly delineated boundaries—the premise on which neoliberal ideology is based. Effective advertising and the social standing of appropriate clothing intrinsically link the participation in the fashion dictate to social success, thus giving enormous social and economic power to the multinational clothing retailers. Rather than consumers dictating to the fashion industry, the momentum works largely the other way around. Consumer power mainly lies in the choice not to buy or to buy selectively. Occasionally it happens that the consumer eschews certain fashions and the producer or retailer is not able to sell them. So the consumer's influence on the production process lies mainly in the ability to reject what is on offer rather than to influence production in the first place (although, of course, rejection of certain types of fashion will lead to the producers taking these rejections into consideration for the next season). In addition, a large part of clothing fashion production is based on the just-in-time method which means that consumer responses can be accounted for even in the same season. Given the substantial advertising budgets that have been used to persuade consumers to keep up their consumption habits, it becomes clear that the structural power of consumers is being suppressed.

This emerging pattern of spiraling consumption draws after it spiraling production to feed consumer demand (but with the producers more or less guiding what is being demanded). This is where the environmental angle on consumption is particularly important. Again, the consumer is removed or alienated from the production process and also from the disposal process of the clothes consumed. Most consumers are unaware of the dramatic social and environmental consequences of the production process of their clothes and fail to respond dramatically when malpractices are occasionally highlighted. However, although environmental degradation is clearly found in the production process, it would be limiting to find the solutions to this form of environmental degradation solely in the production process—as many globalization critics do when they challenge the nature of production in the global economy but not the volume and character of demand that justifies it. In addition, the problem is typically constructed as one of economic organization, which has to be solved at the macro-level alone. The role of consumption and the "collusion" of the consumer in all this is a subject that tends to be ignored by both policy-makers (for obvious reasons) but also civil society.

The existence of sweatshops as a sign of the globalization era and the role of clothing multinationals has been the focus of many activist campaigns, press campaigns, television documentaries, and consumer boycotts. However, the nature of the fashion economy is rarely an issue in these reports or campaigns. Rather, the analytical framework of the problem remains restricted to the relationship between manufacturer and sweatshop worker, the call for the recognition of labor unions and the abolition of debt for developing countries so that they can introduce a fairer wage policy. These debates are surely timely and address important issues, yet they neglect the structure of the system itself.

There is also a social and cultural dimension to this argument. Fashion is not only determined by the industrialized countries but this social and cultural dominance is further reinforced by spreading this fashion globally through cultural leadership and hand-me-downs, and by perpetuating the position of the "poor relative" recipient. To explain this further, there are usually two types of fashion or dress styles in many developing countries, western and local dress. Through the destruction of or competition for local industries and the relative price competitiveness and popularity of the second-hand clothing market, a market for western goods is created and the local product undermined (Hansen, 1999). This is globalization in a different sense than the one put forward by the cultural globalization writers. The structural origins of cultural homogenization are not a move towards a global village but rather the economics of the political economy of textiles.

Furthermore, this second-hand clothing market symbolizes the relative positions of developed and developing world in the global political economy. The developing countries supply raw materials and cheap labor for assembly; the developed countries consume at low prices and then dispose of the garments in order to buy more products at cheap prices in the latest fashion. The disposed garments are then used either by the lowest income groups in developed nations or back in developing countries, where the second-hand clothing market undermines local industries that would be a step away from the dependent position of developing countries in the world economy. Thus the cycle is closed and the relative positions in the world economy are reinforced.

The textile and garment sector provides one of the clearest illustrations of the trend of western consumption and southern production. The main reason for this is the importance of fashion as a primary vehicle of advanced capitalism. This is one dimension of capitalism that is under-researched and neglected, mainly because most research in this field is either economically determinist or culturally determinist but rarely takes account of both.

One extreme illustration of this point is the culture of branding as described in detail in Klein's *No Logo* (2000). Branding is an advertising gimmick that leads to more conspicuous consumption and to the determination of one's personality through the brands one consumes. Brands become lifestyles. The most famous examples of this type of branding are the cases of Nike and the Gap, which have been widely quoted (Bernstein, 2003; Holt, 2002). However, branding goes through all layers of society and is not just a middle-class phenomenon. Even ethical consumption often takes place through branded products, with Patagonia replacing Nike or Ecover replacing Lever Sunlicht. Branding also absolves the consumer from the necessity to think.

Once the consumer has chosen what sort of image s/he would like to project, they only need to shop in the right places. Thus, slowly, consumers are alienated from the ability to think and judge for themselves what constitutes good taste or common sense. By projecting and selling an image, a brand can now create all sorts of behavioral norms. For example, the ever-increasing turnaround of fashions and the need to keep up with them as well as the increasing lack of quality of garments are phenomena that are not questioned by consumers and are fully accepted as entirely normal and even desirable. Although these are producer-led trends, they need the full cooperation of the consumer in order to carry off trends such as branding and fashion. These trends play on the insecurities of human beings to be an acceptable member of their chosen group, to fit in while still being individualistic and competitive. They also buy heavily into the beauty myth, selling an image of beauty that again is fashion-dependent and demands an aestheticism in a beauty-addicted society. Thus the consumer is an integral part of the machinery of garment production as one of the main beauty and style industries.

Many social movements have realized the potential of consumer power and the intrinsic complicity of the consumer in the practices of the global political economy. They have called for more openness about the production processes and more input into the policy-making processes. However, they have rarely called into question the nature of consumption per se unless they come from an environmental perspective. Even church groups have neglected to highlight the relationship between northern consumption and southern production in ethical terms. Rather, most civil society involvement in this field has concentrated on the conditions of production in developing countries in the textile sector. This neglects the understanding that the environmental side of textile consumption manifests itself through the unequal distribution of consumptive power as well as the disproportionate amount of environmental side effects in the developing world as compared to the disproportionate enjoyment of garment consumption in the North.

Conclusion

The study of international environmental politics has focused overwhelmingly on the creation of environmental governance institutions, primarily through treaties, soft law, and interstate bargaining. This approach goes to the heart of the discipline of political science by studying the relationship between structure and agency as well as actor behavior and decision-making. However, it cannot tell us in detail how problems in disenfranchised areas and moral issues of international equity can be addressed with the current analytical frameworks. This chapter does not suggest any political tools to do so, but has sought to provide an illustration of what analytical details are missed by starting off with a traditional actor-centric framework. Thus this chapter has been concerned with highlighting linkages between previously unrelated issue areas, using the example of cotton agriculture and the textile industry. This method of exploring linkages demonstrates that the narrow parameters of environmental institutions capture only a partial glimpse of the intricate network of social, political, and economic dimensions that inform decisions on sustainability. Sustainability in the twenty-first century goes very much beyond the traditional frameworks of the earlier phases of environmental policy-making and requires a broader, more fully integrated policy approach that takes on board the complex interplay between economic and environmental as well as social decision-making.

The alternative approach presented here, focusing on local–global linkages, illustrates that an exploration of a particular commodity and its production-consumption chain offers multiple starting points for action that may not fall under traditional institutional responses but nevertheless offer promising solutions, both as an academic study and in practical and policy terms.

References

Agyeman, Julian, Bullard, Robert, and Evans, Bob (eds.) (2003) *Just Sustainabilities: Development in an Unequal World*, Cambridge, MA: MIT Press.

Banuri, T. (1998) *Global product chains: northern consumers, southern producers and sustainability—cotton and textiles in Pakistan*, prepared for United Nations Environment Programme.

Bernstein, D. (2003) "Corporate Branding—Back to Basics," *European Journal of Marketing* 37,7–8: 1133–1141.

Braudel, Ferdinand (1993) *A History of Civilizations*, London: Penguin.

Clairmonte, F. and Cavanagh, J. (1981) *The World in Their Web: Dynamics of Textile Multinationals*, London: Zed Books.

Dicken, Peter (1992) *Global Shift: The Internationalisation of Economic Activity*, London: Paul Chapman Publishing. Second edition.

Drezner, David (2001) "Globalization and Policy Convergence," *International Studies Review* 3,1: 53–78.

Eisa, H.M., Barghouti, S., Gilham, F. and Al-Saffy, M.T. (1994) *Cotton production prospects for the decade to 2005*, World Bank Technical Paper Number 231.

Featherstone, Mike (1991) *Consumer Culture and Postmodernism*, London: Sage.

Green, D. and Jones, L. (1998) *The Asian Garment Industry and Globalisation*, report of the Catholic Agency for Overseas Development.

Hale, Angela (2002) "Trade Liberalisation in the Garment Industry: Who is Really Benefitting?" *Development in Practice* 12,11: 33–44.

Hansen, K. (1999) "Second-hand Clothing Encounters in Zambia: Global Discourses, Western Commodities and Local Histories," *Africa* 69,3: 343–365.

Harrison, G. (2001) "Administering Market Friendly Growth? Liberal Populism and the World Bank's Involvement in Administrative Reform in Sub-Saharan Africa," *Review of International Political Economy* 8,3: 528–547.

Holt, Douglas (2002) "Why Do Brands Cause Trouble? A Dialectical Theory of Consumer Culture and Branding," *Journal of Consumer Research* 29: 70–89.

Isaacman, A. and Roberts, R. (eds.) (1995) *Cotton, Colonialism and Social History in Sub-Saharan Africa*, Portsmouth, NH: Heinemann.

Keifer, Matthew (1997) "Human Health Effects of Pesticides," *Occupational Medicine* 12,2: 203–411.

Klein, Naomi (2000) *No Logo*, London: Flamingo Press.

Kütting, Gabriela (2003) "Globalization, Poverty and the Environment in West Africa: Too Poor to Pollute?" *Global Environmental Politics* 3,4: 42–60.

Martinez-Alier, Joan (2002) *The Environmentalism of the Poor: A Study of Ecological Conflicts and Valuation*, Cheltenham: Edward Elgar.

Michaelowa, A. and Michaelowa, K. (1996) "Der Seidene (Handels-)Faden," *Politische Oekologie* 14, 45: 49–53.

Miles, S. (1998) *Consumerism as a Way of Life*, London: Sage.

Mshomba, R. (2000) *Africa in the Global Economy*, Boulder, CO: Lynne Rienner.

Murray, Doug (1994) *Cultivating Crisis: The Human Cost of Pesticides in Latin America*, Austin: University of Texas Press.

Murray, Doug and Taylor, Peter (2000) "Claim No Easy Victories: Evaluating the Pesticide Industry's Global Safe Use Campaign," *World Development* 28,10: 1735–1749.

Myers, Dorothy and Stolton, Sue (eds.) (1999) *Organic Cotton: From Field to Final Product*, London: Intermediate Technology Publications Ltd.

Pesticides Trust (1990) "King Cotton and the Pest," briefing paper on *Pesticide use in Cotton*, London.

Ross, Andrew (ed.) (1997) *No Sweat: Fashion, Free Trade and the Rights of Garment Workers*, New York: Verso.

Sanbon, Margaret and Cole, Donald (2004) *Pesticides Literature Review*, Ontario: Ontario College of Family Physicians.

Schott, J. (ed) (1998) *Launching New Global Trade Talks: An Action Agenda*, volume 12, Washington: Institute for International Economics.

Sklair, Leslie (2002) *Globalization, Capitalism and its Alternatives*, Oxford: Oxford University Press.

United Nations Conference on Trade and Development (UNCTAD) (1996) *The Uruguay Round and the World Cotton Market: A Preliminary Overview*, New York: United Nations. UNCTAD/COM/77.

Yang, Y. (1994) "The Impact of MFA Phasing Out on World Clothing and Textile Markets," *Journal of Development Studies* 30,4: 892–915.

5 The marketization of global environmental governance

Manifestations and implications[1]

Peter Newell

Introduction

Despite acknowledgments that accelerating patterns of globalization render the fragile systems of global environmental governance increasingly irrelevant (UNEP 1999), contemporary thinking about the challenge of managing global environmental change continues to look to international regimes for responses to environmental crisis. Increasingly, however, the study of international organizations cannot be divorced from an understanding of the nature of the contemporary global political economy and its implications for the future direction of environmental politics. As Saurin (2001: 80) notes "international political analysis continues to be conducted as if environmental goods and bads are produced, accumulated and therefore regulated by public organizations. They are not."

Taking evidence of the construction of regimes at the international level as an indication of institutional effectiveness, all would appear to be well amid proliferating and denser forms of global cooperation on the environment than at any point in history. When combined with the "success" of the ozone regime, the key elements of which were concluded amid significant scientific uncertainty, the fact that the climate regime has two agreements to its name and managed to conclude them over a relatively short period, the track record appears quite impressive. Yet environmental devastation proceeds apace, apparently unchecked by this flurry of global institutional activity. Given this, the question becomes one of how to account for the ineffectiveness of current policy responses to environmental problems.

There are many possible explanations, but I want to argue that the debate about the types of regulation and political action necessary to tackle many environmental problems is increasingly conducted in the shadow of, and is often trumped by, parallel concerns with trade and global market integration. This narrowing of the terms of the debate to political solutions that can comfortably be accommodated within the business-as-usual model of contemporary neo-liberalism serves to marginalize, delegitimize, or render invisible alternative solutions that may be more effective. While it is increasingly clear that the regulation of the environmental impacts of market actors has to assume heightened importance if we are serious about promoting a meaningful notion of sustainable development, attempts to address this issue have been systematically undermined by state and corporate entities that profit from current patterns of unsustainability.

Calls to regulate trade and the activities of multinational companies, and the flows of finance that impact so greatly on patterns of resource use, in the name of social and environmental ends, have so far been successfully ignored. Instead, there is growing evidence of a staggering and highly damaging degree of policy incoherence whereby there is no integration of environmental goals into mainstream economic, trade, and development policy such that policy in these areas systematically undermines the achievements of environmental policy, rendering it ineffective. The manifestations of this "dialogue of the deaf" are many (Newell 2002). Export credit guarantees and the use of overseas aid money, provided bilaterally and through funding for multilateral organizations such as the World Bank, continue to be allocated to developments with devastating environmental consequences, offsetting the gains made by environmental programs (Newell 2004). Since 1992, the World Bank has spent 25 times more on climate-changing fossil fuels than on renewables. One report found that less than 10 percent of all Bank projects are screened for their impact on the climate (Sustainable Energy and Economy Network 1997). Internationally, lack of policy integration between regimes means that the goals and possible net gains from agreements on climate change, for example, are reduced to nothing because the WTO, at the same time, negotiates increases in trade which will increase emissions of CO_2 well beyond the savings carefully negotiated in the climate treaties, by transporting greater volumes of trade around the world. Similarly, while we talk of the need to promote higher standards of environmental protection among firms, there is simultaneously discussion about concluding an investment agreement, possibly along the lines of the stalled Multilateral Agreement on Investment (MAI), that will allow companies to challenge national and local governments seeking to raise environmental standards in the name of non-discrimination against foreign investors.

What appear to be, from an environmental point of view, cases of alarming incoherence in policy objectives, actually make perfect sense once we understand that discussions about the ecological footprint of market-led globalization are strictly off limits. Reform proposals that deviate from received wisdoms about the pre-eminence of individual property rights and (ostensibly) laissez-faire economics, are discredited and ridiculed. While economic orthodoxies are sacrosanct and protected from scrutiny, environmental measures are always evaluated according to their potential to negatively affect capital accumulation objectives. Likewise, while there is growing emphasis on the deployment of deliberative and inclusive policy-making processes around environmental questions, decision-making around the economic processes which drive environmental degradation remains secretive and closed to public participation, driven instead by the commercial interests it seeks to serve (Newell 2006).

The focus of this chapter is the encroaching *marketization* of environmental governance, a phenomenon whose manifestations and implications are explored and explained below. It refers to

> an ensemble of strategies of market governance including practices of privatisation and commodification of natural resources which derive from a common belief in the ability of markets to provide the public good of environmental protection in the most efficient way. Taken in isolation, none of the individual components of this ensemble of practices provides sufficient evidence of a trend towards marketization. ... Taking the strategies together, however, we can observe the myriad ways in which the possibilities of environmental politics are being defined according to their ability to serve the broader end of global market expansion.
>
> (Newell 2005: 189)

The marketization of environmental policy is certainly not hegemonic, however. It is an expression of the contemporary organization of the global economy and the ideologies that rationalize its operations, failings, and structural inequities. Not only are there deviations from it in the form of different national and regional approaches to regulation, but also in everyday practice around the world, customary patterns of resource stewardship predominate, existing alongside market structures or subversive of them. Marketization, therefore, describes a particular historical juncture already subject to significant contestation and perhaps flexible enough to accommodate challenges to its reach without confronting the relations of power which underpin it, but perhaps also capable of being challenged in more fundamental ways.

Marketizing environmental policy

The purpose of this section is to illustrate the range of forms that "marketization" takes. At the most general level, in this context, it refers to a trend towards viewing the market as the source of innovation, efficiency, and incentives necessary to combat environmental degradation without compromising economic growth. In academic terms, it may be described as one manifestation of "ecological modernization" (Hajer 1995). In turn, as Saurin notes, in many ways, ecological modernization is the environmental face of what has been referred to more generally as "market civilization" (Gill 1995).

Marketization is more than an ideology, however. In policy arenas this belief system is advanced by key actors such as the World Bank that are able to use their economic power to promote the marketization of environmental policy within national systems of environmental governance. It is shown below that the use of market tools and reliance on market actors to deliver environmental improvements are now entrenched characteristics of the contemporary landscape of global environmental politics. The problem is that while the traditional regulatory tools of environmental regulation are increasingly subject to marketization, market actors are not at all subject to the logic or requirements of achieving sustainability. Describing this in terms of a shift in power between the public and private realm, Saurin (2001: 76) shows that while the public realm is left attempting to resolve harms generated by private actors, "the private entities—businesses and corporations—retain authority over production systems."

Market solutions

The privileging of market-based solutions to environmental problems is one obvious manifestation of the trend towards "marketization." From discussions about the use of tradeable permits to tackle regional problems such as acid rain in North America to incentivizing global action on climate change, the exchange of "pollution rights" through the market has become an increasingly popular way of "internalizing" the costs of environmental action. Two recent examples would be the European Union emissions trading system and the Chicago Climate Exchange, which allows companies to trade in carbon allowances.[2] The ideology of market efficiency is invoked to justify the claim that permit trading can produce large cuts in emissions at a lower cost than traditional "command and control" measures by providing financial incentives for heavier polluters to reduce their emissions and a reward system for less polluting countries that are entitled to sell surplus permits (Lunde 1991). While economists recommend the system as a way to bypass the complexities of negotiating pollution reduction targets on an inter-state basis, it is increasingly obvious that market based systems also require careful political negotiation. Environmental markets are no exception to Polanyi's notion that markets always have to be embedded within rules and institutional structures (Polanyi 1944). This is perhaps especially the case in global discussions where questions of equity and historical responsibility assume a high profile. Beyond the unquestioned efficiency of pollution trading schemes, ecologically, such systems allow wealthier countries to buy permits from lower emitting countries rather than reduce the pollution they generate at source, to displace rather than confront the unsustainability of current practices.

Ecological taxation is another market tool that has become popular in academic and policy circles. It is sold as an instrument that can make the polluter pay at source for the production of pollution, thereby incentivizing measures to reduce its generation in the first place. Economic instruments are said to address the under-pricing of resource-intensive goods and services which results in consumers and producers of products failing to receive the correct signals about the true cost of the environmental damage they cause. As Van Dieren and Hummelinck claim in their book *Nature's Price*, "By putting a cash value on nature's gifts such as sun and wind, soil and water, minerals, fossils and wildlife, plants and insects ... industrial man [sic] may be shocked into halting his own self-destruction" (Van Dieren and Hummerlinck 1979). There is now a range of policy tools in place aimed at addressing these "market failures." Taxes on inputs and final products whose production and consumption are associated with pollution externalities are one such means and enjoy the advantage of relying on the administrative backup of the existing tax system. No monitoring of the sources and levels of emissions is needed and product taxes can be easily collected from producers at the time of exchange.

Their ability to act as an incentive for pollution abatement depends on the level of taxation being high enough and the demand for the product elastic enough to discourage the consumption and production of the product. Such approaches are far more popular in Europe than in the USA where opposition to taxes in any form is deeply entrenched. European governments have also encountered political opposition to the implementation of measures, however, given the high rates at which taxes often have to be set in order to generate change in consumer behavior. The European Union's carbon tax ended in spectacular failure after Europe's industrialists mounted a successful offensive to crush the proposal (Newell 2000). Likewise proposals to set and collect carbon and energy taxes at the international level run into governments' reluctance to cede tax collecting and redistributive authority to supranational entities.

While environmental taxation continues to be applied, therefore, it should be considered one of the weaker areas of the marketization of environmental policy, in most cases because of the resistance of the market actors to be taxed even if for some governments it provides a potentially attractive revenue stream. Rather than tax polluters directly, some governments have opted for tax differentiation to discriminate in favor of ecologically benign technology options. For example, buyers of "greener" cars are given a tax advantage and differential VAT (Value-added tax) has been applied to "environmentally friendly" products.

The environmental labeling of products has been another surrogate for environmental regulation, allowing market preferences for greener products to determine acceptance of higher environmental "standards." While exporters often view labeling as a barrier to market access or a way of discriminating against their products, many firms have turned consumer demands for the labeling to their advantage. In the case of biotechnology, labeling has been used to try and reassure consumers about the safety of foods containing GM ingredients. This, and the fact that some firms regard labeling as positive branding of an "improved" product, has allowed the labeling of products to take off (Newell 2003). In this instance, labeling has also served as a post-hoc mechanism for notifying risks associated with products that have been approved by regulatory systems that often lack the trust of the public. In other instances positive brand recognition is sought to reward investment in responsible environmental practice. The Forest

Stewardship Council (FSC) and the Marine Stewardship Council operate in this way, for example, assuring consumers that products have been produced in an ecologically benign way. In the case of the FSC, the scheme substitutes for a lack of effective state action on the issue, a direct response to the "lack of commitment and progress being observed at the international policy level" (Murphy and Bendell 1997: 105).

The market is also held up as the answer to broader questions of global institutional reform in relation to environmental issues. Whalley and Zissimos (2001) call for a World Environment Organization that would internalize environmental costs through global deal-brokering of funds between the developed and developing world. Such proposals have been critiqued on grounds of political practicability and desirability and ecological effectiveness, but reflect nevertheless the pervasive logic of market solutions to problems that are fundamentally political or institutional in nature. The "willingness to pay" formula that such approaches employ for establishing the worth of environmental goods implies that resources are only as valuable as the Organisation for Economic Co-operation and Development (OECD) bidder that wants to pay for them. It assumes, by implication, that those without financial resources either do not care or do not care enough about the environment to pay for it. Problematically, also assumed is a "willingness to accept" environmental damage by those whose environmental assets are not of interest to those with the capital to protect them. Being driven by issues that are of interest to those with the capital to engage in deal-brokering, the body would be in danger of targeting a narrow range of environmental problems (Newell 2001b).

Private regulation

Alongside the trend towards using the market as a tool of environmental regulation, the persistent questioning of the effectiveness of state-based interventions, associated with neo-liberalism, has manifested itself in the environmental field in the systematic privileging in discourse and practice of forms of private and "soft" regulation. This bias, evident in the publications of the World Bank, as well as the reports of bodies such as the Business Council for Sustainable Development, reflects the preferences of many corporations for voluntary, flexible, and market-based forms of regulation (Schmidheiny 1992; World Bank 2000). These have become the favored option of companies themselves; providing for a more rapid process of standard-setting and with the added attraction of offsetting or in many cases, pre-empting, the need for state-based regulation. Companies have explicitly invoked the fact they have adopted voluntary measures to lobby against the need for legally binding environmental legislation. Concrete manifestations include the growth of individual codes of conduct as well as industry-wide standards such as the "Responsible Care" program in the chemical industry aimed at pacifying demands for stringent new controls in the wake of the Bhopal chemical disaster. At the international level examples would include the Business Charter for Sustainable Development and the standards set by the International Organization for Standardization (ISO), which prescribes global standards of environmental management.

For Clapp (1998), such standards amount to the "privatization" of global environmental governance. She shows how the growth of private standards-setting bodies has led to hybrid regimes whereby both states and private authorities are heavily involved in the creation and maintenance of international principles, norms, rules, and decision-making procedures. The ISO 14000 standards, in particular, are being adopted by standards-setting bodies in some states as national standards of environmental management and are now recognized by the World Trade Organization (WTO) as legitimate "public" standards (Finger and Tamiotti 1999), effectively creating an international ceiling for environmental management systems. Industry has been very supportive of ISO 14000 standards, hoping that adherence to them may pre-empt or soften, present and future environmental regulations. The legitimacy of bodies such as the ISO to establish global norms for environmental behavior is in question, however, when developing countries and Small and Medium Sized Enterprises (SMEs) do not have much representation in the organization (Krut and Gleckman 1998). There are also questions regarding the overall effectiveness of standards set *by* market actors *for* market actors, but which carry enormous implications for governments and publics alike.

Setting product standards that facilitate market access is a far cry from effective action to regulate the environmental impacts of business activity. There has been a notable lack of recognition in international environmental agreements of the role of Transnational Corporations (TNCs) in causing environmental problems. Provisions within environmental agreements that question, however implicitly or indirectly, the impact of increased market activity on the environment, have often been subject to veto. The issue of TNC regulation was dropped from the UNCED agenda and while a UN body was set up in 1973 to address the issue, it was unable to conclude negotiations on a code of conduct and was subsequently dissolved (Chatterjee and Finger 1994). This has raised concern about the imbalance between the promotion and protection of investor rights over investor responsibilities in international law; regulation *for* business rather than regulation *of* business (Newell 2001a). The attempt to create a Multilateral Agreement on Investment and the WTO TRIPs (Trade-Related Intellectual Property Rights) agreement are examples of an increase in "market-enabling" regimes aimed at facilitating investment opportunities and creating protection for investments at the expense of "market-restricting" regimes tackling environmental problems for example (Levy and Egan 2001). They are indicative of a broader power-shift in which regional trade organizations, such as NAFTA (North American Free Trade Agreement), permit companies to challenge governments and local authorities about environmental restrictions on their operations. This trend in the environmental arena provides further evidence of what Gill (1995: 413) more generally refers to as the "new constitutionalism" whereby the rights of capital over states are increasingly privileged and protected through international law. He notes that

> Central ... to the new constitutionalism is the imposition of discipline on public institutions, partly to prevent national interference with property rights and entry and exit options of holders of mobile capital with regard to particular jurisdictions.

Property rights

A third way in which marketization is promoted as a solution to environmental problems is through emphasis on the role of property rights in incentivizing action on the environment. In conventional economics, property rights are central to the efficient functioning of the market. In practice, this emphasis takes a number of forms from the protection of investor rights through intellectual property protection to advocacy of the World Bank's (1997) "enabling" vision of the state in which enforcement of property rights becomes a central state function. The importance of property rights to the market actors that worked so hard to secure the TRIPs agreement and the governments that acted on their behalf, is underscored by the fact that TRIPs requires governments to take positive action to protect intellectual property rights rather than merely determine acceptable policies as was the normal precedent with the preceding GATT regime (Correa 2000; Sell 1999). TRIPs-Plus provisions in bilateral trade agreements have further reinforced this trend. As it relates to the environment, Conca (2000: 492) notes that the agreement, "carried to its logical conclusion, ... promises the trade-based dismantling of three decades of global environmental rulemaking and the selling of important dimensions of the global commons." Particularly controversial are provisions in the agreement for the patenting of living organisms. This has prompted debates about the implications for access to genetic resources, especially where the rights of multinational companies are seen to conflict with the traditional rights of farmers and communities to save and exchange seed (Yamin 2003).

The question of the extent to which individual property rights can apply to living resources held on a communal basis tests the limits of the logic of commodification that underpins the ideology of "marketization." The assumption seems to be that resources are worthless unless they are valued in economic terms. As Saurin (2001: 77) notes,

> One of the characteristics of environmental harms is that markets either do not exist or surrogate markets are weak. The consequence is that under capitalism, if harms are to be addressed, "proper" prices need to

be identified and thus if a market did not previously exist then one needs to be created—in other words environmental harms themselves become commodified and subject to the logics of the market.

For resources to be valued in these terms requires the allocation of property rights. Such systems, it is argued, protect resources from exploitation, leading, for example, to community-based initiatives to document and record types of biodiversity and its use to pre-empt patent claims from foreign multinationals. That this is seen as the optimal way to promote the sustainable use of biodiversity given the alien logic it imposes on groups that have stewarded resources on a collective basis for generations, and the near impossibility of attributing particular innovations in their use to the actions of individuals, is testimony to the potency of the discourse and practice of marketization.

Beyond attempts to attribute individual units of value to nature, we have also seen a spectacular growth in the business of pollution: the commodification of pollutants such that rather than being seen as a symptom of an economic system malfunctioning, they become a source of new capital accumulation strategies. The Chicago Climate Futures Exchange and the rise of "carbon brokers" such as the appropriately named Australian company "Emit" provide examples of this. The carbon offsets industry is another growth area where business can profit from pollution: firms and consumers pay a third party to offset their carbon emissions by funding projects in the global South which serve as a sink for that pollution. Tons of CO_2 become the unit of property and international carbon markets the means for trading and capitalizing upon it. Once again, despite claims to the contrary, such market innovations require institutional frameworks even if it is in the form of information and surveillance and the use of "biopower" to sustain the credibility of transactions and to maintain investors' faith in their value (Oels 2005).

Property rights also play a significant part in some versions of proposals for a World Environment Organization (Whalley and Zissimos 2001), discussed above. In order for deal-brokering to proceed along the lines suggested, property rights would have to be allocated and enforced. This has raised concerns about who would allocate and enforce such property rights, particularly in settings where rights of access and use of natural resources are highly contested. Agreeing and resolving property rights issues is particularly difficult at the global level. Even a cursory reading of the history of international environmental cooperation reveals a string of unresolved battles concerning property rights over global public goods. Rights to the use and protection of Amazonian rainforests, Antarctica, and the deep-sea bed show that rights of access in the global commons are strongly contested and that the record of attempts to address them at the international level has been poor. It also raises questions about the effectiveness of marketizing environmental goods in this way, bypassing as it does the need both for

institutional reform and to tackle the causes of environmental degradation
in the more industrialized North (Newell 2001b).

Marketizing environmental rules

Besides the prominence given to market-based solutions to environmental
problems, described above, there has been increasing policy (and academic)
attention given to the relationship between rules aimed at facilitating international trade, investment, and market integration on the one hand, and
those whose aim is to provide a framework for environmental protection on
the other. Despite the explicit, and often implicit, anti-state bias of many of
the solutions proposed above, we have already noted that markets rely not
just on property rights for their operation but also institutions to create and
enforce rules of engagement.

The clearest manifestation of this conflict is the debate about the appropriate relationship between trade rules and MEAs (Multilateral Environmental Agreements). Environmentalists are concerned about the ways in
which the use of policy instruments aimed at protecting the environment are
increasingly questioned on the grounds that they are incompatible with
trade rules and disciplines. Expressing this concern, LeQuesne (1996: 73–74)
notes that

> Current WTO rules provide an inadequate framework for sustainable
> development precisely because they do undermine governments' ability
> to legislate in favour of environmental sustainability ... current trade
> rules discourage governments from pursuing a strategy of internalizing
> costs precisely because they prohibit governments from protecting their
> domestic industry from cheaper competition from countries who have
> not internalized costs to the same extent.

In the past, for example, bans, border taxes, subsidies, and other trade
restrictions have been used to explicitly discriminate between environmentally destructive and environmentally benign activities. While economists
may approve of the use of carrots and sticks to create incentives and disin-
centives regarding behavior towards the environment, they strongly dis-
approve of these forms of direct intervention in the market. As van Bergeijk
(1991: 106) argues "A solution on the basis of trade impediments will waste
the potential contribution that international specialization can make to
global environmental efficiency ... liberalizing trade is probably a necessary
(but not sufficient) condition for sustainable development."

Most problematic for environmentalists is the fact that discrimination on
grounds of production process is denied by trade rules, as the "dolphin tuna"
and many subsequent cases have clearly demonstrated. This is the basis of
their campaign for the incorporation of Process and Production Methods
(PPMs) into trade rules. It is increasingly difficult to maintain a distinction

between the production processes and a final product in the light of growing emphasis on life-cycle approaches, the popular use of eco-labeling and efforts to address the consumption of energy in a product's production, an impact that clearly derives from the production process. As LeQuesne (1996: 81) notes "from an environmental point of view, there is no meaningful distinction to be drawn between environmental harm which is generated by a product, or the harm generated by its process and production methods."

A related concern in this regard is the use of trade-restricting measures in MEAs. Many such agreements, in different ways, employ restrictions on the trade in substances considered to be harmful to the environment. The Montreal Protocol on substances that deplete the ozone layer, for example, restricts the trade in CFCs to those that have signed up to the accord, thereby excluding non-parties from the trade in ozone-depleting substances and therefore violating the most-favoured nation principle (Brack 1996). The rationale behind this is to create positive incentives for countries to comply with the accord and reduce the potential for free-riding by non-parties to the Protocol. Similarly, the Basel Convention on the trade in hazardous wastes outlaws certain forms of trade (Krueger 1999). The use of trade embargoes in these instruments violates WTO prohibitions against quantitative restrictions.

The CTE (Committee on Trade and Environment) of the WTO has identified 22 MEAs that require or cause governments to implement trade measures that may violate their WTO obligations, yet the use of TREMs (Trade-Related Environment Measures) in these MEAs has not been challenged to date (Morici 2002). The 1996 Singapore Ministerial meeting endorsed the CTE finding that members may bring to the WTO disputes concerning MEA-related trade measures, but no conclusions have been reached on proposals to modify article XX of the GATT to incorporate MEAs explicitly (Williams 2001). What is interesting is that their use in new legal instruments has been shaped by the need to anticipate and pre-empt conflicts with trade rules. The 2000 Cartagena Protocol on Biosafety provides a case in point in this regard. The preambular language to the Protocol reflects strong differences of opinion between the European Union and United States over what was known as the "savings clause" determining the extent to which the provisions contained in the Protocol should be subordinate to the trade rules of the WTO. There is growing resistance, however, to the way in which environmental agreements are assumed to be subservient to trade regimes. While some would like to see a general exception for environmental measures from WTO rules (Morici 2002), others endorse a more full frontal attack on the mentality of "the market über alles" (Hines 1997).

It is often also the case that market integration is the driving rationale for environmental measures. The imperative of constructing a "level playing field" often requires harmonized product standards and environmental policy provides a means to this end. Grant, Matthews, and Newell show how key environmental initiatives within the European Union are regarded as valid only to extent that they enable completion of the internal market (Grant *et al.* 2000). European Commission White Papers on energy policy, for example, spell this out explicitly. Policy has to be rationalized in terms of contribution to this aim and, by implication, achievement of economic growth. There is a disturbing irony in the fact that claims for environmental action have to be validated according to their ability to contribute to the very patterns of economic growth that further exacerbate environmental problems.

Accounting for the marketization of environmental policy

This section of the chapter seeks to account for the manifestations of the trend towards the marketization of environmental policy, described above. It is important to understand the conditions in which the marketization of environmental policy has come about in order to understand how deeply and over what time frame it is likely to leave an impression on the conduct and effectiveness of contemporary global environmental politics.

A prevailing context of corporate-led globalization has to feature in any such explanation. To the extent that the forces of globalization constrain state autonomy, this clearly has implications for environmental policy. Businesses fearing the onset of environmental regulation have repeatedly invoked the threat of capital flight and relocation to a less burdensome regulatory climate. Often it is the case that claims regarding the economic impact of environmental regulations on firms bear no relation to the actual costs. The costs of meeting environmental standards constitute a small part of the overall costs faced by industry and certainly pale into insignificance compared with other factors such as labor, with costs to industry from domestic environmental regulation estimated to rarely exceed 1.5 percent of overall production costs (Williams 2001). Nevertheless, the threat of relocating operations has a direct impact on the possibilities of environmental policy. While the extent of this trend and evidence of the resulting "race to the bottom" in environmental standards is contested, depending on the sector and region in question, there is evidence of "regulatory chill" where governments refrain from adopting new environmental regulations or demonstrate a reluctance to enforce existing regulations for fear of deterring potential investors. In this context, it becomes easier to see the attraction of voluntary and market-based solutions that require fewer interventions from government and reduce the risk, therefore, of being disciplined by investors for interventions in the market.

In this regard, we should recall that capital mobility merely adds to a plethora of lobbying tools available to firms seeking to contest regulatory developments that threaten their interests and to promote market solutions. Party funding, contributions to the tax base of governments, and the employment opportunities that firms create, afford corporations extensive structural influence. We are reminded of this by current events in the United States where "roll back" of environmental measures has proceeded apace under President Bush at the behest of firms that contribute significantly to party coffers, most especially the oil companies with whom the President has notoriously close ties. This national level lobbying exists alongside patterns of intense corporate lobbying at the international level, either against types of regulation threatening to their interests or in favor of market-enabling regimes (Levy and Egan 2001). In their efforts to promote the marketization of environmental policy, it is also important to note the supportive role of conservative environmental NGOs that have leant their support to the use of market measures such as permit trading and ecological taxation, for example. Elite NGOs such as Environmental Defense (EDF) and the Natural Resources Defense Council (NRDC), part of the Washington "big 10," have also enabled the growth of voluntarism by working with firms on particular projects, such as the infamous collaboration with McDonalds, for example (Murphy and Bendell 1997). Often these are successful in yielding short-term environmental benefits, but politically they serve to entrench the acceptability of partnership-based voluntarism over state-led regulation. Lending their support to market-based approaches to pollution control also affords legitimacy to such tools in so far as it allows advocates to claim an environmental as well as economic case for their adoption.

Another important development has been the way in which the lack of state capacity to enforce environmental regulation has been invoked as an added validation for marketized environmental policy. This lack of capacity has been used as an argument for self-regulation by industry or for the adoption of private market standards such as IS0 14001 that bypass state authority. The inefficiency of state intervention is also used to underscore the advantages of delivering pollution abatement though broader market reform. The World Bank's (2000) *Greening Industry* report, for example, advocates national-level economic reforms to enable environmental improvements. Unsurprisingly, privatization, liberalizing trade and the removal of subsidies are highlighted as important enabling policies in this regard. What is lacking in such policy recommendations is an acknowledgment of the social and environmental consequences of the macro economic policies that are promoted, particularly in terms of adjustment costs and who bears them, questions of access to resources for the poor and impacts on rural livelihoods.

At a broader level, the shift away from "command and control" measures, on grounds of efficiency and effectiveness, has also been justified by the failure of Soviet-style environmental regulation and the disastrous ecological legacy left by former Communist regimes in Central and Eastern Europe. Such experiences are cited as vindication for the argument that state-led regulation generates waste and inefficiency and fails to harness the power of the market to the goal of environmental reform. While the World Bank recognizes the importance of the state for allocating property rights and providing legal frameworks for the orderly conduct of market transactions, the 2003 World Development Report on "Sustainable Development in a Dynamic Economy" (World Bank 2003) advances the idea that the spectacular failure to tackle poverty and environmental degradation over the last decade is due to a failure of governance, "poor implementation and not poor vision" (Foster 2002). This is indicative of the by now familiar mantra that neo-liberal policies work, the problem lies with governments that do not implement them properly. Reflecting this ideology, the report notes, "Those [poverty and environmental problems] that can be coordinated through markets have typically done well; those that have not fared well include many for which the market could be made to work as a coordinator." The challenge for governments is therefore to be more welcoming of private actors through, among other things, "a smooth evolution of property rights from communal to private" (World Bank 1997: section 3.22). As the Environment Group at the Institute of Development Studies (IDS 2002) comment in relation to the report,

> Looking only at how the "dynamic economy" helps to open up options and not at the ways in which new economic forces and relations also constrain what policy interventions are possible, presents a one-sided reading of the challenges of achieving sustainable development in a context of globalization.

In reflecting on the role of the Bank, we are necessarily drawn to the politics of knowledge production and the knowledge brokers that provide the intellectual legitimation for the project of marketizing environmental policy. Besides the broader political and material shifts described above, the privileging of marketized solutions to environmental problems in policy discourse also results from the increasing salience of economists in environmental decision-making. While the privileged role of scientists in environmental debates has been subject to increasing scrutiny through debates about the sociology of science (Wynne 2001; Levidow 1998), economists have managed to preserve a protected status, despite critiques from academics and activists (Jacobs 1994). The use of conventional cost/benefit analysis as a basis for making judgments about the costs associated with particular environmental policy measures, and therefore for marketizing environmental entitlements, has drawn particular fire. The Global Commons Institute (GCI) became embroiled in a dispute with the IPCC (Intergovernmental Panel on Climate Change) over the use of cost–benefit models which drew on assumptions that the life of people in many less developed countries was worth one fifteenth of the value of someone living in the more developed world. "Willingness to pay" assumptions allowed economists to arrive at such controversial assumptions, dubbed the "economics of genocide" by GCI (Newell 2000). Despite efforts to contest the ethics of rationalizing action and inaction on the environment in such ways, cost–benefit analysis continues to be the most popular way of assessing the costs of environmental policy.

We can see, therefore, how a potent combination of material, institutional, and discursive forces combine to advance the marketization of environmental policy. Capital mobility and demands for global market access place constraints on policy options. The global neo-liberal institutions of the World Bank and the World Trade Organization play their part in creating and institutionalizing the conditions in which interventions in the market are regulated and constrained. The assumptions upon which their policy proscriptions and agreements are founded are supported by the work of neo-liberal economists, privileged in such debates, that serves to reinforce the idea that market solutions to environmental problems are more effective and efficient. In some cases, as we saw above, these proscriptions are leant legitimacy by conservative elements within the environmental movement.

To reiterate, none of these forces is static or uncontested. Global market actors and the institutions that act on their behalf have been forced to accommodate the concerns of environmentalists as well as opposition from many developing countries on the periphery of the world economy. The reality of how markets operate in practice has also brought about a belated recognition of the importance of "governance" and the role of the state, as recent World Bank's World Development Reports, discussed above, make clear. Possibilities for redefining a new environmental politics, one that is not subjugated to the logic of the market or the rules that are created to ensure that environmental goals do not restrict the globalizing ambitions of capital, will continue to proliferate in the future. This can be expected in a context in which popular concern continues to mount about the benefits of a global economic system organized around the principle of "market über alles." As member, negotiator, and implementer of the agreements that circumscribe environmentally motivated interventions in the market, as the source of authority to regulate business actors and in many ways the ideological battleground for policy debate, the state will provide the venue for many of these contestations in the first instance.

Conclusion

The marketization of environmental policy provides an illustrative case of a broader trend whereby the causes of environmental degradation emanating from global economic processes are increasingly protected from policy interference. This trend is manifested in a number of ways. We have seen the increasing use of trade rules and the doctrine of "sound science" to restrict the conditions in which health and environmental concerns can be invoked to justify a barrier to trade. This carries serious implications for governments' autonomy to act on risks, environmental or otherwise, that are of concern to the publics they claim to represent (Newell 2007).

We are also witnessing concerted efforts to reduce governments' scope to use policies that discriminate against environmentally destructive forms of investment. Attempts to conclude investment agreements to secure investor rights and provisions within regional trade accords that permit investors to sue governments for loss of income from environmental regulations provide evidence of this. It is to be expected, therefore, that future environmental negotiations will increasingly be conducted in the "shadow" of the WTO, operating in a constrained space in which trade-restrictive environmental measures that have proved to be so central to the effectiveness of MEAs in the past, will increasingly be off the menu of possible policy options.

It is clear then that the environmental movement cannot afford to focus its attention exclusively on those global actors and institutions that identify themselves as environmental in isolation from the global economic processes in which they are embedded and which ultimately they will have to regulate if they are to make a difference. Environmentalists have been heavily involved in campaigns around global investment accords such as the MAI, in global trade negotiations hosted by the WTO and regional trade negotiations across the world, and in pushing for a global corporate accountability convention. The strategic dilemma is where to concentrate efforts; working with those bodies developing legally binding international environmental law, or mobilizing to influence the activities of firms, banks, and those actors whose day to day decisions impact more directly on patterns of natural resource use than any global institution could ever achieve. Battles to generate consumer pressure, ethical investment, and the like are clearly important to mobilize constituencies that these market actors are responsive to. The corporate accountability movement has a key role to play in exposing misconduct, building new coalitions and lobbying for progressive legislation that regulates directly the actions of major polluters. Ultimately, therefore, we return to the state as an important, if not central, site in the struggle for sustainability. As unreliable an ally as the state can be given the networks of power in which it is embedded and the interests it responds to and represents, it remains a key source of authority and power that can force changes that are almost impossible to imagine by other means. The challenge is to work with progressive elements within the state when it makes sense to, lobby firms and investors directly when such pressure is likely to achieve more, and to form global coalitions to shift the agendas of global institutions when decisions reach beyond the sphere of either of these. In engaging in such short-term politicking, we have to keep alive a vision in which choices about which globalization we want are subject to the imperative of constructing a more sustainable global system and not the other way around.

Notes

1 Some sections of this chapter draw on material published in Newell 2005.
2 See the web site of the Chicago Climate Exchange at www.chicagoclimatex.com/

References

Brack, Duncan (1996) *International Trade and the Montreal Protocol*, London: RIIA/Earthscan.

Chatterjee, Pratap and Finger, Matthias (1994) *The Earth Brokers*, London: Routledge.

Clapp, Jennifer (1998) "The privatization of global environmental governance: ISO 14001 and the developing world," *Global Governance* 4,2: 95–316.

Conca, Ken (2000) "The WTO and the undermining of global environmental governance," *Review of International Political Economy* 7,3: 484–494.

Correa, Carlos (2000) *Intellectual Property Rights, the WTO and Developing Countries: The TRIPS agreement and Policy Options*, London: Zed Books.

Finger, Matthias and Tamiotti, Ludivine (1999) "New global regulatory mechanisms and the environment: The emerging linkage between the WTO and the ISO," *IDS Bulletin* 30,3 (July).

Foster, P. (2002) "The WDR 2003: Greenwashing Globalization," in *Managing Sustainability World Bank Style: An Evaluation of the World Development Report*, Washington: Heinrich Boll Foundation and UK: Bretton Woods Project.

Gill, Stephen (1995) "Globalization, market civilization and disciplinary neoliberal ism," *Millennium: Journal of International Relations* 24,3: 399–423.

Grant, Wyn, Matthews, Duncan, and Newell, Peter (2000) *The Effectiveness of EU Environmental Policy*, Basingstoke: MacMillan.

Hajer, Maarten (1995) *The Politics of Environmental Discourse: Ecological Modernization and the Policy Process*, Oxford: Clarendon Press.

Hines, Colin (1997) "Big stick politics," The *Guardian*, October 8, pp.4–5.

IDS (2002) "From Washington consensus to Washington confusion? Environment Group," in *Managing Sustainability World Bank Style: An Evaluation of the World Development Report*, Washington: Heinrich Boll Foundation and UK: Bretton Woods Project.

Jacobs, Michael (1994) "The limits of neoclassicalism," in M. Redclift and T. Benton (eds.) *Social Theory and the Global Environment*, London: Routledge.

Krueger, Jonathan (1999) *International Trade and the Basel Convention*, London: Earthscan/RIIA.

Krut, R. and Gleckman, H. (1998) *ISO 14001: A Missed Opportunity for Sustainable Global Industrial Development*, London: Earthscan.

LeQuesne, Caroline (1996) "Profits and Pollution Havens," in *Reforming World Trade: The Social and Environmental Priorities*, Oxford: Oxfam Publishing.

Levidow, Les (1998) "Democratizing technology—or technologizing democracy? Regulating agricultural biotechnology in Europe," *Technology in Society* 20: 211–226.

Levy, David and Egan, Daniel (2001) "International environmental politics and the internationalization of the state: The cases of climate change and the Multilateral Agreement on Investment," in Dimitris Stevis and Valerie Assetto (eds.) *International Political Economy of the Environment: Critical Perspectives*, Boulder, CO: Lynne Rienner.

Lunde, Leiv (1991) "Global warming and a system of tradable emissions permits: A review of the current debate," *International Challenges* 11,3: 15–28.

Morici, Peter (2002) "Reconciling trade and the environment in the WTO," *Economic Strategy Institute*, Washington: 1–127.

Murphy, David and Bendell, Jem (1997) *In the Company of Partners*, Bristol: Policy Press.

Newell, Peter (2000) *Climate for Change: Non-State Actors and the Global Politics of the Greenhouse*, Cambridge: Cambridge University Press.
—— (2001a) "Managing Multinationals: The Governance of Investment for the Environment," *Journal of International Development* 13: 907–919.
—— (2001b) "New environmental architectures and the search for effectiveness," *Global Environmental Politics* 1,1: 35–45.
—— (2002) "Globalization and sustainable development: A dialogue of the deaf?," *International Review for Environmental Strategies* 3,1: 41–52.
—— (2003) "Globalization and the Governance of Biotechnology," *Global Environmental Politics* 3,2: 56–72.
—— (2004) "Climate change and development: A tale of two crises," *IDS Bulletin* (special issue on Climate Change and Development) 35,3: 120–126.
—— (2005) "Towards a political economy of global environmental governance," in P. Dauvergne (ed.), *Handbook of International Environmental Politics*, Cheltenham: Edward Elgar.
—— (2006) "Democratising trade policy/ecologising democracy," *Re-Imagining Democracy*, July, 2006. Available www.re-public.gr/en/?p = 42
—— (2007) "Corporate power and bounded autonomy in the global politics of biotechnology," in R. Falkner (ed.), *The International Politics of Genetically Modified Food*, Basingstoke: Palgrave.
Oels, Angela (2005) "Rendering climate change governable: From biopower to advanced liberal government?," *Journal of Environmental Policy and Planning* 7,3: 185–208.
Polanyi, Karl (1944) *The Great Transformation: The Political and Economic Origins of our Time*, Boston: Beacon Press.
Saurin, Julian (2001) "Global environmental crisis as "disaster triumphant": The private capture of public goods," *Environmental Politics* 10,4: 63–84.
Schmidheiny, Stephen (1992) *Changing Course*, Cambridge, MA: MIT Press.
Sell, Susan (1999) "Multinational corporations as agents of change: The globalization of intellectual property rights," in Claire Cutler, Virginia Haufler, and Tony Porter (eds.), *Private Authority and International Affairs*, New York: State University of New York Press.
Sustainable Energy and Economy Network USA, International Trade Information Service, US, Halifax Initiative, Canada and Reform the World Bank Campaign, Italy (1997) *The World Bank and the G7: Changing the Earth's Climate for Business: An Analysis of the World Bank Fossil Fuel Project Lending since the 1992 Earth Summit*, June.
United Nations Environment Programme (UNEP) (1999) *Global Environmental Outlook*, London: Earthscan and UNEP.
van Bergeijk, P. (1991) "International trade and the environmental challenge," *Journal of World Trade* 25,5 (October): 37–55.
Van Dieren, Wouter and Hummerlinck, Marius. G.W. (1979) *Nature's Price: The Economics of Mother Earth*, London: Marion Boyars.
Whalley, John and Zissimos, Ben (2001) "What could a World Environment Organization do?" *Global Environmental Politics* 1,1 (February): 29–35.
Williams, Marc (2001) "Trade and the environment in the world trading system: A decade of stalemate?" *Global Environmental Politics* 1,4 (November): 1–10.
World Bank (1997) *World Development Report: The State in a Changing World*, New York: Oxford University Press.

—— (2000) *Greening Industry: New Roles for Communities, Markets and Governments,* New York: Oxford University Press.

—— (2003) *World Development Report: Dynamic Development in a Sustainable World Transformation in the Quality of Life, Growth, and Institutions,* New York: Oxford University Press.

Wynne, Brian (2001) "Creating public alienation: Expert cultures of risk and ethics on GMOs," *Science as Culture* 10,4: 445–481.

Yamin, Farhana (2003) "Intellectual Property Rights, Biotechnology and Food Security," *IDS Working Paper 203*, Brighton: IDS.

6 Between market and justice

The socio-ecological challenge

Henri Acselrad

The construction of the notion of sustainable development by the Brundt-land Commission (World Commission on Environment and Development 1987) expressed the desire to make a compromise between development and environment. The Commission's report offered a justification both for economic growth in the South (where certainly there were needs to be met) and for technical changes compatible with Northern interests (justified by the need to limit the environmental damage of progress). This apparent mutual concession to the interests of the North and the South overlapped with the desire to solve another kind of dilemma: that related to the scale of economic growth, as stated in the debate of the Club of Rome. In contrast to the "limits to growth" solution put forward during the 1970s (Meadows *et al.* 1972), the conjuncture of the 1980s was characterized by the desire to frame the environmental problem in a way that did not imply limits to the continued earning of economic profits.

The main compromise then being discussed was between the international political community and the complex of economic forces that had led post-war growth for thirty years. What mattered was that environmental concerns should not be an obstacle to expanding the frontier of profit making, which was basic to the reproduction of capitalist economies. From this point of view, two strong arguments for sustaining profit making activities were offered. The first of these was for expanding, through growth, market relations in the Southern peripheries (which economic theory used to call an "extensive-type accumulation," with profits earned by incorporating quantities of sup-plementary workforce and raw materials). The second argument was for investing in new and more efficient technologies (which economic theory used to call an "intensive-type accumulation," with profits resulting from productivity gains through technical innovations in processes and products).

The main concrete outputs of the 1992 Rio conference were all related to technical changes, albeit in different ways. The Biodiversity Convention codified norms in order to deal with a new market frontier—that involving the transformation of genetic information into a commodity. Here, a large part of the discussion refers to the distribution of rights or opportunities for gain by exploiting strategic natural resources. Legal and political frameworks have been created to deal with this new field of market possibilities. In the Convention on Climate Change, on the other hand, the desired technical changes are not quite compatible with current indicators of profitability. The political decisions at stake imply, in fact, economic behavior related to the current energy matrix that disregards indicators of profitability, in order to "uneconomically" protect the global climate. The US position in respect to climate changes shows that conventional economic rationality has been strong enough to resist sacrificing profits for global environmental benefits.[1] The example of these two conventions seems to confirm that there were, from the start, major tensions between the logic of economic liberalization and deregulation and the expectations that international environmental policies would establish heterodox constraints on the operation of economic rationality.[2]

Sustainable development as a discourse, in its Brundtland version, pointed out, by its very definition, a kind of division of tasks between North and South. The discourse simultaneously justified growth and "technified" the environment in the sense of presenting the environmental crisis as manageable through the adoption of technical innovations (Acselrad 1999). The larger UNCED debate, however, brought to the scene issues that were not, in principle, compatible with the expansion of the market and capital accumulation. Examples include financial transfers, international aid, debt reduction, and changes in the energy matrix. These are issues that cannot be easily translated into market terms and the logic of profitability. On the contrary, they have been built with reference to concepts of justice, in order to tackle the complex of causes said to nourish international social and environmental inequalities.

From the point of view of many non-governmental organizations (NGOs) and social movements, the idea was that after UNCED the UN forums would oppose the insensitivity of the Bretton Woods institutions to social and environmental concerns, and their tendency to disseminate inequity and environmental degradation. But against these expectations a new discursive effort has emerged since 1992, presenting free trade as the decisive institutional context able to tackle environmental problems. A major convergence has been created to support the strategic program of so-called "ecological modernization," which envisions existing institutions internalizing environmental concerns by focusing on technological adaptation, the celebration of the market economy, and a belief in collaboration and political consensus (Blowers 1997). In this manner, environmentalism has been translated into an extension of the process of modernization. However, as the discourse and institutionalization of ecological modernization are being disseminated from the top—by the bureaucracies of multilateral agencies and the strategists of major corporations—another discursive coalition has been developed from below, linking, through new frames, environment and justice. Against the effort to put the environment at the service of the market, the many experiences of social movements for "environmental justice" have been building arguments about the inextricable links between the roots of injustice and the roots of environmental degradation. In the Seattle WTO demonstrations and the World Social Forum initiatives, social justice and environmental protection have been shown to be logically compatible, structurally linked, and elements that must be built together. In this framework, the concentration of political and economic power over material and monetary resources, encouraged by the globalization process, is presented as the basis of social and environmental inequities.[3] The debate on social and environmental impacts of globalization has been increasingly one of opposing diagnoses and proposals, between those that justify the market and those that justify justice.

The sustainability debate and the market agenda

Ever since its arrival on the international public agenda, the environmental issue has been presented in two distinct manners, leading to two very different types of action. A first mode of thinking has stressed the need to fight against the waste of matter and energy, disseminating higher levels of efficiency in the use of environmental resources. Framed in this manner, the challenge is one of sustaining the material basis of economic development, making the planet an object of progressively more efficient practices. Subsequent efforts have focused on the search for an economy of means for development. The nature of the ends for which these means were to be mobilized, however, is not discussed. In other words, there is no speculation on the contents of the development project itself. A thriftiness of matter and energy through a revolution in efficiency is proposed to extend in time a form of development that is unquestioned in its own terms (Sachs 1989).

A second type of thinking has made ecology a moment for reflection on the very sense of development: what ends would justify the growing appropriation of environmental space by societies?[4] If the planet has limits, should we not ask ourselves to what purpose we are appropriating it? Would it be to manufacture deadly missiles or food for the hungry? From this second perspective, the very quality of development began to be questioned. In this view the limited resources of the biosphere should be used, of course, but to the utmost of legitimate purposes, made so by a democratic debate and in the manner most consistent with what can be understood as the peoples' well being. Whether to discuss the purposes or only to spare the means of development: there lies the challenge set forth by the ecological issue to all those who feel responsible for the future of our societies.

If we turn our eyes to the late 1960s, we can observe the birth of an ecologism with a clearly countercultural profile, which has criticized systemic consumerism as a project for our societies. The early 1970s, however, saw the beginning of trend toward the economistic appropriation of the environmental cause. After thirty years of the so-called "Fordist" type of growth, the Club of Rome pointed out the need to limit economic growth (Meadows *et al.* 1972). On the other hand, this analysis posed no questions about the underlying sense of development. While countercultural ecologism was temporarily absorbed by the conjuncture of the struggle for peace, the economistic perspective also temporarily lost its momentum, in light of the energy crisis and the cyclic decline of the world economy that started in the mid-1970s.

The beginning of the 1980s was marked by the debt crisis and the imposition of structural adjustments on the less developed economies at the capitalist periphery. These adjustments joined macroeconomic stabilization programs to finance and trade liberalization, market deregulation, and the privatization of public-sector companies. At the time, social movements questioning the content of the developmental project were deeply engaged in the criticism of the adjustment programs with their social and environmental impacts. These movements attained greater visibility by denouncing the effects of capitalistic expansion on areas where traditional populations are settled. The growing perception that social and ecological disaster accompanied huge development projects was the result of successful alliances linking rural and extractive labor unions in peripheral countries to international environmental NGOs concerned with forest preservation and macroclimatic changes.

In this context, the Brundtland Commision report, published in 1987, put forward the notion of sustainable development as a way to achieve a double solution. One aim was to respond to the worries raised by the report of the Club of Rome and the debate over limiting economic growth—seeking, this time, to internalize environmental concerns into prevailing thinking and practices without stopping the wealth accumulation process. The second goal was to allow for the environmental issue to be assimilated into the structural adjustment programs, serving the greater imperative of an efficiency concept that was to be extended to all the resources and recesses of the Earth.

During the preparatory process for the 1992 UNCED conference, when the first efforts were made to implement the Brundtland Report principles, critics of the prevailing development model voiced their expectations that new instruments would coordinate practices with potential impact on the global environment, and that new mechanisms would manage the transfer of resources from the North to the South. The argument was to implement more political regulation to yield environmental protection that addressed social justice concerns.

No more than a year after UNCED, however, the meeting of the so-called Washington Consensus sought to reaffirm the principles of liberal reforms, asserting the need to ascribe to the structural adjustment programs greater credibility and public acceptance. Liberal policies should be applied all over Southern countries, based on the belief that any perverse social, economic, and environmental effects of the neoliberal program were transient, necessary and to be withstood for the greater long-term common good. For the critics of developmentalism, however, this meant not greater political regulation for environmental protection with social justice, but rather less politics for greater economic efficiency. The perception was growing stronger that economic liberalization would bring about quite harmful social and environmental impacts, despite the promises that the market could ensure a more equitable future.

Moreover, after UNCED, the representatives of liberal thought began investing in the depoliticization of the environmental issue, trying to prevent the debate from moving toward the establishment of new regulatory instruments. Ideas were spread according to which "private property ensures better protection of the natural environment" and "stricter regulation does not ensure greater environmental protection, but results instead in lesser protection." Such statements constitute what Albert Hirschmann (1991) called "the thesis of perversity," through which reactionary rhetoric has tried to suggest that any attempt to change society to promote social justice or environmental protection would make it move in the opposite direction. In the rhetoric of free-market environmentalism, environmental policies tend to be detrimental to the environment.

Through the 1990s, neoliberal think tanks have concentrated their efforts on trying to insert the environmental agenda into that of liberalism. It was up to them to show that the conventional political institutions could internalize ecological concerns so as to reconcile economic growth with the solution of environmental problems, stressing their faith in the triad of technology/market economy/political consensus. Rather than legitimize the market as the best instrument to tackle environmental problems, the attempt was being made to turn the environment into one more reason to implement the liberal reform program. The "ecological modernization" proposal gained much of its prestige from being, first of all, a discursive solution that satisfies neoliberal reformism more generally. It added an environmental face to the neoliberal agenda, rather than simply providing a "market solution" for those liberals worried about environmental issues.

The globalization process, in turn, reconfigured the relative strength among social actors, limiting the effectiveness of political regulations and the respect for social rights and environmental patterns. "Globalization" means, in fact, changing the correlation of power between social actors—with mobile agents gaining power and less mobile actors losing it. Liberal reforms favored mobility gains that were decisive to capitalist prosperity in capitalism's new, flexible stage. With deregulation, the cost of the displacement of production units from one point to another in the world productive space dropped considerably. Large corporations were thus enabled to choose at liberty the political and institutional conditions they found more favorable to their spatial location. The earnings associated with the greater spatial mobility of the big companies would come from the huge transfer of power produced by deregulation. As the absence of regulations decreases the cost of companies' displacements, the most mobile economic agents acquire much of the power formerly held by less mobile social players, such as local governments and labor unions. Thus, the economic power of big corporations has been converted into direct political power, as they became able to dictate the patterns of urban, environmental, and social policies and to obtain changes in regulations by stating their decisive ability to generate jobs and public revenues. National states, weakened in their regulatory capacity, have concentrated on assuring the entrance of capital and monetary stability, offering wage restraints and environmental patterns flexibility. Environmental sustainability became dangerously dependent on the financial "sustainability" of banks, meaning the sustained capacity to attract globalized capital.

The growing inter-territorial competition between nations, regions, and cities—associated with the supposed need for localities to "sell themselves" at the lowest cost for the good of the maximum mobility of capital—has given big corporations the power to dictate urban and environmental policies, leading to deepening inequalities and uncontrollable global impacts. As corporations gained larger degrees of freedom to choose where to locate their activities, many local governments began to involve themselves in a predatory inter-local competition, offering subsidies and low environmental and urban standards in order to attract investors. This growing and near-direct political power in the hands of big corporations has been favoring socially and environmentally destructive backlash tendencies in many localities—particularly in Third World countries, where the successful attraction of industrial and financial investments has been increasing urban poverty, social segregation, political violence, and unequal distribution of environmental risks. For instance, it has been largely proven that the siting of toxic wastes resulting from big companies' industrial activities has usually been located in areas inhabited by concentrations of poor people and ethnic minorities. The main "institutional innovation" brought about by this socio-environmental mode of regulation compatible with flexible accumulation is that capital internalized the capacity to disorganize society—"rewarding" with investment resources those places that accept "flexible" social rights and environmental norms, and simultaneously punishing with the withdrawal of investment those places that try to maintain social and environmental regulations.

In parallel with the disorganizing effects of the new spirit of capitalism, the sustainability agenda came largely to be taken in at the rhetorical level by the market agenda during the 1990s. Subjective conditions were favorable to liberal reforms, and large corporations were strengthened relative to those players who were more qualified to implement socially and regionally redistributive practices and to set forth environmental standards that would converge progressively toward higher requirements. Consequently, it is almost unanimously acknowledged that the 1990s emphasized the social distances within the countries, increasing the gap between richer and poorer countries and between the more affluent and less prosperous regions inside each country. Instead of promoting greater corporate environmental and social responsibility, globalization disseminated the idea of the environment as a business opportunity. Meanwhile, the notion of "corporate self regula-tion" sustained the concentration of wealth in the hands of global interests, with no accountability to governments and communities for social and environmental practices.

The absorption of environmental issues by the market agenda has mani-fested itself through the harmful dissociation between the environmental agenda and the social agenda, whose docket has done nothing but increase cumulatively. The perception that the liberal reforms have contributed to worsen social inequalities and environmental indicators seems to have touched even some portions of the World Bank and International Monetary Fund. The concern for some sort of re-regulation by multilateral organizations does not have the same meaning, of course, as the agenda put forward by social movements committed to democratic social changes. For the former, to regulate means to stabilize social conflicts and modernize the channels that sustain political hegemony. For the latter, however, to strengthen the poli-tical sphere means to develop spaces for democratizing social debate and to implement decision-making processes from an emancipatory perspective. As Boaventura de Sousa Santos (2000: 1) reminds us, "The occidental moder-nity emerged as an ambitious and revolutionnary socio-cultural paradigm based on a dynamic tension between social regulation and social emanci-pation." As hegemonic forces tend to absorb social struggles through the creation of new regulations, emancipation invests in new social spaces, jus-tifying the emergence of new transformative social actors and developing the political sphere outside the frame of the state apparatus alone.

Environmental justice versus consensual post-democracy

The end of Latin American military dictatorships and the democratizing wave of the 1980s gave rise to general expectations that there would be advances in the double process of democratizing the state and socializing politics. This would imply more transparency in public management and greater involvement of society in the political debate and the process of sharing the resources of power. It was then assumed that the growing adherence to the project of building democracy as a form of existence of society, and not merely as a political regime, in conjunction with the revival of social movements, would allow the emergence of what was called a "new politics." Essentially, this was understood as a type of merger of the political and non-political spheres, of the state and civil society. In this process, citi-zens were supposed to participate in the control of political elites through the new channels of communication with the state. Matters that were once private, moral, or economical would be introduced into the public sphere. The citizen's action in the sphere of government authority would spread, the non-political institutions in civil society would be politicized, and society would question the values and cultural models in which diverging interests had traditionally been established. The nature, profile, and direction of political control would be themselves subjects of political conflict, which would be expected to occur in a broader public sphere than that of the state alone.

In the beginning of the twenty-first century, a very different paradigm has emerged, in which the disqualification of politics justifies the spread of non-political space. Formerly political themes are depoliticized and moved to the private sphere. Government practices are transferred to non-state actors through new channels, such as forums and councils that are considered to be exempt from the evils of politics. The political sphere is now said to be left to the arbitration of elites, given the supposed irrelevance and ineffectiveness of politics. Private civil institutions are now expected to express unity, which was once the prerogative of the state political authority. The values, cultural models, and rules of the social game in which interests are defined are now considered indisputable, and the various interests are symbolically united. Lastly, politics is "economized" through economic metaphors such as "entrepreneurial-city" for urban policies, "entrepreneur-employee" for the management of public investment programs, "competitiveness of the nation" for the country's international strategies, the attribution of prices to non-mercantile elements of the environment, the consideration of the selling capacity of science as an expression of the value of the knowledge produced in the universities, and so on.

This model, which Jacques Rancière (1995) called "consensual post-democracy," is becoming increasingly visible. It is characterized by the concealment of litigation, the "disappearance" of politics, and the designation of certain social groups as appropriate negotiating partners for the state. The so-called "good social practices" presume the "good poor," which do not present demands on the political system. "Good environmental practices" presume that NGOs will disseminate expertise and good behavior without reference to power structures that subordinate the environment to the dynamics of capital accumulation. If the councils and forums include entrepreneurs and workers, polluting agents and the victims of pollution, these hybrid mechanisms between state and society assign to them the homogeneous status of "partners," in a way that dilutes any difference in social roles, responsibility, or power. The liability for pollution and its solution is frequently shared equally, for instance, in settings such as the so-called local Agendas 21. Nevertheless, polluters tend not to disclose information about the hazards they cause, much less authorize social control of these hazards. The councils may be increasingly "participatiory" in their composition, while having less decision-making power by the very content of their agenda and a greater likelihood of being taken over by a kind of "show-politics." The wish for social non-differentiation inside the spheres of "partnership" tends to benefit the development of a democracy strongly based on images. The apparent stability achieved by symbolic consensus becomes an essential element of the policies to attract international investment. The need to offer international advantages for investors—social consensus, security, ecological sustainability—justifies that all projects in dispute are obscured in favor of inter-local or inter-urban competition. However, the fictional character of many of these consensus processes will be felt in the increasing visibility of the symptoms of a break in the linkages of sociability, increasing socio-spatial segregation, and political violence within cities.

Consensus-building technologies are then developed in order to char-acterize all litigation as a problem to be eliminated. Every remaining dis-pute, consequently, will tend to be regarded as a result of the lack of training for the consensus and not as an expression of real differences between social actors and social projects—differences normally to be trea-ted in the public sphere. To fill the political void and create democratic legitimacy, a discourse on "local citizenship" is provided in which commu-nity ties are presented as indicators of the unitary self-comprehension of society. An attempt will then be made to compensate the real trend toward social fragmentation by seeking to integrate the excluded in local collectiv-ities. A sort of "democracy of proximity" is presented as a remedy for social breakdown. However, the most deep-rooted causes for social exclusion and political violence are not found at the local level. The very idea of "urban violence," for instance, territorializes a social crisis whose origins are extra-local, to be found in social inequality and the ongoing global redistribution of power. The subordination of social rights to competitive rationality, for instance, makes the local place itself an inevitable expression of "globali-tarian" reasoning.

Consensual post-democracy also suggests the corporation as a model for the organization of society. The idea is that the logic of efficiency, measured by strictly monetary criteria, is from now on a guide to all aspects of social life—from public administration to the management of genetic information. But no process of democratic construction would survive the shaping of social life in the model of business with its non-discussed hierarchies. The democratic project is, on the contrary, committed to constantly recalling the ancient Polis, a sphere which is at once multiple, in that it reflects the dif-ferent citizens' perspectives, and common, because it is shared by all.

This is exactly the challenge that environmental issues bring to the poli-tical system: environmental "externalities" are strictly political issues, resulting from the structural dynamics of markets and not circumstantial "market failures." The environment is threatened not only by inefficiency but also by the lack of social justice. This is why, in the face of worsening of social and environmental inequities, social movements have been denoun-cing these outcomes as inherent to the market logic. Local claims for a better distribution of environmental resources have been unified at national levels and also begun to be internationalized as an integral part of politics. Their emergence derives from the development of an environmental aware-ness in the traditional social movements, whether on behalf of civil rights or the democratization of land. But they are also due to the worsening envir-onmental destitution of the most poverty-stricken populations, either in the peripheral countries or within the wealthier nations themselves.

Environmental justice is at its heart an expansion of the arena of environmental concern to address the spatial and social distribution of environmental goods and bads, the sharing of burdens inevitably associated with environmental protection, and, perhaps most important, the loci of environmental decision making. As we turn our attention to these distributional issues, our field of vision expands to include the local as well as the global, and urban as well as rural regions. We need to ask about the distribution of environmental burdens within cities and among them; between cities, their peri-urban regions, and hinterlands; and among the regions of the world. From this perspective, pollution in a specific area that puts workers and their neighborhoods at risk is as much a global problem, by its logical interlinkages, as is biodiversity loss, climate change, and ozone depletion (Lynch 1999).

The inequitable distribution of environmental goods and ills reflects broader economic inequities that are closely tied to a region's integration into the global economy as well as structural factors within individual countries. Because these economic inequalities are so often reinforced by international development policies, an effort to achieve environmental justice in Southern countries will require attention to these inequities and policies designed to reduce them. As criticism of global trade policy grows stronger, it just may be possible to do this. Considering that international development agencies have perpetuated environmental injustices in less developed countries, the pursuit of environmental justice entails innovations in environmental policy making as well as higher levels of linkage among social movements around the world.

If, as Low and Gleeson (1998: 203) suggest, "environmental justice is about the distribution of environments to humans," then environmental justice can be thought of as the spatialization of distributional justice. This means that questions of property and access are fundamental to environmental justice agendas. One set of questions has to do with the *allocation* of environmental goods and ills: privatization of profits gained by fouling the commons; transnational allocations of environmental ills, including transnational trade in toxic wastes and semi-spent equipment and the creation of pollution havens; and decisions to preserve landscapes of consumption while destroying the landscapes of production that enable places and cities to survive and grow.[5]

Another set of questions has to do specifically with access to land and the destructive impacts of the reduction of complex social relations to property and exchange. The *commodification* of space leads to the enclosure and simplification of landscapes and ecologies. This in turn makes them inherently unstable and favors their use in ways that imperil the health of workers on the land, local residents, and non-human life. Almost inevitably, it leads to eviction and the alienation of rural peoples from their resource base. Land concentration and environmental injustice in rural areas are also linked to the production of equally unjust urban spaces.

Another set of issues has to do with the way polluting facilities and people are located within urban space. Real estate markets, employment opportunities in the formal and informal sectors, housing, and transport affect the distribution of both people and risk. The effects of these policies are likely to be most pernicious where they are informed by racial and ethnic as well as class biases (Lynch 1999). Health and sanitation have been concerns for urban policy makers in Third World countries since the mid-nineteenth century. In recent years, these problems have been "environmentalized" and problems of access to water, sewage, and solid waste collection are cast, increasingly, as environmental justice issues. All too often, however, they are seen as the only urban environmental issues. Latin America, for instance, has long been both overwhelmingly urban and fully integrated into the global economy; its citizens are routinely exposed to the risks of late modernity—air and water pollution and exposure to toxic substances in the workplace and the neighborhood. These risks are not confined to the region's megacities, but also are experienced in the smaller cities and peri-urban fringes where industries are more often sited. The environmental hazards associated with these industries can be thought of as imported byproducts of international commerce in toxic substances and technology transfers. Many environmental hazards are experienced locally, most often in older working class neighborhoods and newer informal settlements (Lynch 1999).

In this context, the environmental justice paradigm was forged by activists who came to the environmental arena with a long history of engagement in civil rights struggles. In the case of United States, the movement was sufficiently compelling to propel environmental justice into the mainstream of policy making. The report of the Commission on Racial Justice on toxic waste and race in the United States (Lee 1987) offered hard quantitative evidence to show that toxic facilities were concentrated not only in low-income neighborhoods, but in communities of color. The publication of toxic release inventory data by the US Environmental Protection Agency further assisted activist efforts to collect and disseminate information on the spatial distribution of risk in US cities. In the United States the environmental justice issue has developed closely linked to the denunciation of "environmental racism" by movements of people of color. In Southern countries such as Brazil, the discursive linkage between environment and justice is being made mainly by urban workers and settlers' associations as well as social movements placed in the expanding territorial frontier of capitalistic social relations—for example, the Movement of Dam-Affected Peoples and the family-based agriculture and extractivist movement in the Amazon region. These movements understand environmental injustice as an outcome of the evil logic of a system of production, land tenure, ecosystem depletion, and spatial location of pollutants, which directly penalizes the labor and health conditions of the working population living in the poor districts and threatened by the big projects of development. While higher-income populations can afford to move away from areas of environmental depletion toward more protected areas, the poorer are spatially segregated, living in valueless and unsafe urban plots, often in abandoned industrial areas contaminated by illegal toxic wastes, or left to cultivate less fertile pieces of land. Urban and rural workers are often exposed to hazards originating from dirty technologies that distribute cumulative pollutants that endure in the environment for ages. Many of these technologies, already forbidden in the more industrialized countries from which they came, cause diseases in their workers and sometimes fatal "accidents" among children who walk around in the areas where illegal waste disposal occurs. In this perspective, the environmental justice movements tend to contest the fundamental locational logic through which the market mechanisms reproduce spatial inequalities.

Conclusion

As we have seen, the growing inter-territorial competition between nations, regions and cities, associated with the supposed need for cities and places "to sell themselves" at the lowest cost for the good of the maximum mobility of capital, has given to big corporations power to dictate urban and environmental policies. The results are deepening inequalities and uncontrollable global impacts. With the processes of economic globalization, corporations gained larger degrees of freedom to choose where to locate their activities. As a result, many local governments began to involve themselves in predatory inter-local competition, offering subsidies and low environmental and urban standards in order to attract investors. This growing and almost-direct political power put into the hands of the big corporations has been favoring socially and environmentally destructive backlash tendencies in many localities, particularly in Third World countries, where the successful attraction of industrial and financial investments has been increasing urban poverty, social segregation, political violence, and unequal distribution of environmental risks. The main "institutional innovation" brought by this aspect of the socio-environmental mode of regulation compatible with flexible accumulation is that capital has been internalizing the capacity to disorganize society—"rewarding" with its investment resources the places that accept "flexible" social rights and environmental norms, and punishing with the withdrawal of its investments those places that try to maintain social and environmental regulations. Using the power to locate its investments, the corporations not only maximize profits but, simultaneously, penalize the more organized communities and reward less organized localities.

In conclusion, a new type of articulation, grounded in social movement intiatives and associating environmental and social issues, has emerged to contest the absorption of an environment reduced to mere quantities by the logic of efficiency and against the disqualification of politics by the "post-democratic consensus." This new articulation provides political support and a renewed moral force to the ecological cause, questioning the cultural values and the ends that justify the planet's appropriation. From this point of view, the international debate should recognize that environmental resources are unequally distributed and that exposure to environmental hazards across different social groups is also quite unequal. Through their locational practices, multinational corporations have made it increasingly evident that the market logic (as formally justified in the controversial Summers Memorandum diffused inside the World Bank in 1992),[6] tends to distribute polluting processes and environmental damage, both within national space and at the international level, in a manner that jeopardizes the poorer populations. This systematic transfer of environmental damage to less powerful social groups results mostly from the delocalization strategies through which corporations impose risks and social-rights regressions as conditions to locate their investments resources in countries facing a crisis of unemployment. As long as environmental justice movements resist these delocalization strategies, their collective action appears as a means of not only limiting environmental degradation but also placing obstacles in the path of large corporations using their economic power to disorganize society.

Notes

1 It is now clear that for a long time, in the words of Taylor and Buttel (1992: 406)

> a moral construction of the global environmental problems emphasizing the common interest in the efforts to face up to them has prevailed, diverting the attention from political setbacks resulting from the diversity of social interests and nations involved in this confrontation.

2 The political dilemma referring to global environmental changes affects, certainly, the scientific debate itself: "global change research is part of a contested science in a contested political arena." See Krueck and Borchers (1999: 123).

3 In the words of Amartya Sen, "The real debate associated with globalization is, ultimately, not about the efficiency of markets, nor about the importance of modern technology. The debate, rather, is about inequality of power" (IIED 2001: 9).

4 Georgescu-Roegen (1971) had already resorted to the problem of entropy to put the ecological question as an ethical choice: given the irreversibility of entropic processes, the choice has to be made between producing ploughs or tanks, for example.

5 As Concepción (1995) shows, transnational allocations of environmental ills are interconnected with the history of anti-colonial struggles.

6 A well-known memo written by Lawrence Summers, when the ex-US Secretary of the Treasury was chief economist for the World Bank, suggested that poor countries should be pollution havens. Summers argued that the environment is an aesthetic concern only for the well-off, that most Third World residents do not live long enough to experience the ill effects of pollution, and that even if they did, their lives are worth less in monetary terms than those of their counterparts in developed nations. Although Summers denied the seriousness of his assertions, the logic there exposed is currently at work in the real economy.

References

Acselrad, Henri (1999) "Sustainability and Territory: Meaningful Practices and Material Transformations," in E. Becker and T. Jahn (eds.) *Sustainability and the Social Sciences: A Cross-disciplinary Approach to Integrating Environmental Considerations into Theoretic Reorientation*, London: Zed Books.

Blowers, Andrew (1997) "Environmental Policy: Ecological Modernization or the Risk Society?," *Urban Studies* 34,5–6: 845–871.

Concepción, C. (1995) "The Origins of Modern Environmental Activism in Puerto Rico in the 1960s," *International Journal of Urban and Regional Research* 19,1: 112–128.

Georgescu-Roegen, Nicholas (1971) *The Entropy Law and the Economic Process*, Cambridge, MA: Harvard University Press.

Hirschmann, Albert (1991) *A Retórica da Intransigência*, São Paulo: Compania das Letras.

International Institute for Environment and Development (IIED) (2001) *The Future Is Now: For the UN World Summit on Sustainable Development*, Vol. 1, April, London: IIED.

Krueck, Carsten P. and Borchers, Jutta (1999) "Science in Politics: A Comparison of Climate Modelling Centers," *Minerva* 37,2 (summer): 105–123.

Lee, Charles (1987) *Toxic Wastes and Race in the United States: A National Report on the Racial and Socio-Economic Characteristics of Communities with Hazardous Waste Sites*, United Church of Christ, Commission for Racial Justice.

Low, Nicholas and Gleeson, Brendan (1998) "Situating Justice in the Environment: The Case of BHP at the Tedi Copper Mine," *Antipode* 30,3 (July): 201–226.

Lynch, Barbara Deutsch (1999) "International Institutions for Environmental Protection: Their Implications for Environmental Justice in Latin American Cities," paper presented at the *International Meeting on Democracy, Equality, and the Quality of Life: The Challenge for Cities in the 21st Century*, Porto Alegre, Brazil, December 5–8.

Meadows, Donella H., Meadows, Dennis L., Randers, Jørgen, and Behrens, William W. III (1972) *The Limits to Growth*, Washington, DC: Potomac Associates.

Rancière, Jacques (1995) *La Mésentente: Politique et Philosophie*, Paris: Galilée.

Sachs, Wolfgang (1989) "Le Culte de l'Efficience Absolue: A propos du rapport Worldwatch sur l'état du monde et de quelques autres," *La Revue du MAUSS* 3: 85–95.

Santos, Boaventura de Sousa (2000) *A Crítica da Razão Indolente: Contra o Desperdício da Experiência*, Volume 1, São Paulo: Cortez Editora.

Taylor, Peter and Buttel, Frederick H. (1992) "How Do We Know We Have Global Environmental Problems? Science and the Globalization of Environmental Discourse," *Geoforum* 23,3: 1–11.

World Commission on Environment and Development (1987) *Our Common Future*, New York: Oxford University Press.

7   Sustainable consumption?

Legitimation, regulation, and environmental governance

Matthew Paterson

An emerging element in global environmental governance is a focus on "sustainable consumption" (French 2004; Fuchs and Lorek 2002). A range of international agencies has articulated the notion of sustainable consumption (SC) as a key element in the broader discourse of sustainable development. It has the potential to become in the long term one of the central general elements in the post-Rio map of global environmental governance, one able to articulate a broad range of specific regulatory or governance projects under its wing. Thus, the usefulness or lack thereof of SC as a concept is crucial in terms of the pursuit of sustainability.

I would argue that SC should be interpreted as a principal regulatory element in the accumulation regime envisaged by proponents of sustainable development or ecological modernization. As with other such regimes, a mode of regulation[1] to shape, normalize, and regularize the patterns of accumulation, and to regulate individual behaviors to conform to the systemic requirements of particular accumulation regimes, is an essential element in capital's projects to legitimize and stabilize capitalist societies. In this context, ecological modernization can be seen as the project to develop an accumulation regime that responds to the twin pressures of mobilization around the "environmental crisis" and economic globalization (Mol 2001; Barry and Paterson 2004). SC governance is the element in this regime that aims to shape consumer practices to meet these twin (and often contradictory) sets of pressures.

But SC is interesting in this context as it emerged out of radical challenges to the basic logic of capitalist societies. While sustainable development emerged more out of reformist elements in environmentalist ideology, relatively accommodated to capital, consumerism, the state, and so on, articulations of consumption and consumerism as a fundamental aspect of precisely what is unsustainable about contemporary societies, are more commonly associated with the more radical end of environmental politics. SC thus has the potential to get to what is for many the heart of the problem—overconsumption by most people in the affluent industrialized countries and a growing consumer class in the "global South." The project of cooptation by capital is thus simultaneously more ambitious, audacious, and contradictory than with sustainable development.

This chapter explores the dynamics and politics of the contemporary discourse of SC. It starts by outlining the institutional contexts within which SC is being articulated, the particular discourse of SC being developed by those institutions, and the academic arguments being developed around it by those who can be associated with the "SC project." The chapter then discusses the intellectual and political origins of SC, showing how it has been shaped in particular ways to defuse its radical potential and act as part of the general legitimizing strategy of global capital in relation to the "environmental crisis." As the editors suggest in their introduction, one of the central political processes surrounding the development of global environmental governance has been the marginalization of what they call "serious approaches to global sustainability," of which the critique of consumption and consumerism is an important element. But this marginalization is not only, as they suggest, because of "opposition from powerful interests." It is also because of the way that consumption has become constitutive of individual and collective identities across much of the globe. The third part of the chapter shows that as practices and policies are developed to put into practice SC as it has been articulated in the UN Environment Programme (UNEP), the Organization for Economic Co-operation and Development (OECD), and other such institutions, these then appear as a technocratic, rationalizing governmentality, which acts on individuals in progressively more intrusive ways precisely because of the way the notion has been shaped as it was articulated to fit with dominant political-economic discourses. This is precisely because of the prior importance of consumption in daily lives, and its "unquestioned" character. The chapter concludes with a theoretical elaboration of the argument outlined in the first two paragraphs—of SC in the context of the regulation of global capitalism.

The institutionalization of sustainable consumption

Sustainable consumption has become institutionalized in a range of international agencies during the 1990s. It has been principally developed in the OECD, the UN Commission on Sustainable Development (UNCSD), UNEP, the Division of Sustainable Development of the UN's Department of Economic and Social Affairs (UNDESA), and the international non-governmental organization Consumers International.[2] Scandinavian countries, particularly the Norwegians, have led development of the idea. As with sustainable development, a dominant definition of SC has emerged which has Norwegian origins. Following a conference in Oslo in February 1994, it has been ubiquitously defined in these institutional contexts as

> the use of goods and services that respond to basic needs and bring a better quality of life, while minimizing the use of natural resources, toxic materials and emissions of waste and pollutants over the life cycle, so as not to jeopardize the needs of future generations.[3]

In the standard presentation by proponents, sustainable consumption arose out of the UNCED conference (UNEP/Manoochehri 2001: 11; Murphy and Michaelis 2003). At UNCED, consumption was made part of the problem. Chapter 4.3 of Agenda 21 states that "The major cause of the continued deterioration of the global environment is the unsustainable pattern of consumption and production, particularly in industrialized countries, which is a matter of grave concern, aggravating poverty and imbalances" (UN 1992, Chapter 4.3).

UNEP presents the following as the major events in the development of SC (UNEP/Manoochehri 2001: 24); the elaboration of the need to consider SC by the Commission on Sustainable Development in 1994; the UN Economic and Social Council (ECOSOC) requesting that SC be incorporated in the UN Guidelines on Consumer Protection (originally developed by the UN General Assembly (UNGA) in 1985); the beginning of work on SC by the OECD in 1995 with a major report in 1997 (OECD 1997); the beginning of the UNEP SC program in 1998; a significant discussion in the 1998 Human Development Report of the UN Development Programme (UNDP 1998); and the discussion of SC at the World Summit on Sustainable Development (WSSD) in Johannesburg in 2002.[4] Through this institutional development, it has gone from processes of issue definition and articulation through to the sophisticated elaboration of a set of strategies and policy tools for implementation. It also entailed a certain movement through various international bodies—with the CSD playing an important role in the mid-1990s before a coalition of UNEP and Consumers International became the lead agencies by the late 1990s (UNEP/CI 2004: 9). At the WSSD one of the outcomes in the Plan of Implementation was a ten-year program on sustainable production and consumption (UN 2002: paras 14–23). The concept has also spread out into other areas of global governance, notably being discussed by participants in the Global Compact, the UN's institutional format for developing ideas about Corporate Social Responsibility at the international level, but also widely interpreted as a process of corporate capture of the UN (Global Compact 2004; Hughes and Wilkinson 2001). It has also been paralleled in many countries by concrete policies to promote SC.[5]

The present focus of international organizations is on implementation. This implementation can be usefully divided into two elements—one focused on widening participation and building partnerships, and one based on developing information concerning specific sectors and issues.[6] Concerning the first, UNEP and the UNDESA started co-ordinating a series of meetings and other "multi-stakeholder" processes (see Whitman, this volume) in 2003 for the ten-year program on Sustainable Consumption and Production mentioned above, which became known also as the "Marrakech Process." These meetings are organized on a variety of bases—meetings organized regionally (e.g., a European meeting in Ostende, Belgium, in November 2004 (UNEP 2004)), or on the basis of expertise (UNDSD 2003) or social/economic sector, notably advertising and "youth."[7]

Regarding the development of information, UNEP and Consumers International have produced two "tracking progress" reports, surveying activities of governments in relation to the development of policies to implement the principles of sustainable consumption (UNEP/CI 2004), and in particular in relation to the SC dimensions of the UN Guidelines on Consumer Protection. UNEP and UNDESA have also developed a series of programs to analyze the policies necessary to implement the principles of SC. The Marrakech Process has been organized around four clusters: "human settlements"; "general policy measures and analytical tools"; "tools for changing consumer behavior"; and "tools for changing production patterns."[8] One of the principal UNDESA contributions has been a report on the current activities of a wide range of UN agencies that are pertinent to SC and through which SC programs could be developed (UNDSD 2003). UNEP's own programs appear more ad hoc, comprising a focus on government policies, in particular procurement policies and the adoption of the UN Guidelines on Consumer Protection; the development and dissemination of a range of tools for product life cycle analysis and management (organized jointly with the Society for Environmental Toxicology and Chemistry, or SETAC); and two programs under the heading "Sustainable Products and Services," one of which is on "ecodesign" and one on "product services and systems."[9]

SC governance is still in an early stage of development, and the manner in which it becomes further institutionalized is likely to develop and shift. Nevertheless, a few preliminary points can be made concerning the nature of this institutionalization. First, concerning a mode of governance, it is clearly not something based on highly formalized rules, norms, and so on, as in most accounts of international environmental regimes.[10] There is no international treaty on Sustainable Consumption, and no impulse within the Marrakech process to suggest that such a treaty is necessary. Rather, SC governance operates through a combination of entrepreneurial leadership by the agencies involved, clearinghouse and information exchange processes, and the development of partnership arrangements. Thus, the institutionalization of SC can be regarded more in terms of a range of mechanisms through which more diffuse and general goals may be pursued than could be done through formalized, legalistic processes, a form of informal process-based governance which operates through incorporating agents into the process, attempting to re-articulate their interests and thus their practices through the act of deliberation and information sharing. It may be possible to claim that such forms of governance are likely to become more prevalent in global environmental governance, on the one hand as a consequence of neoliberal patterns of governance (in effect, SC is a series of global "public–private partnerships" and "voluntary agreements") and on the other as the elements of social behavior being regulated shift from the relatively discrete (CFC use, sulfur dioxide production) to the general and diffuse (whole patterns of consumption). One central element here is the discursive dimensions of governance, to which I now turn.

Contradictions of sustainable consumption discourse

UNEP's document "Consumption Opportunities: Strategies for Change" is a useful and very full outline of SC as it is articulated in these institutional contexts, and worth using to examine the discourse (UNEP/Manoochehri 2001). It reveals the complexities and the contradictions entailed within SC discourse, as well as the elisions and occlusions it produces in order to present SC as a coherent discourse.

Perhaps the first thing to note is the properly radical intent maintained in much of the UNEP discourse. It is clear that for the authors of the report, the implications of referring to SC are clearly to argue for "radical reductions in aggregate material throughput in developed economies" as one of the key "immediate goals" of SC (UNEP/Manoochehri 2001: 14). The general question involved in SC is "to take standard economic 'consumption', the purchase of goods and services, and to examine how this can be made environmentally 'sustainable'" (UNEP/Manoochehri 2001: 12). But "sustainable" itself is never explicitly defined, and at the same time as this radical intent is maintained, the space is thus there for rather different interpretations, and much of the productive potential of the report depends (as for sustainable development discourse more generally) on the slippage between these usages, enabling it to speak simultaneously to different audiences with different agendas.

But immediately after the focus on making consumption sustainable, which invokes radical claims about radically reducing aggregate throughput, comes the "Oslo definition," which only focuses on "minimizing" resource use in production and consumption. This may seem small, but immediately a sense of the quantitative limits on overall throughput that ecosystems can withstand, usually invoked by the notion of sustainability (whether weak or strong), is lost.

This slippage away from its radical implications also occurs as SC becomes in the report "ultimately" about "quality of life" (UNEP/Manoochehri 2001: 10, and *passim*). While in part this invokes a shift in focus away from valuing the quantity of goods consumed and is potentially consistent with reductions in aggregate throughput, it simultaneously removes the reference point (sustainability) against which such reductions may be judged. There is recognition that for some, "this may include a questioning of the role of consumption in delivering quality of life," that "people's needs can also be satisfied in other ways than by more goods" (UNEP/Manoochehri 2001: 10, quoting Rensvik 1994: 91). But shortly after, with the effect of marginalizing this position, the section headed "what is sustainable consumption?" starts with a bald quote from the director of UNEP's Division of Technology, Industry and Economics that "sustainable consumption is not about consuming less" (UNEP/Manoochehri 2001, quoting Aloisi de Larderel 1999).

Thus a discourse that contains implicitly within it a notion of limits and reductions in consumption, becomes a looser, vaguer term with this radical implication only being one among a range of possible interpretations. The rest of the quote from Aloisi de Larderel discloses the range well: "Sustainable consumption is not about consuming less, it is about consuming differently, consuming efficiently, and having an improved quality of life. It also means sharing between the richer and the poorer" (UNEP/Manoochehri 2001: 12).

Differently, efficiently, improved quality of life, more sharing. All readily presentable as desirable, all of course possible without being in a strict sense sustainable. As environmental discourse, then, SC operates, like sustainable development, to obscure its radical potential, and to undermine the "sustainable" element. This is at times recognized by its advocates, when the telling term "more" occasionally appears as a qualifier to the term "sustainable consumption" (UNEP/Manoochehri 2001: 6 and 11)—we know we can't really expect to get to sustainable consumption, but we can aim to make it "more sustainable," or perhaps "less unsustainable."[11] That sustainability might be an either/or rather than something with gradations is not entertained in that phrasing.

The contradictions in SC discourse appear at their most stark when discussed in contexts like the Global Compact, or in UNEP's attempts to engage the advertising industry. For corporate participants in the Compact's policy dialogue on the topic, SC ends up having to be presented as an opportunity, while its risks are evident. The slippage from "sustainable" to "more sustainable" is immediate in the first paragraph of the report of the Global Compact's meeting on SC (Global Compact 2004). Alongside this, however, SC is discussed as a marketing opportunity, an official from the Global Compact suggesting that "there is real opportunity to build brands around the concept of sustainable consumption" (Global Compact 2004: 1). At the same time, the contradictory nature of the attempt to think about SC from this perspective is readily apparent, workshop participants musing seriously (and confirming the suspicion that these days, satire is redundant) about how and whether it might be possible to "advertis(e) to consume less" (Global Compact 2004: 7). UNEP's Advertising and Communication Forum on Sustainability extends this contradictory discourse and takes it to its (il) logical extreme.[12] Not content with asserting that advertising cannot be associated with overconsumption in the North, it manages to rearticulate the imperative of SC to being not only not about reducing consumption, but actually about increasing it: "the first priority of sustainable consumption is to provide access to consumption for all."[13]

Sustainable consumption as legitimation strategy

The internal tensions and contradictions within sustainable consumption discourse as shown above suggest that it can be interpreted principally as a legitimation strategy. The emergence of sustainable consumption in the early 1990s is interesting as it appears as the outcomes of specific compromises and attempts by dominant political forces to co-opt radical elements within western environmentalism and contain geopolitical conflict in the run up to and aftermath of Rio. The discussions of the concept by the Global Compact participants show this element most clearly. The official presentations of SC (reasonably enough, it is not their concern) obscure this history, but it is worth elaborating a bit on the conflictual history of consumption in global environmental politics.

SC discourse presents a myth of origins concerning when consumption appears on the global environmental agenda, suggesting that UNCED in 1992 is where consumption became "recognized" as problematic.[14] As already quoted, Chapter 4 of Agenda 21 was entitled "Changing consumption patterns," and located the origins of environmental degradation in consumption patterns. But in practice, consumption was politicized at the beginning of the articulation of global environmental politics in diplomatic forums and elsewhere. There were two principal elements in this contestation over consumption.

At the Stockholm Conference (UNCHE) in 1972, the principal element in North–South conflict at the conference was over consumption. Developing country delegates fiercely resisted narratives of common global responsibility for the "environmental crisis," focusing specifically on the unequal patterns of consumption across the globe (Thomas 1992: 25). Attempts to place equal responsibility were interpreted widely in the South (and have been since) as a project of "environmental colonialism," with the North/West using the environmental crisis to re-impose control over patterns of development in the South, or even to stop development altogether. By contrast, Southern negotiators wanted to place the responsibility for the environmental crisis squarely on "overconsumption" in the North.

This notion of "environmental colonialism" became particularly sharp in relation to a focus by many environmentalists (and some governments) in the West on population growth. The emerging environmental studies at the time made much of an equation I = PCT (or sometimes I = PAT, the effect is the same), where overall environmental Impact is equal to Population × Consumption (or Affluence, if the A was used) × Technology. For some, most famously Paul and Anne Ehrlich (1968), the population element in this equation was the most important, and the most important determinant of environmental degradation was the level of human populations and/or rates of population growth. This became popularized in the Ehrlichs' term the "population bomb." In geopolitical terms, however, what this did was place attention firmly on developing countries, where rates of population growth were highest, population levels in many industrialized countries having more or less stabilized. The conflict over this also went on within Western environmentalism, notably in well-publicized debates during the 1970s between Paul Ehrlich and Barry Commoner, the latter resisting the wholesale focus on population. Since that time, the North–South dimension to consumption-environment politics has generated a range of responses within the North. These include the developments of the notion of "environmental space" (Friends of the Earth Netherlands 1990), "ecological shadow" (MacNeill *et al.* 1991), and "environmental footprint" (Wackernagel and Rees 1996), which all arise out of attempts to account for the differential ecological impacts of consumption levels of societies around the world, both in technical and ethical terms. The focus on consumption levels has also influenced the way that some in the North have resisted the assumption that what is needed is a geopolitical bargain involving large-scale North–South financial and technological transfers, which in this view often take away the attention from the levels of Western consumption, and in favor of the North/West "getting its own house in order" by reducing its overall ecological impact (Sachs *et al.* 1998). Finally, these academic/think tank accounts of consumption's global environmental politics have their counterpart in the emergence during the 1990s of social movements in the West focusing on the global justice dimensions of consumption—anti-sweatshop movements, fair trade movements, and ethical/green consumption movements, in particular.

Thus in geopolitical contexts, developing countries have focused on consumption, and have had some solidaristic responses from environmentalists in the West. But many Western environmentalists identified consumption and consumerism as part of the causes of environmental degradation and the more general cultural malaise of Western societies. There are two principal modes here. One is more technical or rationalist in orientation, generating a range of analyses of how specific consumption practices, and aggregate consumption more broadly, generate environmental degradation. The work of the Worldwatch Institute is perhaps the best-known example of this.[15] A key element in such critiques is that technological change is ineffective at reducing overall ecological impacts in the face of rising overall consumption levels. But alongside this is a strand of critique that focuses on the broader cultural dimensions of consumer societies. At times such critiques are spiritual or religious in orientation, in terms of objections to materialism (Gardner and Peterson 2002), but they are also often social objections to inequalities involved in consumption (as in the global justice arguments already discussed, but also in terms of the status competition involved in consumption) or to the domination of the life-world by commercial culture. In this latter mode, the critique is frequently about how consumption has become a site not where human freedom is to be pursued (as in neoliberal ideology) but rather where human creativity and freedom is quashed by the all-encompassing scope of commercial culture, and where the potential for human freedom is limited through its channeling in consumerist directions (Bordwell 2002; Purkis 2000; Klein 2000; Lasn 1999). The magazine *Adbusters* is the best-known contemporary site for this sort of counter-cultural critique of consumption.

What has essentially happened since the early 1970s is an attempt by Western (and increasingly global) elites to marginalize such critiques through a range of strategies: displacement through techno-fixes, outright denial and backlash, recycling, co-optation (Karliner 1994). The response to the Southern critique has been different, and by the time of Rio, a geopolitical compromise emerged which resulted in the discourse of SC. While the discourse has not fully ended such conflict (UNEP/Manoochehri 2001: 12), it has perhaps contained it. But underlying this geopolitical compromise is the other response to critiques of consumerism, missed by SC discourse.

What this alternative history of SC shows us is that while consumption was articulated as environmentally problematic, a series of moves have been made to render this articulation marginal. The principal reason for this, missed by SC discourse, is that increased consumption is widely understood to be a necessary condition of economic growth, and thus to call consumption into question is to call the very condition of possibility of capitalist society into question. Much of the discursive/ideological effort of capital since the early 1970s (when, bizarrely perhaps, transnational capital, in the form of the Club of Rome, funded the *Limits to Growth* study (Meadows *et al.* 1972)) has sought to shape the environmental agenda in terms that deny a limits to growth interpretation, in favor of focuses on "global equity" (initially emphasized in *Mankind at the Turning Point* (Mesarovic and Pestel 1974), the follow-up to the *Limits to Growth*), "sustainable development" (WCED 1987) and "ecological modernization" (Mol 1995; Hajer 1995). These discursive moves are accompanied by, for example, the development of recycling, specifically developed by Western industry in order to displace arguments for reductions in consumption (Karliner 1994).

This point is perhaps usefully underscored by considering more generally the contemporary place of consumption in political-economic discourse. Western economies have undergone a transition since the end of the 1970s from the management of economic cycles through Keynesian techniques of *public* borrowing in times of downward cycles, towards a management system predicated on rising levels of *private* debt to finance private consumption.[16] It is virtually ubiquitous in the business pages of newspapers to assert the centrality of private consumption in keeping growth going since September 11, 2001 at least, if not since the Asian financial crises of 1997–8 (or even earlier—one could in fact argue it is a central element in the neoliberal regime of accumulation). Especially in the aftermath of the September 11 attacks, public agencies and private agencies alike adopted a range of measures designed to stimulate private consumption in order to prevent economic collapse. Many of these measures were in highly ecologically destructive activities (specifically car use and aviation) for their economic benefits and, in the context of the attacks, symbolic importance.[17] As one further consequence, consumption has taken on moral-political overtones, in that the act of consumption has become, in for example the phrase attributed to George W. Bush (but probably apocryphally), the "patriotic duty to consume" (McFeatters n.d.).

At the same time, and conversely, consumption has become a site where individuals are integrated into the circuits of capital, and disciplined into practices that promote accumulation. For example, while the rise in private debt has been in part stimulated by relatively low interest rates and the development of easy technical means of credit creation (the rise of the credit card, in particular), it has also for many been rendered necessary in order to get access to basic services. Credit-worthiness has become an important component of economic citizenship and thus a means of disciplining individuals in relation to the workplace (Gill 1995).

In this context sustainable consumption appears as an uneasy, unstable suture. Rendered politically necessary to respond both to the geopolitical conflict over environmental degradation and to the articulation of consumption as problematic by environmentalists, it contains the contradictory elements outlined above, where it has both the potential for a radical interpretation emphasizing reductions in consumption in rich countries, but the dominant effect is to negate such an interpretation, emphasizing instead "different, efficient, quality of life oriented, equitable" consumption. SC discourse insists on disaggregating consumption to emphasize that different forms of consumption have different ecological consequences. Manoochehri for example discusses the importance of conceptualizing *patterns of consumption* rather than consumption per se (UNEP/Manoochehri 2001). Burgess *et al.* (2003: 287) conclude by suggesting that "capitalism and industrialization lie at the heart of increasing consumption although ... consumption meanings and practices are both context-specific and dynamic," to emphasize the possible detachment of aggregate consumption (as GDP) from aggregate consumption (as materials/energy throughput) via different consumption (as individual practice). While this is clearly not the explicit intent of Burgess *et al.*, nevertheless the attention is drawn away from reduced consumption (as aggregate GDP, material throughput and/or as individual practice), while no evidence is given for the viability of this decoupling.[18] Such a discourse can be seen fundamentally to help reveal the nature of the "environmental crisis" as a legitimation crisis, where states are required (individually and collectively) to intervene to promote accumulation to stabilize capitalist society, and at the same time to intervene in response to environmentalism to legitimize itself, but where the two sets of interventions frequently are in contradiction with each other (Hay 1994).

Sustainable consumption as governmentality

As sustainable consumption discourse acts to shape the understanding of the "consumption problem" in ways consistent with capitalist imperatives for accumulation, it thus simultaneously displaces attention from imperatives to reduce overall levels of consumption in industrialized countries, but, perhaps more importantly, effects a kind of "green governmentality" (Luke 1998).

To elaborate this, it is perhaps necessary to elucidate an essential (and often productive) ambiguity in the meaning of consumption. In environmental contexts, consumption is used to refer simultaneously to the aggregate throughput in materials and energy, and at the same time to the individual acts of consumption—purchasing and use of goods.[19] This conflation can be seen throughout in the official documents on SC (UNEP/Manoochehri 2001) as well as in broader literature on consumption and environment (Cohen 2001; Princen *et al.* 2002). But what tends to happen as institutions act on SC is that the two get conflated. In formal discourse, what is impressive in many ways in "Consumption Opportunities" is the explicit denial of this conflation—that consumption, if it is to be understood in terms of its environmental impacts, is not just about individuals, that governments, industries, and so on, are themselves consumers in ecological terms. The document also talks about "systemic" consumption, emphasizing this broad understanding (UNEP/Manoochehri 2001). Thus to act on consumption is to involve a wide range of activities designed to reduce the material throughputs in the economy. But when it comes to practical activities, it is most commonly individual consumers who are invoked, and thus consumption as aggregate throughput and consumption as individual practice that is invoked.

For example, when the OECD starts discussing SC, they precisely and explicitly reduce it to "household consumption" (OECD n.d.) It is precisely this displacement that is necessary to obscure the relation where consumption (as aggregate throughput) is a synonym for growth and therefore structurally required for capitalist legitimacy, and the indicator of the ecological impacts of the economy. Shifting the meaning of consumption to that of individual practices, the link to overall ecological impacts is obscured.

This problem is also evident in the more sophisticated academic literature on the subject. In one of the most thorough reviews, Burgess *et al.* state again that focusing only on domestic or individual consumption is inevitably limited:

> Consumption practices are fundamentally political. Large organizations, public authorities, the military, and commercial companies, are largely responsible for the bulk of human-environment transactions which lead to damage to bio-physical systems, as Stern *et al.* acknowledge. But the focus of attention in terms of achieving changes in consumption practices has remained firmly on individual consumers and thus domestic consumption.
>
> (Burgess *et al.* 2003: 268, citing Stern *et al.* 1997)

But then Burgess *et al.*'s review again accepts this narrow focus and concentrates on empirical work (including their own) and the methodological/interpretive debates underpinning explanations of (individual) consumer behavior. There is a concern to move from rationalist accounts of behavior where either (a) information or (b) norms are held to affect the sustainability or otherwise of consumer behavior, to an account emphasizing the embeddedness of individual practices in "collective socio-material networks," but the practices focused on remain those of individuals and households.[20]

Tellingly in this context, as SC moved through the UN system, one of its routes was to become incorporated into the UN Guidelines on Consumer Protection. These had been established through a UNGA resolution (39/85) in 1985 to provide guidelines "for use by governments in developing and strengthening national consumer protection legislation and regulation" (Bentley 2002: 12). Consumers International got involved in discussions, organizing a conference on "the transition to sustainable consumption" in 1993 (Bentley 2002: 10), and interestingly argued that the concept should be incorporated into the UN guidelines. Consumer protection thus became articulated to include shaping consumer behavior in particular ways. UNEP and the CI conflate these two thus:

> The extension of the Guidelines to include sustainable consumption provided an important opportunity both to update consumer protection policies to include environmental protection and sustainable development, and to strengthen the linkage between consumer interests and sustainable consumption, thereby stimulating national policy making to promote more sustainable consumption.
>
> (Bentley 2002: 12)

The move made to conflate the protection of consumer interests with the promotion of particular consumption patterns is not explained in the document cited above, but two years later, UNEP and CI make this more explicit:

> There is wide global recognition that unsustainable patterns of consumption have serious social and environmental impacts. ... Protecting consumers from impending environmental and social catastrophes is an integral responsibility of governments all around the world.[21]

In other words, consumers are the root cause of the environmental changes and degradations which in turn cause potential disasters for consumers themselves (conflated in the minds at least of the heads of CI and UNEP with citizens), and the role of governments is in effect thus to shape consumer behavior to protect consumers from themselves. What emerges is a transformation from regulation for consumer protection to the governance of consumers themselves, legitimized by those who are in principle organizing to protect consumer interests.

In part as a consequence of this displacement of attention, SC thus appears as a power/knowledge formation. It has a set of technocratic tools to rationalize and ascribe responsibilities. Much of the efforts of institutions like the OECD in relation to SC have been to "track consumption patterns," and to generate new forms of knowledge concerning consumption and its environmental consequences. Again, tools developed to articulate more radical agendas have their legacies, as concepts such as "ecological footprints" (Wackernagel and Rees 1996) and "environmental space" (originally developed by Friends of the Earth Netherlands), appear, albeit unacknowledged, in "Consumption Opportunities." Much attention is on developing indicators for the sustainability of consumption, and tracking patterns in order to provide for policy intervention.

Alongside this exercise in knowledge generation, classification, and so on, is a de facto individualization and a concurrent attempt at subject formation. The opening paragraph of "Consumption Opportunities" is instructive in this regard: "Sustainable consumption is possible. But it requires *change*—change that can be a positive, innovative experience. To effect this change, it calls for knowledgeable and committed agents at all levels of decision-making" (UNEP/Manoochehri 2001: 10).

Acting to undermine the focus later on where individualization is resisted (see above), this passage expresses perfectly governmentality as, in Ian Douglas's (1999: 138) useful phrase "the passing of the command structure into the very constitution of the individual." Power is organized to effect changes not only in a regulatory sense, to restrict and channel individual behavior, but to act on how individual subjectivities are formed, to shape who people are and how they orient themselves to the world.

When implemented, SC strategies reveal this governmentality more clearly, as shown for example by Hobson's study of the United Kingdom (Hobson 2002). First, when put into practice, SC focuses on household and individual consumption (despite the recognition of the limits of this by UNEP) and thus misses the bulk of consumption understood as aggregate throughput. Second, SC practices involve the attempts to shape behavior along rationalized lines. Neoliberalism as a form of rule invokes personal freedom (conceived of as lack of state interference) as one of its principal norms, and thus direct restrictions on behavior are politically difficult (Hobson 2002: 99). Simultaneously, consumption becomes a principal means of articulating citizens into a social/political whole (Hobson 2002: 100; Paterson 2002). As a consequence, to promote changes in consumption patterns involves attempts to shape the preferences of consumers by creating means of getting them to articulate environmental concerns into their purchasing preferences (Hobson 2002: 100). Hobson then shows a range of processes through which such concerns have been pursued in the United Kingdom, principally through the program called "Action at Home," through which participants were given a range of materials regularly with information about the impacts of different forms of their consumption and the possibilities of alternative practices.

The review of implementation of SC programs by UNEP and Consumers International (Bentley 2002) also shows this individualization and focus on shaping consumer preferences and identities. In Australia, all of the concrete actions focus on individuals and households and mechanisms to change their behavior, with the exception of the Sydney Olympics (Bentley 2002: 30–37). In China, the government began a "Green consumption" campaign in 2001, which involved getting people to make pledges about changes in personal consumption patterns (Bentley 2002: 42–45). In Germany, most of the programs focus on individual consumption, with the rationale easily understood in terms of governmentality: "the challenge we face is the question of how we can reorient existing lifestyles towards sustainability" (Bentley 2002: 50). Overall, UNEP/Consumers International regard the principal success that governments have had in implementing a sustainable consumption agenda as in the realm of consumer information (Bentley 2002: 61).

This focus of SC governance strategies on technocratic development of indicators and tracking of patterns, and individualization, acting on individual subjectivities, occurs precisely because of the way in which it has been shaped to respond to the legitimization requirements of capitalist societies and away from a serious analysis of the role of consumption in environmental degradation. Rajan's (1996) analysis of the regulation of automobiles to improve air quality in California is an instructive analogy here. Given the taken-for-granted nature of automobile use in California, intervention to respond to the air quality problems created by mass automobility began with simple technological fixes—small changes in engine design, addition of filters, catalytic converters—then moved to inspection and maintenance regimes, and then focused on a discourse about "sick cars." At each stage, the level of intrusion into the daily activities of car drivers increases (even while car use itself is principally understood in terms of individual liberty). The combination of a set of technocratic tools to monitor the situation, and a set of individualizing strategies designed to produce new sorts of subjects, is resonant with the form SC takes as a governance strategy. SC discourse is at an earlier stage, but the dynamics are very similar. In Rajan's case, it is the political impossibility (as he sees it) of challenging car use per se that generates the forms of intervention that ensue. Regarding SC, it is the political imperative to avoid arguments for reducing consumption that generate the focus on individual households and consumers and a set of disciplinary and pastoral practices to shape their practices and subjectivities. Given its mis-specification of the problem however, such intervention will become progressively more intrusive as each stage of intervention will necessarily be insufficient to deal with the impacts of consumption, thus justifying yet more intrusive regulation.

Conclusions: sustainable consumption as a mode of regulation

But the focus on legitimation and governmentality give perhaps only a partial picture. While SC governance is both of these things, it can also be seen as the way in which an emerging ecological regime of accumulation is being shaped and governed. In regulation theory (Aglietta 1979), modes of regulation are referred to as the socio-political institutions and ideologies through which capital attempts to smoothly reproduce a specific regime of accumulation, the "mechanisms which adjust the contradictory behavior of individuals to the collective principles of the regime of accumulation" (Lipietz 1992: 2). The latter refers to the historically specific way in which surplus value is extracted and realized, and a long-term model is articulated which creates a general consistency between conditions of production and "the conditions under which production is put to social use (household consumption, investment, government spending, foreign trade)" (Lipietz 1992: 2). The need for such strategies and policies arises out of the contradictions internal to capitalist society's basic structure. In particular, capitalism has a tendency towards underconsumption crises, because of the contradiction between the interests of individual capitalists (in maintaining wage levels at a minimum, ideally as close to subsistence levels as possible) and those of capital collectively (in maintaining sufficient aggregate demand for its products). Regimes of accumulation are precisely means of overcoming this tendency, by finding ways of producing aggregate demand.[22]

In the context of ecological crises, the discourse of ecological modernization (Mol 2001) can be regarded as an attempt to articulate a possible regime of accumulation consistent with environmental limits of various sorts. For many, this is becoming an important element of accumulation strategies in many countries, especially in continental Europe (Paterson 2001; Barry and Paterson 2004; Dryzek *et al.* 2003; and Eckersley 2004). Ecological modernization entails a set of shifts in terms of state economic management techniques and goals, as well as state–business and state–civil society relations, which would be designed to realize the technical potential for decoupling economic growth (in monetary/GDP terms) from its ecological impacts, as noted above. Interpreting it thus as a (incipient) regime of accumulation seems thus reasonable. Sustainable consumption can be regarded thus as an element in the regulation of such a regime; it is the project to shape the lifestyles, aspirations, and practices of individuals in ways which would foster enhanced consumption of goods and services and thus enable continued accumulation, while responding politically to the articulation of environmental degradation as a political crisis. Occasionally the articulation of this by SC advocates is explicit. In the words of the German government in their response to UNEP's report on progress in implementing SC, which could almost have been written by a regulation theorist,

> The issue of sustainable production and consumption should be seen as a long-term process of social innovation and cultural reorientation, because the idea emerged that an "ecologization" of patterns of production and consumption could also be seen as a new stage in the modernization of societies and cultures. Here, it became clear that political objectives were required for the whole of society, and that it cannot simply be a question of cultivating a particular "ecological lifestyle" in society niches.
>
> (Bentley 2002: 50)

Both regimes of accumulation and modes of regulation contain within themselves, however, contradictions which arise out of the basic contradictions of capitalist societies (between modes and relations of production, and perhaps in ecological contexts, between the combined mode/relations of production and the conditions of production, referred to by eco-Marxists such as O'Connor (1988) as the "second contradiction") and the specific ways each attempts to suture these contradictions. SC is in this context no different. It is contradictory in part because of the environmental contradictions entailed in the dependence of ecological modernization on the assumption that efficiency gains from technological change can be effected fast enough (and permanently enough) to overcome the increased consumption which is a corollary of growth. But it is also contradictory in terms of its internal relation as simultaneously a moment in the circulation of capital (the site where new commodities are consumed and accumulation effected), and a site of the legitimation of capitalism. In other words, (sustainable) consumption is legitimized in terms of individual freedom (to consume) while, at the same time, entailing ever-greater regulation of and self-discipline by consumers themselves. As emphasized in the introduction to this book, much of this is because of the basic mis-specification of the nature of the environmental problematic—the failure to realize (or perhaps more precisely, an attempt to create a discourse which insists on forgetting the realization of) the origins of environmental degradation precisely in industrial capitalist development and its legitimation through consumer culture.

Notes

1 I should emphasize perhaps the specific usage of the term regulation here, which differs from the more everyday usage in terms of specific interventions to control, or "regularize," particular activities. The term "mode of regulation" is specific to regulation theory, and refers to an overall pattern by which states shape and attempt to control practices across the social totality in line with the needs of a regime of accumulation. I try to use the term regulation in this specific manner throughout the chapter. See also Brand, this volume, for an elaboration of a regulation-theoretic account of global environmental governance. See the conclusion for more elaboration here.

2 Consumers International is an interesting organization in this context. It is formally an International NGO, but (like a number of such NGOs) is composed of members from states around the world, some of which are state consumer protection agencies, others more strictly "non-governmental." In addition to membership fees, CI gets funding directly from governments and from intergovernmental organizations, further complicating the "non-governmental" identity (see its website at www.consumers international.org/about_CI/, for a description of its organization). I have not been able to find any academic research specifically on CI, but it would seem fair to characterize it as a hybrid organization, much in the manner of analyses of the International Standardization Organization or the International Council of Scientific Unions, for example. On the former, see Clapp 1998 or Finger and Tamiotti 2002.

3 UNEP/Manoochehri 2001: 12. Many others also give this definition: see, for example, OECD n.d.; UN 1999: Section G, paragraph 42; Bentley 2002: 10.

4 For a fuller history see UNEP/Ryan 2002; Cohen 2001.
5 For reviews of its development in the United Kingdom (as one example) see for example Hobson 2002 or DEFRA 2003. For a general review of implementation by various countries, see OECD 1998; OECD 2002. For a review of other sorts of organizations involved, see French 2004.
6 These elements of course overlap and interact, but it is useful perhaps to keep them separate for analytic purposes; as noted later on, they entail different modes of governance.
7 On the former, see WFA/EACA 2002. The Youth part of the program no longer appears to exist, although a link to such a program remains on UNEP's main SC site, at: www.uneptie.org/pc/sustain/home.htm.
8 UNDSD 2003. It is not especially important or interesting in my view to dwell too much on the substance here; for the most part these documents contain the usual wish-list of policies and management techniques which have become familiar in the environmental politics/policy domain over the last 20 years. What is novel is their packaging in terms of "sustainable consumption and production."
9 See UNEP's SC website at: www.uneptie.org/pc/sustain/home.htm. SETAC is a professional association of biologists, chemists, and toxicologists working in the environmental field. See www.setac.org.
10 Haas *et al.* 1993; Vogler 2000; and Young 1989. It is, however, consistent with the definition of such a regime, which does not require that the "principles, norms, rules, and decision-making procedures" be formalized in treaties (Krasner 1983: 2).
11 The concept is similarly weakened in some of the academic literature on sustainable consumption; see for example Spaargaren 2003.
12 See generally the forum web pages at: www.uneptie.org/pc/sustain/advertising/advertising.htm.
13 WFA/EACA 2002: 6. Of course the immediate objection to this critical comment is that in effect the claim is "true"—there are many people in the world for whom the meeting of their basic needs does entail an increase in consumption. But of course what the discourse here misses is that such consumption is in terms of material needs—foodstuffs, clean water, and so on—while the accelerated commodification of such materials in fact entails a denial of access to their consumption for those without the cash income to pay. The slippage (or basic mistake in understanding, perhaps) is the conflation of consumption as simple use, and consumption via the marketplace.
14 For example, UNEP/Manoochehri 2001: 11; and Bentley, 2002: 9. For an exception, which recognizes the longer history, see UNEP/Ryan 2002: 9.
15 As, for example, in Durning 1992. But see also for example Westra and Werhane 1998; Redclift 1996; or, in a Marxist mode, Trainer 1985.
16 For a particularly sophisticated economic history of the period, which shows this shift from public to private financing of economic cycles (although this is not his principal purpose), see Brenner 2002.
17 For example, the US Federal Reserve reduced real interest rates to zero in the aftermath of the attacks, and GM introduced a zero percent financing scheme on new cars in "an unabashed appeal to the patriotism of US consumers" (Teather 2002).
18 I do not wish here to give myself the task of arguing the opposite—that such meanings of consumption cannot be so decoupled. The point here is simply to show that in taking for granted that they can, SC discourse should be understood ideologically. The ecological modernization discourse of which SC can be regarded as the "mode of regulation" similarly tends simply to assert the possible decoupling of GDP growth from material throughputs (see for example Mol 2001), while the strongest attempts to demonstrate it are in the "factor 4/10" writers (Hawken *et al.* 1999; Von Weiszäcker *et al.* 1998 or Ekins 2000). Two key

points often made are, first, that the simple technical possibility of eco-efficient performance does not take into account that technologies are always deployed in a social setting—it is more appropriate to talk of socio-technical systems than simply technological possibilities; and, second, that at least in terms of our historical experience, but also arguably logically, in a continually growing system, efficiency gains are usually countered by increases in aggregate consumption (with energy efficiency in cars a paradigmatic example). For a good critique of these attempts to demonstrate the potential decoupling of growth from environmental impacts, see White 2002.

19 This is different to the attempt at conceptual clarification by UNEP/Ryan (2002: 11) which distinguishes between "the economic focus on *consumption of goods and services* (demand and volume) and the ecological focus on *consumption of resources and generation of waste* (ecological impact)". This distinction is of course crucial to establishing the viability of sustainable consumption and ecological modernization, that is, it is the basis for attempting to show the potential decoupling of the former from the latter. But of more interest here is the distinction between consumption as aggregate throughput (whether measured economically or ecologically) and as an individual practice. Later, Ryan does distinguish in this manner (p. 39), and, like Manoochehri, as noted already, attempts to make clear that "consumption" does not reduce to "consumer behavior." It is also worth distinguishing this sort of critique from that which focuses on the explanation of individual consumption underpinning models of policy-making, as for example developed (brilliantly) by Shove (2003).

20 Burgess *et al.* 2003: 275. A similar narrowing to individuals is effected by Murphy and Cohen (2001: 8), who recognize the problem more explicitly, and rationalize it as a scoping problem. Similarly, Spaargaren (2003) recognizes the limits of understanding individual's consumption in terms of individual agency, and invokes the notion of "systems of provision" to discuss the structuring of individual consumption and thus the mechanisms by which sustainable consumption might be pursued. See also Fine and Leopold 1993 and Van Vliet *et al.* 2005. But while Spaargaren illustrates the importance of this notion well in relation to the development of photovoltaics in the Netherlands, the focus is still on the ways in which individual decisions towards sustainable consumption might be enabled.

21 Sylvan and Töpfer 2004: 3. There is a very nice slippage between the second sentence quoted here, and the main body of this document (UNEP/CI 2004). In the main body, it is "citizens" who have to be protected from "environmental and social disasters," while in the foreword, it is "consumers."

22 The ideal-typical instance is the Fordist–Keynesian regime which involved a combination of the direct raising of wages by some firms and sectors (paradigmatically the emerging car industry), and the development of the welfare state, both of which spread the potential for private consumption, alongside the disciplining of the labor force through organized trade unionism which produced enhanced productivity gains and labor stability, and the management of aggregate demand through public deficits by the state.

References

Aglietta, Michel (1979) *A Theory of Capitalist Regulation*, London: New Left Books.

Aloisi de Larderel, Jacqueline (1999) *Speech to the 4th International Business Forum*, October 1999.

Barry, John and Paterson, Matthew (2004) "Globalization, ecological modernization and New Labour," *Political Studies* 52,4: 767–784.

Bentley, Matthew (2002) *Tracking Progress: implementing sustainable consumption policies: A global review of the implementation of the United Nations Guidelines on Consumer Protection (Section G: Promotion of Sustainable Consumption)*, Geneva: Consumers International/United Nations Environment Programme. Available www.uneptie.org/pc/sustain/guidelines/guidelines.htm (accessed February 14, 2005).

Bordwell, Marylin (2002) "Jamming Culture: Adbusters' Hip Media Campaign Against Consumerism," in Thomas Princen, Michael Maniates, and Ken Conca (eds.) *Confronting Consumption*, Cambridge, MA: MIT Press.

Brenner, Robert (2002) *The Boom and the Bubble: the US in the World Economy*, London: Verso.

Burgess, J., Bedford, T., Hobson, K., Davies, G., and Harrison, C. (2003) "(Un)Sustainable Consumption," in F. Berkhout, M. Leach, and I. Scoones (eds.) *Negotiating Environmental Change: New Perspectives from Social Science*, Cheltenham: Edward Elgar.

Clapp, Jennifer (1998) "The Privatization of Global Environmental Governance: ISO 14000 and the Developing World," *Global Governance* 4: 295–316.

Cohen, Maurie (2001) "The Emergent Environmental Policy Discourse on Sustainable Consumption," in M. Cohen and J. Murphy (eds.) *Exploring Sustainable Consumption: Environmental Policy and the Social Sciences*, Oxford: Elsevier.

DEFRA (2003) *UK Government Framework for Sustainable Consumption and Production*, London: Department for Environment, Food and Rural Affairs.

Douglas, Ian R. (1999) "Globalization *as* Governance: Toward an Archaeology of Contemporary Political Reason," in Aseem Prakash and Jeffrey Hart (eds.) *Globalization and Governance*, London: Routledge.

Dryzek, John, Downes, David, Hunold, Christian, and Schlosberg, David, with Hernes, Hans-Kristian (2003) *Green States and Social Movements*, Oxford: Oxford University Press.

Durning, Alan (1992) *How Much Is Enough?* Washington: Worldwatch Institute.

Eckersley, Robyn (2004) *The Green State: Rethinking Democracy and Sovereignty*, Cambridge, MA: MIT Press.

Ehrlich, Paul and Ehrlich, Anne (1968) *The Population Bomb*, New York: Sierra Club.

Ekins, Paul (2000) *Economic Growth and Environmental Sustainability: The Prospects for Green Growth*, London: Routledge.

Fine, Ben, and Leopold, Ellen (1993) *The World of Consumption*, London: Routledge.

Finger, Matthias, and Tamiotti, Ludivine (2002) "The Emerging Linkage between the WTO and the ISO: Implications for Developing Countries," in Peter Newell, Shirin M. Rai and Andrew Scott (eds.) *Development and the Challenge of Globalization*, London: Intermediate Technology Development Group Publications.

French, Hilary (2004) "Linking Globalization, Consumption, and Governance," in Worldwatch Institute, *State of the World 2004*, New York: WW Norton & Co.

Friends of the Earth Netherlands (1990) *Action Plan for a Sustainable Netherlands*, Amsterdam: Vereniging Milieudefense.

Fuchs, Doris and Lorek, Sylvia (2002) "Sustainable Consumption Governance in a Globalizing World," *Global Environmental Politics* 2,1: 19–45.

Gardner, Gary and Peterson, Jane (eds.) (2002) *Invoking the Spirit: Religion and Spirituality in the Quest for a Sustainable World*, Washington, D.C.: Worldwatch Institute.

Gill, Stephen (1995) "The Global Panopticon? The Neoliberal State, Economic Life, and Democratic Surveillance," *Alternatives* 20,1: 1–50.

Global Compact (2004) "Global Compact Policy Dialogue on 'Sustainable Consumption: Marketing & Communications'," *Meeting Report*, Paris, France April 5–6, 2004. Available www.uneptie.org/pc/sustain/events/gc_meetingreport.pdf (accessed August 30, 2004).

Haas, Peter, Keohane, Robert, and Levy, Marc (eds.) (1993) *Institutions for the Earth: Sources of Effective Environmental Protection*, Cambridge, MA: MIT Press.

Hajer, Maarten (1995) *The Politics of Environmental Discourse: Ecological Modernization and the Policy Process*, Oxford: Oxford University Press.

Hawken, Paul, Lovins, Amory, and Lovins, Hunter (1999) *Natural Capitalism: The Next Industrial Revolution*, London: Earthscan.

Hay, Colin (1994) "Environmental Security and State Legitimacy," in M. O'Connor (ed.) *Is Capitalism Sustainable? Political Economy and the Politics of Ecology*, New York: Guilford Press.

Hobson, Kersty (2002) "Competing Discourses of Sustainable Consumption: Does the "Rationalization of Lifestyles" Make Sense?," *Environmental Politics* 11,2: 95–120.

Hughes, Steve and Wilkinson, Rorden (2001) "The Global Compact: Promoting Corporate Responsibility?" *Environmental Politics* 10,1: 155–159.

Karliner, Joshua (1994) "The Environment Industry: Profiting from Pollution," *The Ecologist* 24,2: 59–63.

Klein, Naomi (2000) *No Logo: Taking Aim at the Brand Bullies*, London: Flamingo.

Krasner, Stephen D. (1983) "Structural Causes and Regime Consequences: Regimes as Intervening Variables," in Stephen D. Krasner (ed.) *International Regimes*, Ithaca, NY: Cornell University Press.

Lasn, Kalle (1999) *Culture Jam: The Uncooling of America^{TM}*, New York: Eagle Brook.

Lipietz, Alain (1992) *Towards a New Economic Order: Fordism, Ecology and Democracy*, Cambridge: Polity Press.

Luke, Timothy W. (1998) "Environmentality as Green Governmentality," in Eric Darier (ed.) *Discourses of the Environment*, Oxford: Blackwell.

MacNeill, Jim, Winsemius, Pieter, and Yakushiji, Taizo (1991) *Beyond Interdependence: The Meshing of the World's Economy and the Earth's Ecology*, New York: Oxford University Press.

Marrakech Report (2003) *International Expert Meeting on the 10 Year Framework of Programs on Sustainable Consumption and Production*, Marrakech June 16–19, Summary by the Co-Chairs of the Meeting. Available www.uneptie.org/pc/sustain/10year/international.htm (accessed February 14, 2005).

McFeatters, Ann (n.d.) "Your patriotic duty to consume." Available www.smirkingchimp.com/article.php?sid=3148 (accessed May 13, 2002). Originally in the *Pittsburgh Post-Gazette*.

Meadows, Donella, Meadows, Dennis, Randers, Jørgen, and Behrens, William (1972) *The Limits To Growth*, London: Pan.

Mesarovic, Mihajlo and Pestel, Eduardo (1974) *Mankind at the Turning Point*, London: Hutchinson.

Mol, Arthur (1995) *The Refinement of Production: Ecological Modernization Theory and the Dutch Chemical Industry*, Utrecht: Van Arkel.

—— (2001) *Globalization and Environmental Reform: The Ecological Modernization of the Global Economy*, Cambridge, MA: MIT Press.

Murphy, Joseph and Cohen, Maurie (2001) "Introduction: Consumption, Environment and Public Policy," in M. Cohen and J. Murphy (eds.) *Exploring Sustainable Consumption: Environmental Policy and the Social Sciences*, Oxford: Elsevier.

Murphy, Joseph and Michaelis, Laurie (2003) "Consumption, Environment and Sustainability," in Ed Page and John Proops (eds.) *Environmental Thought*, London: International Library of Ecological Economics, Edward Elgar.

O'Connor, James (1988) "Introduction: Capitalism, Nature, Socialism: A Theoretical Introduction," *Capitalism, Nature, Socialism* 1: 11–38.

Organisation for Economic Co-operation and Development (OECD) (n.d.) *Conceptual Framework and Definition: What is Sustainable Consumption?* Paris: OECD. Available www.oecd.org/oecd/pages/home/displaygeneral/0,3380,EN-document-496-nodirectorate-no-no-18914-21,00.html (accessed July 8, 2003).

—— (1997) *Sustainable Consumption and Production*, Paris: OECD.

—— (1998) *Towards Sustainable Consumption Patterns: A Progress Report on Member Country Initiatives*, Paris: OECD.

—— (2002) *Towards Sustainable Household Consumption? Trends and Policies in OECD Countries*, Paris: OECD. Available www.oecd.org/EN/home/0,EN-home-468-nodirectorate-no-no-no-21,00.html.

Paterson, Matthew (2001) "Climate policy as accumulation strategy: the failure of COP6 and emerging trends in climate politics," *Global Environmental Politics* 1,2: 10–17.

—— (2002) *Shut up and shop! Thinking politically about consumption*. Available www.theglobalsite.ac.uk/press/211paterson.htm.

Princen, Thomas, Maniates, Michael, and Conca, Ken (eds.) (2002) *Confronting Consumption*, Cambridge, MA: MIT Press.

Purkis, Jonathon (2000) "Modern Millenarians? Anticonsumerism, Anarchism and the New Urban Environmentalism," in B. Seel, M. Paterson, and B. Doherty (eds.) *Direct Action in British Environmentalism*, London: Routledge.

Rajan, Sudhir Chella (1996) *The Enigma of Automobility: Democratic Politics and Pollution Control*, Pittsburgh: University of Pittsburgh Press.

Redclift, Michael (1996) *Wasted: Counting the Costs of Global Consumption*, London: Routledge.

Rensvik, H. (1994) "The Role of Authorities: From Pollution Watchdog to Catalyst for Sustainable Development," in *Symposium: Sustainable Consumption*, Oslo: Norwegian Environment Ministry.

Sachs, W., Loske, R., Linz, M. *et al.* (1998) *Greening the North*, London: Zed Books.

Shove, Elizabeth (2003) "Changing human behavior and lifestyle: a challenge for sustainable consumption?" paper for the Economic and Social Research Council's Environment and Human Behaviour program. Available www.psi.org.uk/ehb/docs/shove-changinghumanbehaviourandlifestyle-200308.pdf.

Spaargaren, Gert (2003) "Sustainable Consumption: A Theoretical and Environmental Policy Perspective," *Society and Natural Resources* 16: 687–701.

Stern, P.C., Dietz, T., Rutter, V.W., Socolow, R.H., and Sweeney J.L. (eds.) (1997) *Environmentally Significant Consumption: Research Directions*, Washington: National Academy Press.

Sylvan, Louise and Töpfer, Klaus (2004) "Foreword" to UNEP/CI, *Tracking Progress: Implementing Sustainable Consumption Policies*, 2nd edition, Paris: United Nations Programme Division of Trade, Industry, and Economics.

Teather, David (2002) "Motor city kingpin who kept America rolling: Interview, Richard Wagoner, CEO, General Motors," The *Guardian*, July 20, p. 30.

Thomas, Caroline (1992) *The Environment in International Relations*, London: Royal Institute of International Affairs.

Trainer, F.E. (1985) *Abandon Affluence!* London: Zed Books.

United Nations (UN) (1992) *Agenda 21*, New York: United Nations.
—— (1999) *United Nations Guidelines on Consumer Protection (as expanded in 1999)*, New York: Commission on Sustainable Development. Available www.un. org/esa/sustdev/sdissues/consumption/cpp14.htm#report.
—— (2002) "Plan of Implementation of the World Summit on Sustainable Development," in *Report of the World Summit on Sustainable Development*, UN Document A/CONF.199/20*, New York: United Nations.
United Nations Development Programme (UNDP) (1998) *Human Development Report*, New York: UNDP.
United Nations Division of Sustainable Development (UNDSD) (2003) *International Expert Meeting on the 10 Year Framework of Programs on Sustainable Consumption and Production*, Marrakech, June 16–19, background paper prepared by the United Nations Division for Sustainable Development. Available www.un.org/esa/sustdev/sdissues/consumption/Marrakech/conprod10Yglobmeet.htm (accessed February 14, 2005).
United Nations Environment Programme (UNEP) (2004) *European Stakeholder Meeting on Sustainable Consumption and Production: Meeting Report and Co-Chairs Summary*, Ostende, Belgium, November 25–26, 2004, Paris: UNEP Division of Trade, Industry, and Economics.
United Nations Environment Programme/CI (2004) *Tracking Progress: Implementing Sustainable Consumption Policies*, 2nd edition, Paris: UNEP Division of Trade, Industry, and Economics.
United Nations Environment Programme/Manoochehri, John (2001) *Consumption Opportunities: Strategies for Change*, A Report for Decisionmakers, Geneva: UNEP. Available www.uneptie.org/pc//sustain/.
United Nations Environment Programme/Ryan, Chris (2002) *Sustainable Consumption: A Global Status Report*, Geneva: UNEP.
Van Vliet, Bas, Chappells, Heather, and Shove, Elizabeth (eds.) (2005) *Infrastructures of Consumption: Environmental Innovation in the Utility Industries*, London: Earthscan.
Vogler, John (2000) *The Global Commons. Environmental and Technological Governance*, Chichester: John Wiley.
Von Weizäcker, Ernst, Lovins, Amory, and Lovins, Hunter (1998) *Factor Four: Doubling Wealth, Halving Resource Use*, London: Earthscan.
Wackernagel, Mathias and Rees, William (1996) *Our Ecological Footprint: Reducing Human Impact on the Earth*, Gabriola Island, BC: New Society Publishers.
Westra, Laura and Werhane, Patricia (eds.) (1998) *The Business of Consumption: Environmental Ethics and the Global Economy*, Oxford: Rowman & Littlefield.
White, Daman Finbar (2002) "A Green Industrial Revolution? Sustainable Technological Innovation in a Global Age," *Environmental Politics* 11,2: 1–26.
World Commission on Environment and Development (WCED) (1987) *Our Common Future: Report of the World Commission on Environment and Development*, Oxford: Oxford University Press.
World Federation of Advertisers/European Association of Communications Agencies (WFA/EACA) (2002) *Industry as a Partner for Sustainable Development: Advertising*, London: WFA/EACA. Available www.uneptie.org/outreach/wssd/contributions/sector_reports/sectors/advertising/advertising.htm (accessed February 14, 2005).
Young, Oran (1989) *International Cooperation: Building Regimes for Natural Resources and the Environment*, Ithaca, NY: Cornell University Press.

8 Transnational transformations

From government-centric interstate regimes to cross-sectoral multi-level networks of global governance

Sanjeev Khagram and Saleem H. Ali

Much scholarly and public policy attention has focused on the contestation around older intergovernmental agencies such as the United Nations, World Bank, and International Monetary Fund, as well as newer ones such as the World Trade Organization and the International Criminal Court (Woods 1999 and 2002).[1] But far too few of these, even scholarly versions, examine the relations between these organizations and the broader underlying institutional arrangements, that is interstate regimes, let alone perhaps a world society, of which they are constitutive elements, central actors, and core symbols (Rittberger 1995).

Even fewer rigorous analyses based on in-depth empirical research have been offered of the various new forms of "supra-state" and "trans-territorial" organizations that have been described by others as global policy or action networks (Reinecke and Deng 2000; Waddell 2003).[2] Although not fully satisfactory, we will utilize the label of "global governance networks" in this chapter for this category, which is not synonymous with intergovernmental organizations, multinational corporations, transnational professional associations, epistemic communities, or even transnational nongovernmental organizations (NGOs) by themselves, but rather novel arrangements *among* these various and other constituents including governmental agencies across sectors and levels of governance.[3] Identifying the core features, genesis, effects, and emerging roles of these global governance networks is critical for many reasons, not least of all because of their rapid proliferation over the last decade, from virtually zero to several dozen, and associated claims that they are the most potentially transformative new entrants in world affairs today.

Once again, it is not surprising that negligible scholarship can be found that conceptualizes the relationships between these novel global governance networks and changes in broader underlying institutional arrangements such as, for example, changes within, of, or perhaps even away from interstate regimes. Regimes are understood as "sets of implicit and explicit principles, norms, rules and decision-making procedures around which actor-expectations converge in a given issue area," and the actors that count for interstate regimes are governmental (Krasner 1983, 3–4).[4] Changes in rules and decision-making procedures are considered changes *within*, whereas changes in principles and norms are seen as changes *of*, these interstate regimes. But there is also the possibility that these global governance networks are a semi-formalization of "transnational organizational fields" and correspondingly an increasingly structured, albeit contested, world society.[5]

Why have these global governance networks emerged, what are their defining features, and are they efficacious? Do global governance networks signal a possible shift underway from the predominance of government-centric interstate regimes in world affairs? Are these novel global governance networks constitutive elements of a new cross-sectoral, multi-level world society composed of transnational organizational fields, or merely epiphenomena soon to be forgotten for all empirical and practical purposes?

In the next section we briefly identify some broad conceptual arguments—all in their infancy—that have been formulated to better explicate these novel and rapidly mutating phenomena and dynamics of world affairs. We then conduct a structured, focused comparison of four ostensible global governance networks, focusing on their historical genesis, organizational elements, potential impacts, and implications for broader and deeper institutional arrangements that shape their issue areas. We conclude with some tentative findings and hypotheses on the framing questions laid out in this introduction, as well as avenues of research that will be required in the future.

Theoretical foundations

Some rationalist scholars of world politics suggest that a "more complex political geography" is emerging globally in which the actors of governance stretch beyond the confines of states to where governmental, civil society, and private sector actors form functional coalitions and broad horizontal networks, and the institutions of governance include not only international laws and treaties, but also the use of norms, codes, and voluntary standards (Keohane and Nye 2000). Stepping back from this empirical claim, they subsequently identify five possible ideal types of global governance that might be envisioned: 1) a state-centric model, 2) an intergovernmental organization model, 3) a transnational private actors model, 4) a global governance networks model, and 5) a world state model (Keohane and Nye 2003).

The ideal-typical "state-centric model" is derivative of the conventional rationalist, neo-realist perspective that identifies anarchy with the lack of a world state, postulates states focused on survival (and possibly power maximization) as the primary actors, and views the distribution of power among states as fundamental elements of world affairs and constraints on transstate authority relations. Powerful states create intergovernmental organizations to achieve their interests and undermine those that do not (Waltz 1979). The "intergovernmental organization" model is the neo-liberal rationalist variant in which governments as principals appoint intergovernmental organizational agents to whom they delegate tasks that will generate mutually beneficial gains for states by reducing uncertainty and transaction costs (Axelrod and Keohane 1985; Oye 1986; Milner 1992). But intergovernmental organizations can produce outcomes that would not be expected under the "state-centric" model as a result of their relative autonomy from the imperfect monitoring by governmental principals as well as their relative capacity to act derived from various types of resources they garner and deploy.[6]

The rationalist "transnational private actors" model entails the recognition that a host of private, non-state actors increasingly act autonomously and generate outcomes in a range of issue areas of world affairs. Most of the activities of non-states actors condition governance by prompting the actions of governments or by reshaping their interests, but there are emerging interactions and institutional arrangements that marginally involve either governments or relatively autonomous intergovernmental organizations, and often bypass them altogether, such as corporate codes of conduct (Keohane and Nye 1972; Risse-Kappen 1995; Keck and Sikkink 1998; Sklair 2000, Khagram *et al.* 2002; Hall and Biersteker 2002). A "global governance networks model" is a theoretical, empirical, and practical extension of this rationalist approach in which governance involves the authoritative negotiation among the various governmental and/or non-state based actors that have interests at stake and capabilities to shape processes and outcome in particular issue areas. The most formal of these governance structures are said to entail trans-territorial, tri-sectoral initiatives that bring together actors from the public, private, and not-for-profit sectors in the form of loose issue-based inter-organizational networks (Rhodes 1997; Reinecke and Deng 2000; Waddell 2003).

These rationalists discard the "world state" model as a matter of fact, noting the historical absence of such an entity as well as the unlikely prospects for one to be established for the foreseeable future.[7] But they do suggest that the other four models are not necessarily mutually exclusive but rather "layered" versions of the progressively more complex reality of world affairs—with global governance networks complementing the others. On the other hand, they radically downplay an "interstate regime" model of world affairs—despite acknowledging that norms, standards, and laws are increasingly important in world affairs—by focusing almost entirely on intergovernmental organizations in their theoretical and empirical analyses.

That rationalists miss the possible importance of interstate regimes is not surprising given the neo-utilitarian, actor-centric assumptions that limit their approach. In the words of the broadly constructivist argument about "structuration processes," there are agents without structures. To the extent that there are structures, they are understood as incentives or constraints on means to ends, not constitutive of interests, preferences, identities, rules of appropriateness, or power relations (Ruggie 1998; Wendt 1999; Wendt and Fearon 2002). Correspondingly, the possibility that global governance networks are elements of change within or of interstate regimes, let alone of altogether novel transnational social fields potentially (re-)constituting a partially structured world society, is not examined.

Other scholars have formulated elements for understanding global governance networks derived from an ostensibly more "constructivist" approach that historically has posited the importance of broader and deeper institutional and societal "structures" that shape and are shaped by the identities and actions of governments and intergovernmental organizations (Kell and Ruggie 1999; Ruggie 2002). Perhaps the most powerful argument offered along these lines is that the forward march of globalization is threatened by the fact that global markets are not sufficiently embedded in a universally shared system of social values, a dangerous gap between market forces and social expectations reminiscent of Karl Polanyi's (1944) *The Great Transformation*. Specifically, the interstate regime of "embedded liberalism" that historically under-girded political stability and economic expansion for at least the states of the industrialized West is becoming unraveled by globalization with nothing to replace it (Ruggie 1982). A second piece of the argument is that the gaps in global norms and institutions or, in other words, failures *of* extant interstate regimes brought about by globalization, will stimulate the creation of new, more robust interstate regimes or perhaps altogether new forms of complex institutional arrangements.

More specifically, globalization—conceptualized as economic and political liberalization along with rapid technological change that has spurred greater degrees of market integration—has undermined the capacities of states and the interstate system. As a result, a set of operational gaps in governance have emerged: 1) between the territorial basis of the state system and the trans-border nature of many, if not most, problems; 2) between the need to take speedy actions and to take into account long temporal periods that run counter to state-based electoral time-cycles and bureaucratic decision-making; 3) between the complexities of cross-border problems and the information and knowledge that governmental and intergovernmental actors possess to address them; and 4) between growing social expectations and global market expansion. In addition, a two-fold participatory gap has emerged between those who are benefiting from the processes of globalization and those who are not, and between the demands for and the availability of opportunities for participation in authoritative decision-making (Reinecke and Deng 2000; Witt *et al.* 2000).

Global governance networks—identified once again by these authors as loose trans-territorial, multi-stakeholder arrangements that bring together organizations from the public, private, and not-for-profit sectors—fill these gaps. To be fair, it is noted that these novel organizational forms emerge not only to fill the functional gaps in governance generated by more simplified or complex processes of globalization. Like rationalists, they identify that these networks emerge in a context in which governments and intergovernmental organizations are no longer the sole actors or forces with trans-territorial interests or capacities. Also, they suggest implicitly that some—although unidentified—actor or actors are aware of these governance gaps and note that other, newer trans-territorial actors that now are relevant, consciously create global governance networks by linking the latter in novel organizational arrangements to address the former.

But despite their "constructivist" orientations, the arguments that are offered from this work remain broadly (neo-)functionalist in orientation, focusing primarily on system-level failures, necessary responses, and the actors that already have the capacities to act in the requisite ways. Adequate explanations of why these agents—either the supposed "conveners" or the emergent trans-territorial constituents—who are engaged in global governance networks act as they do are not offered. Why the particular organizational form of a global governance network emerges or is chosen is not addressed. Finally, why and how these global governance networks might actually perform these gap-filling functions, and what broader and deeper institutional ramifications they might have, are not examined empirically or explored theoretically.

To sum up, the key hypotheses that emerge from this theoretical review are twofold: first, that global governance networks are functional responses to gaps generated by processes of globalization that states and the extant inter-state system cannot fill; and second, that various new organizational actors besides governments and intergovernmental agencies, with trans-territorial reach and/or identities and interests for which states and the interstate system are not sufficient, are critical to the functioning of these networks. There seems to be implicit agreement that these global governance networks are not replacing or superceding governmental and intergovernmental action or state institutions and interstate regimes—but rather complementing or supplementing them by filling in for their inadequacies. While these ideas do offer some basis of understanding and explanation, they remain elementary, particularly in terms of their analysis of the complex political interactions and potential broader institutional implications of these networks.

Comparative empirical analysis

In order to begin deepening our understanding, we now examine four ostensible and quite recent global governance networks that have been identified by various actors as particularly noteworthy: the World Commission on Dams; the Minerals, Mining and Sustainable Development Initiative; the Global Reporting Initiative; and the Global Compact. The first two were global governance networks designed as short-term strategic interventions, whereas the latter two continue to grow and become more institutionalized. In order to increase the rigor of this relatively inductive analysis of a small number of cases, we employ the method of structured, focused comparison. We first ask similar questions of each case. How did it emerge? What were its espoused goals? How was it structured organizationally? How has it evolved? What have been its effects? What role does it play in the institutional arrangements that shape its domain?[8] We then compare and contrast our results across cases, to derive findings and potential hypotheses that address the themes from the preceding theoretical exploration.

We can offer at best simplified overviews of these extremely complex cases, which can provide a basis for preliminary analysis. In particular, the sections on the origins of these experiments do not delve deeply into their longer historical genesis, and the sections on the evolution of their structures and processes do not convey the dynamism each has entailed. Moreover, the sections on their impacts and roles are highly speculative because the cases are so recent in origin, and all ongoing in some fashion. Finally, it should be noted that in-depth investigation (including archival research, interviewing, and participant observation) on these and other global governance networks is ongoing.

The World Commission on Dams (WCD)

The WCD is an example of a cross-sectoral, multi-level initiative in global governance, the creation of which was driven by progressively more organized and effective transnational coalitions of NGOs and social movements. Increasingly intense conflicts over large dams emerged worldwide at the local, national, and international levels from the 1950s onwards. By the 1980s, transnational coalitions of domestic NGOs and social movements with foreign and international counterparts began to effectively block the construction of new large dams out of concern for the destructive effects on both ecosystems and the lives and livelihoods of affected peoples, their disappointing economic performance, and the broader models of development in which they were embedded.

Genesis

Motivated by their increasing successes in individual campaigns against large dams as well as larger policy and institutional reform efforts, opponents of large dams gradually ratcheted up their demands for the creation of an independent body to conduct a comprehensive review of the performance of large dams that had been built with the support of international aid agencies. The opportunity to achieve this goal presented itself at an April 1997 workshop in Gland, Switzerland on the future of large dams, sponsored jointly by the World Bank and the World Conservation Union (IUCN) and attended by a wide group of representative stakeholders.

After a recently produced World Bank evaluation of 50 large Bank-supported dams around the world was reviewed and critiqued—most intensely, but not exclusively, by members from transnationally allied opponents—the latter demanded an independent and comprehensive "audit" of the performance of large dams that had been built with the support of international agencies. But proponents of large dams—particularly those representing private-sector dam-building companies and professional technical and industry associations—proposed that a set of criteria and guidelines for the future also be formulated. And representatives of intergovernmental agencies such as the World Bank called for a review of all large dams built—not just those supported by aid agencies.

In highly contested exchanges, the assembled participants concluded that no existing group or organization had broadly recognized legitimacy to evaluate the historical experience with large dams worldwide or to propose recommendations for the future. The participants converged on the establishment of an independent world commission with a two-year mandate to review the development effectiveness of large dams worldwide and generate new criteria and guidelines for these projects—both to be published in a final report. The World Commission on Dams (WCD) would be "governed" by a number (initially set at eight) of commission members, including a chair, selected from the range of stakeholders involved in large dam issues. A secretary general and secretariat would be appointed as the administrative apparatus of the WCD. An expanded "forum" of stakeholder representatives, including many but not all of those at the Gland meeting, would be created to monitor and contribute to the work of the commission. Perhaps most importantly, the guiding principles of the new entity would be independence, transparency, participation, and inclusiveness.

In order to determine who specifically would be selected as commissioners, the chair, and secretary general of the WCD, the Gland workshop participants agreed on an interim group of key stakeholder representatives. During a negotiation process that took more than a year, each of these decisions was hotly contested. At several points, deadlock seemed to foreshadow an end to the process. Eventually, 12 commissioners, including a chair, vice-chair, and 13th ex-officio commissioner/secretary general, were selected, rather than the initially envisioned eight.

Thus, the WCD was created from an intense political process in which virtually every aspect of its mandate, organizational structure, and funding was negotiated. Each actor attempted to advance its own agenda in shaping the WCD. It became even more global in orientation as a result of the shift in focus from World Bank-funded projects to all large dams. It became multi-stakeholder partly as a result of the absence of other politically acceptable alternatives, and partly as a result of the broadly accepted premise that a multi-stakeholder orientation would increase the likelihood of success.

Structures and processes

All significant aspects of the WCD, its membership, structure, work program, and sources of financing, were envisioned to be cross-sectoral, multilevel, and global. The 12 commissioners ranged from a South African Minister of Water Affairs (the WCD Chair) to the leading social movement activist around large dams in India, to the CEO of one of the largest energy multinational corporations in the world. The 10-plus member secretariat, headed by the secretary general, included individuals from all over the world, from different disciplinary backgrounds, and with extremely varied professional histories. A WCD Forum, as mandated, eventually was broadened into a much wider range of 60 members, including representatives of national ministries of water/power, national and international aid agencies, heads of professional industry associations, private sector firms, and leaders of international NGOs, community-based organizations, and indigenous peoples groups.

The central activities of the WCD, elaborated in a work program, were also to be cross-sectoral, multi-level, and global. The work program activities included nine in-depth case studies (seven river-basin and two national in scope) in countries ranging from China to the United States to Zimbabwe to Norway, a "cross-check" survey of more than 125 dams located in more than 50 countries worldwide, and 17 cross-cutting thematic reviews on issues ranging from the impacts of large dams on indigenous peoples to options for water resources development and management. The work program also envisioned an extensive "stakeholder consultation/communication" effort that included several regional consultations, an active solicitation of submissions from any interested person or organization from all over the world, a regular newsletter eventually published/translated into three (or more) languages, and a state-of-the-art website.

The principles of independence, transparency, openness, and inclusiveness guided both the formulation and implementation of the WCD. The commission's perceived independence partly depended on its adherence to an informal norm that no more than 10 percent of the operational budget would come from any single actor, and none of the funding of nearly $10 million could be "tied." Each of the work program activities—case studies, cross-check survey, thematic reviews—was pushed and pulled continually by both internal and external actors around the degree to which it was transparent, participatory, and inclusive in greater breadth and depth.

The earliest, most powerful and sustained criticism of the WCD came from particular governments from some developing countries, such as Indian federal authorities, that argued that the commission was a self-appointed body with no legitimacy. Less vocal in their criticism but increasingly disengaged was the Chinese government, which quietly compelled the Chinese commissioner to disengage midway through the process. By the end of its life, however, the WCD was able to complete a national case study in both countries and the Indian government sent a representative to the WCD Forum. Private sector companies were more cautious than critical early on, but increasingly became engaged with the WCD over time. Among the critics of large dam building, the Brazilian movement of dam-affected peoples (MAB) had an extremely volatile relationship with the WCD from the time of its establishment through the publication of its final report, but still considered it one of the most accessible global entities with which it had engaged.

Outcomes and effects

The final report of the WCD was completed in September and issued in November 2000, three months behind schedule. It was presented to the WCD Forum and the broader "international community" as required by its mandate. Eleven commissioners and the secretary general signed the report (the commissioner from China had withdrawn without replacement). One of the remaining 11 commissioners—the leading Indian social activist—signed, but only with the inclusion of a note of dissent that the WCD report did not go far or deep enough in its recommendations.

The report satisfied the first part of the WCD mandate with an extensive review of the effectiveness of large dams, including their financial, economic, environmental, and social impacts; an assessment of water and energy options; and an analysis of the state of governance arrangements in this area. It claimed neutrality on the subject of whether large dams should be built in the future, but urged strongly that these projects be considered as only one of many options for water and energy development—including the option of improving the utility of already built large dams. The final report very consciously embedded its review of the pros and cons of large dams in a wider discussion about options for water and energy development.

For some actors, with a range of perspectives on large dams, the report did not adequately fulfill the second part of the WCD mandate. Guidelines were formulated for decision-making processes in which large dams may potentially be built, but stringent economic, social, environmental, and technical criteria for the sanctioning of large dams were not offered. Nevertheless the WCD process achieved enough legitimacy that all relevant groups have reacted to its report and recommendations.

Many large-dam critics from civil society, concerned about governance and a voice in decision-making processes, welcomed the report. A letter from a transnational coalition of 109 NGOs, community-based groups, and social movements from 39 countries noted that the report vindicates many of the concerns they had previously raised and called upon decision-makers to incorporate all the recommendations of the report before funding more large dams. Many aid agencies, especially European funders, and regional development banks were generally publicly supportive. The World Bank did not adopt the WCD's recommended guidelines but did accept the WCD normative framework of "recognizing rights and risks," arguing that high high-risk, high-reward projects such as large dams were sometimes necessary to achieve development goals.

Some of the most powerful proponents of large dams, primarily from associations of industry professionals and private sector firms as well as some developing country governments, leveled criticism at the final report, including its accuracy and the emphasis of the recommendations on the decision-making process. The International Hydropower Association objected that the overall tone of the report cast a negative light on large dams and claimed that its conclusions were based on inadequately researched data, in that only a fraction of the world's 45,000 dams were studied. An early posting from the International Commission on Large Dams (ICOLD) protested that in only offering guidelines for "consultations" with stakeholders, the report failed in its mandate to offer technical criteria and standards for the planning, construction, and operation of dams. Moreover, it argued that the kind of negotiation and decision-making process proposed in the report would be so cumbersome that it would stall any new large dams.

Nevertheless, the United Nations Environmental Programme constituted a Dams and Development Project (DDP) to formalize a follow-up process to the WCD in which even the most ardent critics of the final report participated. The first phase of the DDP from 2001 to 2004 involved extensive communication of the WCD's report in global, regional, national, and local dialogues all around the world. The report and recommendations of the WCD were translated into multiple languages and disseminated widely. The second phase of the DDP, from 2005 to 2007, involved the promotion of policy and procedural reforms as well as practical tools to improve decision-making around the planning and management of large dams in light of the WCD recommendations.

As a result, the WCD process and final report became a central focal point in the dynamics around large dams, and reoriented the debates about large infrastructure projects as well as sustainable development more broadly. For example, the very same professional associations that criticized the WCD's report revised their own guidelines concerning large dams in relation to the WCD's recommendations. In addition, the analysis and the recommendations of the commission were introduced into the discussions about the social and environmental guidelines to be adopted by export credit agencies. As with all of the global governance networks examined in this chapter, a definitive evaluation of the WCD's impacts is yet to be produced. One lingering question is whether the WCD would have been even more effective had it not been a time-bound initiative like the Minerals, Mining and Sustainable Development Initiative discussed in the next section, as opposed to a longer-term entity such as the Global Reporting Initiative or Global Compact, which are the subjects of the subsequent two sections.

The Minerals, Mining and Sustainable Development Initiative (MMSD)

The Minerals, Mining and Sustainable Development Initiative is an example of a recent multi-actor, multi-level global governance network initiated by a coalition of private sector firms, led in this case by the Global Mining Initiative (GMI). The GMI was established in 1998 by a group of ten leading private sector, multinational mining firms that are members of the World Business Council for Sustainable Development (WBCSD). The WBCSD, in turn, is a global umbrella association of hundreds of transnational corporations united by an ostensible commitment to sustainable development via the three pillars of economic growth, ecological balance, and social progress. Along with the International Chambers of Commerce and World Economic Forum, WBCSD is one of the three key global multi-sectoral business associations involved in world politics.

Genesis

According to the GMI, the mining and minerals sector, and individual companies within it, faced a number of challenges to their own individual and collective survival and growth, chief among which were pressures from financial markets regarding risks and returns; rising public criticism of the industry's social and environmental performance, particularly from local communities linked to indigenous peoples, labor, environmental and human rights organizations around the world; and the increasing trend towards greater governmental intervention in the sector. But the ten business executives who established the GMI espoused the view that the organization's mission entailed more than just ensuring the short-term survival and growth of their companies and the industry. Rather, it would seriously explore proactive options for a global transition to sustainable development in the mining sector.

In July 1999, The GMI commissioned the International Institute for Environment and Development (IIED) to undertake a "scoping project" on possible means by which to move the mining sector towards sustainability and thus increased legitimacy. IIED is a well-established, leading independent non-profit research institute that works in the field of sustainable development, based in London. The scoping project consisted of three main objectives: to offer an external view of the global challenge of sustainable development facing the mining sector; to propose the scope of investigations on these challenges and strategies for addressing them; and to suggest an organizational arrangement for carrying this out. According to IIED, the three-month scoping project involved consultation with multiple actors at multiple levels as well as a review of existing initiatives and research on mining around the world.

In its October 1999 scoping report, IIED recommended that GMI under the auspices of the WBCSD support the creation of a two-year initiative of participatory analysis and action strategy formulation for the mining sector, much like the WCD. The guiding principles of the proposed MMSD initiative would be strategically focused on the long term, global in reach, balanced in substantive issues addressed, comprehensive in investigatory scope, inclusive of a range of actors, reinforcing of existing work, professionally organized and managed, realistic of the possible achievements given time and scope, and action-oriented towards concrete changes in practice.

The work of the MMSD would involve high levels of expert research and participatory consultation to generate a technically sound and politically legitimate final report identifying how the mineral sector could make a transition to sustainable development, what principles and practices should guide the sector, what mining companies in particular could do, and how ongoing and newly emergent initiatives in this area could be strengthened and coordinated—particularly through the planned 2002 World Summit on Sustainable Development. The scoping report laid out a three-tier governance structure composed of a sponsoring group, assurance group, and working group (see next section for more details).

The IIED scoping report was approved by the WBCSD/GMI in December 1999. The original member firms of GMI persuaded 14 other mining companies to join them in sponsoring the MMSD initiative. These companies, again under the umbrella of WBCSD, commissioned and pledged the initial 60 percent of the funding estimated to implement the MMSD to IIED. Eventually a total of 28 corporations pledged at least $150,000 each to the project. IIED's executive director was designated as the project coordinator, and IIED was to deliver a final report and recommendations for follow-up activities by December 2001.

Thus, the MMSD was constituted as a global, cross-sectoral and multi-level initiative as a result of a number of interacting factors. First, leading mining companies took a political decision to proactively shape the institutional context in which they had to work, rather than continuing to react defensively to the mounting pressures they faced. Second, rather than develop only in-company policies or industry codes of conduct independently, they engaged a non-profit think tank to provide advice on an appropriate course of action. Third, the non-profit think tank, as a matter of normal operations, engaged in a multi-stakeholder consultation process to produce the advice that generated a recommendation for an independent and transparent initiative that would balance expert knowledge and multi-stakeholder participation, and which would be global and multi-level in orientation. The MMSD was an organizational arrangement for negotiating and developing recommendations for the norms and principles as well as procedures and decision-making structures of a long-term global institutional mechanism for the mining sector, potentially involving actors with a wide range of understandings and interests with respect to these elements.

Structure and process

The MMSD consisted of a three-tier organizational structure and involved the execution of a two-year work plan. The "work group" was responsible for developing and executing the work plan, as well as for drafting and completing the final report, with the advice and support of the assurance and sponsoring groups. The head of the work group was a project director who was selected by the IIED project coordinator. The project coordinator and director selected a dozen or so senior research and administrative staff from various disciplinary and institutional backgrounds to manage the day-to-day operations of the MMSD. In the last resort, the work group retained the right to publish all its findings independently if no consensus was found with the assurance and/or sponsoring groups.

The multi-actor "sponsoring group" included the organizations financing the project, particularly those that contributed $150,000 or more. MMSD did not meet its target ratio of funding—the envisioned ratio of 60 percent private sector and 40 percent non-corporate funders—and the GMI and other mining firms dominated the list of sponsoring group members. Even the "non-corporate" funders were primarily international and governmental aid agencies such as the Canadian International Development Research Centre (IDRC). Not surprisingly, there was not a single labor union, nongovernmental, or community group among the members of the sponsoring group.

The multi-actor "assurance group" was responsible for advising, peer reviewing, and ensuring the integrity of the overall MMSD initiative. It ranged from between 12 and 25 members during the life of the MMSD. More reflective of the wide array of actors with stakes in mining issues, its members were initially selected by the project coordinator and director based on consultations they conducted and recommendations they received during the early stages of the formal initiative. Over the life of the MMSD, more transparent and formal procedures for selection were developed, and several assurance group members were added to broaden the range of views and regional backgrounds around mining issues globally. For at least half of the assurance group's official life, its chair was a former president of both the US National Wildlife Federation and IUCN.

The MMSD project strategy and work plan consisted of four primary sets of activities—research and analysis, information and communication, stakeholder engagement, and planning for outcomes. Each of these activities was undertaken by both the work group at IIED and regional MMSD partners constituted during the course of the initiative. The idea to form regional partnerships was generated during the early months of the initiative as a result of feedback from various multi-actor meetings. The regional partners were established primarily in the principal mine-producing regions of the world. It seems that more of the research activities were solicited by IIED to "globally recognized expert institutions," while the regional partners increased the breadth and depth of the participatory activities of the overall initiative.

The most vocal and sustained opposition to the MMSD initiative came from critical nongovernmental, community-based, and social movement organizations, coalitions, and networks around the world—many of which refused to participate at all. Others became more engaged over time in response to perceived greater transparency, openness, and responsiveness of the initiative—particularly the regional processes but also the nature of the work program, which evolved from a primarily technical, environmental, and economic focus to engage more directly social, institutional, and governance themes. It seems that various labor organizations were generally more involved throughout and that the original private sector companies have remained committed to the process with some additional firms joining from time to time. The evolving regional processes seem to have engaged governmental actors much more, whereas the IIED work group was able to develop strong links with various intergovernmental organizations such as the UN Global Compact and the World Bank mining unit.

Outcomes and effects

The MMSD's final report was completed several months behind schedule and was formally launched at the World Summit on Sustainable Development in August 2002. The actual impact of the MMSD's output on day-to-day mining operations or the actual policies and practices of mining companies will not be realized for several years. However, even the mining companies have criticized the report for not having concrete and actionable recommendations.

Perhaps most notably, the mining industry established a permanent new umbrella organization, the International Council on Metals and Mining (ICMM), building on an earlier industry association known as the International Council on Mining and the Environment. The ICMM is to be a more independent entity than its predecessor, to continue to facilitate engagement among the multiple actors across sectors with stakes in the issue area of minerals and mining, and to offer more concrete recommendations to the mining industry in four key areas: environmental stewardship, product stewardship, community responsibility, and general corporate responsibilities. ICMM's first director was Dr. Jay Hair, a former leader of various NGOs and chairperson of the assurance group during the initial six months of the MMSD initiative.

Although the formal MMSD initiative ended following the publication of the final report, informal networks and other institutional arrangements that developed through the MMSD may have a much longer life and greater impact than the initiative itself. For example, most of the groups that boycotted the MMSD did attend the culminating conference of the initiative in May 2002, suggesting more engagement among the range of actors at the back end than at the front. The construction of inter-organizational networks seems to have progressed furthest, however, through the activities of the regional MMSD partner organizations, and it may be at that level that the most important long-term effects of the initiative will be seen.

The opposition of many segments of civil society to MMSD remained a continuing theme in many subsequent efforts, including the World Bank's Extractive Industries Review.[9] The irony of the MMSD initiative was that in its attempt to be multi-level and cross-sectoral, the organizers actually distanced many of their potential constituents who perceived their participation to be tantamount to cooptation. Indeed, the criticisms to this effect caused substantial rifts between the NGOs that boycotted the process and those that joined in. The NGOs that boycotted the initiative wrote an open letter to the industry indicating their reasons for taking this decision and largely predicated their resistance on the perception that the outcome of the process had been predetermined by the funders and would characterize mining as "sustainable" under mildly mitigating circumstances. Some of the NGOs that have resisted this effort have a normative stance with regard to mining as being inherently unsustainable and thus would label any attempt at defining "sustainable mining" as "greenwash."

In a five-year retrospective the executive director of MMSD, Luke Danielson, prepared an institutional history of the initiative after deliberating with a group of stakeholders initiated by the Global Public Policy Institute in Berlin (Danielson and Digby 2006). A major challenge identified in this report is differentiating between "deadline-driven" policy forums and "consensus-driven" forums. Ostensibly, deadlines may expedite consensus and hence the two modes could be conflated. However, civil society groups in the case of MMSD were intent on focusing on consensus, as noted:

> One of the major points of negotiation in the development of the MMSD project was precisely that NGO representatives wanted the Assurance Group charter to provide that there would not be a report without consensus. Industry representatives insisted that there had to be a report, one way or another. It was a true point of cleavage, and it is understandable why it was so. The attempt to have an Assurance Group that was neither a Board of Directors with legal authority and control nor simply an advisory group with no control at all was one of the innovations of the MMSD project.
>
> (Danielson and Digby 2006: 73)

At the end of the day, the deadlines prevailed and the Assurance Group focused on getting a report ready for the WSSD in 2002. Nevertheless, the process of constructive confrontation that MMSD facilitated transcended states and paved the way for newer efforts such as the Extractive Industries Review (EIR) of the World Bank. While the EIR was largely coopted by NGOs and many of the recommendations were deemed unacceptable by the World Bank leadership, the process of engagement helped to set boundaries of negotiation for all sides. This may have led to institutional learning, which resulted in the most recent manifestation of a global governance network in the extractive sector—the Extractive Industries Transparency Initiative (EITI). This effort, which was promoted by the British government at the WSSD, has allowed for greater space for civil society, while recognizing the continuing salience of the state. Membership of the initiative is still delineated at the national level. However, the governance structure of the initiative is managed largely by civil society, most notably, the founder of Transparency International, Peter Eigen. Recognizing the continuity of this matter, the Norwegian government offered to provide a long-term secretariat for this initiative in 2007.

The MMSD initiative perhaps did not have as great an effect in the developing world relative to its potential, but acted as a catalyst for other efforts that followed a process of institutional learning about the creation and effectiveness of global governance networks.

The Global Reporting Initiative (GRI)

The GRI is a cross-sectoral and increasingly multi-level permanent initiative that is developing and disseminating globally applicable guidelines for reporting information on the environmental, social, and economic performance of organizations. While intended for any type of organization, including those in the public and not-for-profit sectors, the GRI's initial focus has been on formulating "sustainability" guidelines for "triple-bottom line reporting" that are as generally accepted as conventional financial reporting standards, to be utilized by transnational and large national corporations.

Genesis

The broad justification offered for the GRI's founding is three-fold: 1) accepted guidelines for disclosure of economic, social, and environmental performance are critical to measuring and verifying the actual success of private sector firms and other organizations in executing policies and programs supportive of sustainable development; 2) the information generated from the utilization of the reporting framework will allow private sector firms in particular to identify and improve their internal practices, as well as make it easier for external actors—such as socially and environmentally responsible investors and analysts, activists of critical NGOs, government officials, and others—to evaluate these practices; and 3) a generally recognized framework is required because the current extra-financial reporting practices of corporations are inconsistent, incomplete, and non-comparable. Taken together, these three rationales are linked to a claim that improved sustainability reporting is a crucial part of addressing the problems produced by current processes of globalization, particularly by filling associated gaps of governance with respect to the transparency and accountability of multinational corporations.

But in-depth empirical research suggests a much more circuitous and political genesis of the GRI in which idiosyncratic events, actor characteristics, and broader political-economic factors were important. In 1990, a US-based non-profit organization called the Coalition for Environmentally Responsible Economies (CERES) drafted a set of environmental principles that corporations should adopt, following an oil spill disaster known as the Exxon-Valdez. Another, proximately-based US non-profit think tank called the Tellus Institute developed an environmental reporting toolkit to assist corporations in measuring and reporting their success with implementing the principles. Major US corporations produced over 1,500 environmental reports based on the CERES principles and Tellus disclosure guidelines over the subsequent six years.

In 1997, CERES decided that reporting had to go global. The pivotal incident was a meeting in which senior managers of a major US corporation told representatives of CERES that they needed a single globally accepted reporting standard that included not only environmental but also social and economic performance. The broader political pressures for corporate responsibility and demands for disclosure had grown exponentially, the managers lamented, and costs of providing different sets of information were becoming prohibitive. An initial partnership between CERES and the United Nations Environmental Programme (UNEP), which had become increasingly involved in engaging corporations on environmental issues; the advice of a cross-sectoral "Steering Group" for the start up phase; and growing funding donated by the United Nations Foundation, along with several other philanthropic organizations, eventually led to the decision to establish a permanent independent organization called the GRI.

GRI was conceptualized as global from its inception because of a demand by a particular set of actors—private sector corporations—who were both responding to the rise of broader contextual pressures and advancing an institutional arrangement that fit their political and economic interests. The institutional arrangement was a generally accepted global voluntary reporting scheme. Indeed, it was never really questioned that it should be a global *voluntary* reporting scheme—it was assumed that this feature was critical to success because corporations would oppose other possibilities such as an interstate treaty with government-based regulation (e.g., an interstate regime), the prospects for success of which were seen as not very high.

However, non-profit business service organizations such as CERES, intergovernmental agencies such as UNEP, and the various stakeholders that were selected for the interim steering groups (including representatives from professional accountancy associations and advocacy social movement organizations, among others) were convinced that the organization that would drive this institutional mechanism should be multi-stakeholder and, over time, multi-level in orientation. CERES was itself a cross-sectoral initiative. UNEP, along with other UN agencies, had explicitly begun to adopt a "multi-stakeholder" approach to its work during the 1990s. The philanthropic organizations that funded the GRI increasingly prioritized support for "multi-stakeholder," "multi-level" global initiatives. Linked to the cross-sectoral orientation was a commitment to be independent of any particular stakeholder, while transparent, accessible, and inclusive of all.

Correspondingly, during the start-up period of GRI managed by CERES for the first five years, sets of reporting indicators and guidelines were generated by various cross-sectoral groups consisting of researchers and practitioners, tested by growing numbers of companies from more and more sectors, commented on by a wide range of actors representing different types of organizations and political interests, and revised in several iterations.

Again, actively lobbying governments to include these in state policies or interstate regimes was not considered a high priority—participating in GRI and/or utilizing the GRI reporting framework would be a quasi-voluntary act of organizations. It was postulated that sustained, broad and deep engagement with all relevant and critical actors was the key organizing principle that would lead to the guidelines' continual improvement, acceptance, legitimacy, and, thus, success.

Structures and processes

Thus, virtually from the start, it was clear to the founders that the GRI would actively involve the participation of a wide range of actors including private sector firms, business associations, human rights and environmental organizations, religious groups, labor unions, professional accountancy associations, think tanks, and university research institutes, as well as, albeit with not much focus, governmental and intergovernmental agencies. There was no overt or outside political pressure to do so, but a cross-sectoral multi-stakeholder model was seen as the most legitimate and effective organizational form available. In addition, wide-ranging investigations and consultations on the appropriate future organizational structure of GRI reinforced and deepened this framework.

The first official GRI guidelines were launched in June 2000, after nearly 15 months of dialogues and consultations that proceeded the public debut of the GRI at its first international symposium, held in London the previous year. Thirty-one companies agreed to pilot-test the GRI inaugural guidelines while at the same time a process for developing the next generation of them commenced. The second iteration of the guidelines was unveiled at the World Summit on Sustainable Development two years later. A number of sectoral supplements and additional technical protocols and toolkits were developed over the next several years, leading up to the launch of the G3 guidelines in October 2006.

An interim secretariat to administer the GRI, and especially its numerous multi-stakeholder working groups, was established in early 2000. The secretariat was advised by a cross-sectoral and multi-stakeholder Steering Committee that included 17 members, of which only two were from the developing world (one from India and one from Colombia). Recognizing that a global entity could not be so Northern dominated, the interim secretariat ensured that there was broad representation from outside the OECD at the second GRI international symposium held in November 2000 and subsequently held meetings in all corners of the globe. As a result, the GRI's global network grew from 200 members to over 2,000 within a span of two years.

In March 2002, a Board replacing the Steering Committee was announced, with Judy Hendersen (who brought with her the experiences of a former Commissioner at the WCD) as chair. Two months later, the GRI was formally inaugurated at the United Nations with the approval of the UN Secretary General. The GRI shifted from a CERES-based program with technical support leadership provided largely by the Tellus Institute to a stand-alone entity headquartered in Amsterdam. Legally incorporated as a non-profit organization in the Netherlands with official political and also some financial support from the Dutch government, the fiduciary responsibilities of the GRI were given to a "Board of Directors" of 14 (and subsequently 16) members chosen to represent the widest possible cross-section of constituencies, experiences, expertise, and geographical origins.

Board members are appointed individually and the Board is collectively advised by the "Stakeholder Council," a policy forum of 60 registered stakeholder organizations of the GRI. The 60 organizations were selected to be formally representative of the broad array of actors—similar to those identified previously—that would have interests and capabilities linked to the GRI mission. An unlimited number of organizational stakeholders are also invited to participate voluntarily in the council on a non-voting basis.

The Board appoints the chief executive officer of the GRI and approves the various appointments to a 25- to 30-person secretariat staff, relatively small given its global mandate. The idea is to "leverage" the interests and resources of an ever-expanding global network of organizations and individuals supporting and interacting with GRI, through the Board, Stakeholder Council, Technical Council, Charter Group of Funders, consultation events, reporting and review processes, and so on. The "Technical Council" consists of 10 to 15 Board-appointed experts who provide strategic direction to the work program—particularly the development and dissemination of the reporting indicators and guidelines—managed by the secretariat staff.

The Charter Group of Funders was the set of large donors that have donated more than $3 million collectively to the GRI. An expansion of this group beyond the primarily US-based philanthropic organizations that initially constituted it was expected, given the projected annual GRI budget of approximately $5 million over the short term. However, the idea of retaining an expanded version of the Charter Group was quickly discarded. There was also a proposal to establish several offices in each geographical region of the world to make the GRI more formally multi-level, but these have never materialized, partly due to the scarcity of resources. Revenue generation activities that supported the independent, transparent, cross-sectoral, and multi-level approach of the GRI were also envisioned, but to date have not been developed.

Outcomes and effects

It is difficult to evaluate the outcomes and effects of the GRI because of its relative youth, the complex mechanisms by which these impacts are likely to occur, and, somewhat ironically, the absence of a baseline standard for comparison. The level of contestation around the GRI is minimal compared with the other global governance networks examined in this chapter, not to mention many conventional intergovernmental organizations—although some actors do question the value of voluntary reporting without verification or even certification. Nevertheless, in a relatively short period of time, the GRI has become the unquestioned focal point for the development of globally accepted, voluntary, triple-bottom-line reporting standards and indicators. A World Bank survey of over 100 multinationals in 2002 found that the GRI guidelines were second only to the ISO 14000 in influencing their investment and purchasing decisions.

The GRI is contributing to and being empowered by the growing political momentum for institutional arrangements that constitute corporate citizenship, accountability, responsibility, and sustainability (CCARS) at the trans-state level and in countries around the world. Experts and long-time observers of CCARS as well as business–society–governmental relations concur that, partly due to GRI's efforts, non-financial reporting is higher on the agenda for and altering the behavior of multiple types of actors, from corporations to investment agencies to nongovernmental advocacy groups to labor unions to even governments and intergovernmental organizations. For example, the French Parliament recently passed legislation requiring French corporations to produce triple-bottom-line reporting, the European Union included a similar recommendation in its White Paper on corporate citizenship, and the Japanese Government promulgated a set of official guidelines with similar objectives. All identified the GRI framework as an acceptable standard. The Johannesburg Stock Exchange in South Africa and a new stock exchange in Brazil now require corporations that list with them to do triple-bottom-line reporting; the New York Stock Exchange considered a similar requirement after corporate scandals in the United States. Again GRI is featured prominently in those efforts.

Groups identified the GRI as one of the most important and innovative global governance networks from across the functional and political spectrum at the 2002 World Summit on Sustainable Development in South Africa. Furthermore, over six hundred corporations were utilizing the GRI framework at least partially, if not in its entirety, by 2004. Most recently, the 16 top minerals and mining companies of the International Council on Mining and Minerals, which emerged from the MMSD process, announced that they would all produce sustainability reports based on GRI guidelines for the sector. While many practitioners in developing countries such as Brazil find the GRI guidelines too onerous, when the International Organization for Standardization began a process to establish corporate social responsibility guidelines in 2005, it adopted the GRI's cross-sectoral, multi-stakeholder working group process. And utilizing the reporting framework is considered an acceptable mechanism by which corporations can meet their obligations to the United Nations Global Compact—another global governance network focusing on CCARS, and the global governance network examined in the next section.

The Global Compact

The Global Compact is an example of a cross-sectoral, multi-level global governance network initiated by an interstate body, in this case the Secretary General's office of the United Nations. Launched in July 2000 by Secretary General Kofi Annan, the Global Compact invites and encourages private sector companies—particularly multinational corporations—voluntarily to adopt universal principles of human rights, labor rights, environmental stewardship, and anti-corruption, and to incorporate them into their business practices. It further engages companies in dialogue with other "critical stakeholders" such as labor unions and large nongovernmental advocacy and service organizations to maximize learning on how the principles can best be implemented.

Genesis

Senior advisors in the UN Secretary General's office justified the idea of a voluntary initiative in which corporations adopt universal principles out of a conviction that the current globalizing economy was in jeopardy as long as its fruits were not adequately shared and global markets not sufficiently embedded in broadly shared social values. In papers and speeches published on the Global Compact, Annan and his chief advisors, John Ruggie and Georg Kell, argued that by the end of the twentieth century far more effort in global rule-making had gone into securing the rights of multinational corporations and creating the conditions for free flows of trade and finance than into protecting the environment, labor and human rights or eradicating poverty around the world (Kell and Ruggie, 1999). Unless the growing gap between market expansion and social concerns were addressed, they warned, "rejectionist criticisms" of globalization would grow into a full-scale backlash. This would lead local and national communities to turn inwards and become protectionist, which, in the view of Annan and his colleagues, would be disastrous for the economies of developing countries and the world more generally.

But while this justification of the Global Compact's importance was developed early on in the initiative's life, the emergence of this global governance network was hardly an orderly or strategically planned affair. Indeed, at first it was just a line concocted to add spark to a speech the Secretary General was invited to give at the World Economic Forum. Kofi Annan simply wanted an idea that would be pro-active and innovative in terms of the UN's role in economic globalization, which had been relatively marginal compared to the World Bank, International Monetary Fund, and World Trade Organization. In the January 1999 speech, Annan rhetorically challenged businesses to promote and apply nine universal principles in the areas of human rights, labor standards, and environmental practices, all drawn from international agreements including the Universal Declaration of Human Rights, the Fundamental Principles and Rights at Work of the International Labor Organization, and the Earth Summit's Agenda 21. Annan argued that together these principles constituted a widely shared set of values to underpin the new global economy, put a human face on the global market, and stave off reactionary backlashes or restrictions that would hamper free trade.

Indeed, prior to the actual speech there were absolutely no plans to operationalize the Compact. A completely surprising strong and favorable response from CEOs of multinational corporations, the International Chamber of Commerce, and some labor leaders, however, led to the decision to give the Compact more coherence and legitimacy by creating a formalized organizational structure, with the Secretary General's office acting as convener. Efforts were made to develop policy coordination among UN agencies that represent the areas that the nine principles address; the ILO, UNEP, and UNHCR in turn formulated programs to support the Compact's success. The growing involvement of labor and other "civil society" organizations in the initiative came from the vocal criticism leveled by groups (some calling for inclusion and others completely against the Global Compact), and from companies for whom dialogue and cooperation with other "stakeholders" seemed politically essential to advancing their interests. In July 2000, after two consciously assembled cross-sectoral, multi-stakeholder meetings, the Global Compact was formally launched with letters of commitment from a range of companies, labor organizations, and a handful of prominent international NGOs such as Amnesty International. A secretariat was established within the UN Secretary General's office that November.

The Global Compact thus emerged as a conjunctural outcome of several factors and not just as a functional but relatively spontaneous response to fill a self-evident gap in global governance. These included: 1) the political and bureaucratic interest of the UN Secretary General's office in becoming a more central actor with respect to "managing" economic globalization; 2) the "conveners'" particular analysis of globalization, in which free flows of trade, finance, and investment are by and large positive forces if embedded in certain social and environmental norms—norms that already existed in interstate (UN) agreements but which were not efficacious; 3) a set of political dynamics in which particular multinational corporations and other actors pushed for an institutional mechanism that was voluntary, other transnational actors such as international labor unions and NGOs pushed for the creation of a formal organizational arrangement that was cross-sectoral in orientation, and yet others criticized either/both the institutional mechanism or/and organizational arrangement; and 4) the belief by those actors who supported the ideas of the Global Compact in the value of the UN hosting the initiative.

The net result—a new organizational arrangement in which a set of extant social norms of the interstate system would now be implemented by multinational corporations and other non-state actors—could entail not a change *of* but *within* interstate regimes. But the addition of a novel set of "distributed implementation" procedures and rules to operationalize the principles involving primarily and predominantly non-state actors might signify a broader shift in the nature of underlying institutional arrangements as well. And the question of whether or not the Compact could adopt additional norms and principles over time in addition to the original nine was left open.

Structures and processes

The organizational structure of the Global Compact has evolved in a punctuated manner responding to political pushes and pulls from various network actors as well as to unplanned or unanticipated opportunities. While the overall architecture of the Global Compact remains fluid, procedures, structures, and concrete activities are gradually taking shape. To join, companies must publicly state support for the principles and annually post on the compact website an example of progress made or lessons learned in implementing the principles (Communication of Progress or COP). In its literature the Compact repeatedly emphasizes that it is not a regulatory instrument, a code of conduct, or a vehicle for performance review, but rather "a value based platform designed to promote institutional learning." Tobacco and arms companies have been excluded, while the only original criterion for inclusion is professed support for the principles and collaborative learning model.

The Global Compact secretariat, under the leadership of top advisors to the UN Secretary General, initially undertook four primary, cross-sectoral and multi-level sets of activities: annual Policy Dialogues, the Learning Forum, Partnership Projects, and Regional/Country Outreach. Annual Policy Dialogues were designed to bring together representatives from business, NGOs, and public policy institutes among others to develop collaborative solutions to specific challenges posed by globalization. The first of these dialogues, held in September 2001, focused on the ethical and practical dilemmas faced by businesses operating in zones of conflict and spawned a number of multi-actor, multi-level working groups. A set of dialogues on implementing corporate responsibility for sustainable development was held in 2002. Subsequent themes included business and development, HIV-Aids in the workplace, business and conflict, and anti-corruption.

The Learning Forum is a vehicle for encouraging companies to continually improve practices in keeping with the nine principles. It features a databank and Internet platform for sharing good practices and in-depth case studies that are ostensibly critiqued by academics, NGOs, and other actors and ultimately reviewed at an annual conference. Partnership projects encourage companies to collaborate with UN agencies on specific projects in the developing world in areas such as child labor, the protection of non-renewable resources, literacy, health care, and discrimination.

Finally, the Regional/Country Outreach program actively recruits companies from around the world to join the Compact, and fosters regional partnerships based on multi-actor participatory engagement activities. As mentioned earlier, various UN agencies support and complement these activities: for example, UNDP holds multi-stakeholder consultations in dozens of countries around the world that further add to the multi-level focus of the Compact. To date over 50 country-level Global Compact Networks have been established around the world.

The Compact office defines its task as providing a sustainable organizational infrastructure and coordinating effective delivery systems for the four sets of activities. It does not supervise the projects themselves. The office is financed by voluntary, unrestricted donations from UN member-states and philanthropic foundations; to avoid possible conflicts of interest, it accepts no financial support from companies. As a result, development of Compact initiatives has been constrained by limited resources. In April 2006, an official non-profit foundation was established to raise funds for the Compact from a broader array of potential donors.

As the Compact has grown, policy and governance questions have multiplied; to address them an advisory board has recently been created. It is as yet unclear how board members are selected and what their ultimate role will be. A "Leaders Summit" focused on the future of the Compact, and particularly its governance, was held in June 2004 and a second one was held in 2007. Based on the former meeting and a November 2004 workshop of representatives from the Compact's country networks, a governance reform process resulted in dramatic changes.

A major item on the agenda of the Compact was the question of whether to introduce more robust standards for inclusion and exclusion of companies and other actors. In this regard, a potentially crucial policy decision was taken to require that all companies involved would have to produce a COP describing how they have attempted to implement practically their commitment to the Compact's principles. Over the past three years, hundreds of companies have been made "inactive" from the Compact for not submitting updated COPs over a two-year period. However, many critics are still not satisfied that this new requirement was stiff enough for companies to be able to deploy the brand of the United Nations.

As a project of the Secretary General's office, the Global Compact did not require official sanctioning by the UN General Assembly or Security Council because the original nine principles were derived from already ratified interstate conventions. Proposals to include additional norms were not considered early on, primarily as a result of the political calculation of not opening the Global Compact to a debate of member governments in the UN General Assembly. But the adoption of the UN Convention Against Corruption and the persistent lobbying of anti-corruption NGOs such as Transparency International involved in the Compact led to the adoption of a 10th Global Compact Principle on Anti-Corruption in mid-2004.

Beginning in 2005, the Compact implemented far-reaching governance reforms, responding in part to the criticisms that were being leveled against it (see below), and established six key entities in its new frameworks. A board was created with 20 full members from across business, civil society, labor, and UN sectors. The board became the primary strategy and policy-making body of the Compact. The Secretary General of the UN, the chair of the Compact's foundation and the executive director of the Compact are additional ex-officio members of the board. The board meets annually, with its first meeting held in 2005.

The Global Compact Office, led by the Executive Director, is the secretariat that administers daily affairs and implements the various activities. It works closely with the Inter-Agency Team comprised of representatives from the various UN agencies that are engaged with the Compact, including the UN Environment Programme (UNEP), the UN Development Programme (UNDP), the UN Industrial Development Organization (UNIDO), the Office of the UN High Commissioner for Human Rights (OHCHR), and the UN Office on Drugs and Crime (UNODC). The sixth agency is the International Labor Organization (ILO).

Local networks around the world are a fourth pillar of the Global Compact. These groups focus on promoting the Global Compact at regional and country levels, advise the Global Compact Office on strategic opportunities, nominate members for the board, and hold an annual Local Networks Forum (a fifth governance pillar) to share experiences with one another from around the world. The last and perhaps most visible of the governance structures is the tri-annual Global Leaders Summit which is focused on highlighting achievements, reenergizing commitment, and identifying new strategic directions for the Compact.

Outcomes and effects

As is the case with the GRI, it is difficult to specify, and even more difficult to evaluate, the outcomes, effects and broader emerging role of the Global Compact. Nearly 3,000 organizational stakeholders from all corners of the world have engaged in the Compact since its founding in 2000. The Compact has "recruited" hundreds of transnational corporations as well as hundreds of large national companies, particularly from the developing world, to its network—all of which have agreed to honor the now ten universal principles. Recruiting major US companies, however, has proven difficult until the recent corporate scandals because many had already adopted the Global Sullivan Principles[10] and/or, perhaps more importantly, feared that formally adopting the principles would expose them to lawsuits given the nature of US law. It seems that some corporations have letters from the Global Compact assuring them that the adoption and implementation of the principles is purely voluntary. It remains to be seen whether external pressure or competitive interactions within the private sector will be a significant factor in the adoption and/or implementation of the principles.

The Policy Dialogue seems to have generated some substantive cross-sectoral, multi-level efforts. For example, several companies agreed to focus their energies through partnerships in one of the 40 lowest-income economies in the world and contribute to social development in that country. The normative appropriateness of such a project has not been debated. The Learning Forum has proved more challenging, as it invites companies to be publicly self-critical in evaluating their attempts to implement the principles—an endeavor that is not high on their agendas. Examples and cases presented so far have tended to read like press releases touting good works.

The role of "civil society" organizations in the Compact remains diverse and controversial. Large labor, human rights, and environmental NGOs with trans-territorial reach in particular are urged to work cooperatively with companies to help implement the principles effectively and to comment on specific cases; however, they do not have any mechanisms through which to raise substantive concerns about corporate practices that blatantly violate one of the principles. Thus far, civil society has been mostly represented in the Compact by large Northern-based international NGOs. Save the Children in its initial letter of support warned that the Compact's constituency should expand to include more direct representatives of groups whose basic needs are denied. The US-based organization CorpWatch has been highly critical of the Compact, as has the developing world-based Third World Network of nongovernmental advocacy organizations, among many others.

The Compact has been criticized for supporting token efforts towards corporate responsibility through its "learning environment" approach, while many groups argue that it offers very little real scope for internal debate (an informal rule is that organizations participating in Compact activities cannot criticize each other during the interactions). The scope of the Compact is also growing exponentially due to the breadth of the principles and the number and variety of companies and organizations encouraged to join. It remains uncertain whether the Compact will become a central organizational arrangement linked to a broader and deeper institutional framework of meaningful and sustainable relationships that fosters substantive change in corporate practices and its view of sustainable and inclusive economic globalization. But it does seem that the Global Compact's centrality continues to grow, as exemplified by its connection to the GRI and the MMSD analyzed previously.

Tentative findings, hypotheses, and future research

What are the defining features of these global governance networks and why have they emerged? Do they signal a possible shift away from the predominance of government-centric interstate regimes? Are these novel global governance networks constitutive elements of a new form of multi-actor, multi-level global governance?

These particular cases all attempt to link and even integrate social, economic, and environmental foci (or human rights, labor, and the environment) and, increasingly, anti-corruption in their agendas. Also, as seems to be the case with most global governance networks, they all legitimate themselves as transparent, participatory, and accountable initiatives to all stakeholders, but independent from the dominance of any single stakeholder or set of stakeholders. These stakeholders, however, often come from much more complex sectoral and political origins than tri-sectoral (government, business, and nonprofit/NGOs) perspectives can explain. For example, scientists and technical professionals, identity groups such as indigenous peoples or religious communities, labor organizations that often disagree with NGOs, and numerous other constituencies that do not fit in to or cut across these three sectors often actively shape and participate in these networks.

Moreover, the emergence of these experiments was clearly not simply a functional response to the gap between global governance arrangements and transboundary problems or needs driven by broadly accepted views of globalization. Rather, several factors—complex processes of conflict and negotiation among wider sets of (usually) trans-territorial actors, growing cognitive and normative beliefs in cross-sectoral and multi-level, multi-stakeholder models as appropriate organizational forms, and broader contextual political and economic factors—contributed to their genesis and even idiosyncratic events. Contested meanings of globalization, development, sustainability, and even governance (for example, voluntary versus mandatory approaches) are part of the genesis and constitution of these arrangements, as well as their evolving dynamics and effects.

It may be likely, however, that the creation of future global governance networks will be increasingly justified and legitimated by this type of neo-functional argument. Indeed, our study reveals that global governance networks increasingly exhibit tendencies towards institutional isomorphism—the core features identified above. Yet despite broad isomorphic tendencies, significant differences exist across these experiments in terms of politics, organizational arrangements, and effects. What is particularly interesting is that even though the driving "actors" behind the constitution of each were different, and they were organized in very different ways, they have been pushed and pulled in strikingly similar directions. In addition, there are growing attempts to build linkages among global governance networks such as those examined in this chapter—for example, between the MMSD, Global Compact, and GRI.

Thus, there is suggestive evidence that a contested reconfiguration of the *legitimate* actors that constitute world affairs is underway: from a twentieth-century world of states and IGOs to a twenty-first century world consisting of multiple actors with trans-territorial constituencies, capacities, and world views. Contested transnational structuration processes now more visibly involve multiple sets of actors attempting to enact novel scripts of norms, principles, rules, and decision-making procedures that could very well be signaling a longer-term shift away from government-centric interstate regimes—certainly changes *within* some and *of* other interstate regimes. Perhaps most profoundly, *global governance networks have also themselves become sources of novel "organizational scripts" for the reconstruction of global governance*—they have put into play the possibility that multi-stakeholder networks, as opposed to either unilateralism or multilateralism, could be the future of world affairs.

Certainly, the cases examined herein are primarily about the global political economy and its potential re-embedding into social structures and natural environments. It is important that future research examine global security issue areas in addition to further deepening the analysis of these and other cases. Moreover, these cases certainly are located at one end of the continuum of governance ideal types—relatively formalized, cross-sectoral, multi-level organizational forms. Nevertheless, it may actually be that most issue areas in the global arena are informally cross-sectoral and multi-level in nature—consider anything from trans-border crime and terrorism to finance.

Cross-sectoral, multi-level models of and for world affairs may just be the institutional formalization of already existing, underlying, albeit asymmetric and contested, structural realities (Braithwaite and Drahos 2000, Simmons and Oudraat 2001). Institutional stickiness, entrenched political-economic interests, and failures of imagination will certainly challenge the future of global governance networks. But no one predicted that the entire globe would become organized around mutually exclusive territorially bounded and formerly sovereign states during the twentieth century. It is certainly possible that overlapping and interlocking global cross-sectoral and multi-level governance networks could similarly broaden and deepen during the twenty-first century.

Notes

1 In this chapter, governments and intergovernmental agencies are actors while states and interstate regimes are institutional arrangements. As is evident, we find the terms "nation," "nation-state," and "international" problematic and thus refrain from using them. We correspondingly use awkward but still more meaningful terms such as "government-centric, interstate regimes."

2 Part of our discomfort with this appellation is that policy might be narrowly construed and networks have become more a "fad" concept over time. Moreover, calling all of these organizations "networks" under-emphasizes their differing organizational structures and potential political significance.

3 Among the most celebrated of such efforts is the Global Fund for Aids, Tuberculosis and Malaria.

4 There has been much debate about the definition of governance in recent years. It seems that the definition of an interstate regime offers an excellent starting point, particularly for scholars concerned with global governance.

5 In broadening the focus from just the more formal global governance networks to the broader, underlying institutional arrangements of global governance, we are attempting not to repeat the analogous mistake of scholarship that equates intergovernmental organizations with interstate regimes. For one of the best theoretical treatments of a "world society" approach, see Meyer *et al.* (1997).

6 Barnett and Finnemore (2004) argue that intergovernmental organizations are "Weberian" bureaucratic organizations whose primary goals, somewhat similar to states, are first survival and then growth.

7 Wendt (2003) argues that a world state is a teleological necessity.

8 On the method of "structured, focused comparison," see George and Bennett (2005). The comparative analysis is based on archival research, participant observation, and interviews with key actors who have either chosen to be part or not, as well as those potentially affected by or expert watchers of these global governance networks. We have deliberately not referenced the sources of these case reconstructions for readability purposes, but welcome any queries about the research that generated them. The empirical research is ongoing.

9 World Bank president James Wolfensohn established the Extractive Industries Review (EIR) in 2001, in response to criticism from civil society about the Bank's investment in extractive industries without appropriate review of its own guidelines. The Bank attempted to learn the lessons of the MMSD and the WCD by appointing an eminent person to lead the effort and by fully funding it. The choice was Dr. Emil Salim, the former environment minister of Indonesia. However, and interestingly, the EIR recommendations, which propose that the World Bank should no longer fund any oil or mining projects, are considered to be far more radical than those of the WCD or MMSD.

10 The Sullivan Principles, named for founder Rev. Leon Sullivan, were created in 1977 to apply pressure to promote racial equality on firms doing business in apartheid South Africa. Rev. Sullivan and UN Secretary General Koffi Annan launched an updated set of Global Sullivan Principles on corporate social responsibility in 1999.

References

Axelrod, Robert and Keohane, Robert O. (1985) "Achieving Cooperation under Anarchy: Strategies and Institutions," *World Politics* 38,1 (October): 226–254.

Barnett, Michael and Finnemore, Martha (2004) *Rules for the World: International Organizations in Global Politics*, Ithaca, NY: Cornell University Press.

Braithwaite, John and Drahos, Peter (2000) *Global Business Regulation*, Cambridge: Cambridge University Press.

Danielson, Luke and Digby, Caroline (2006) *Architecture for Change: An Account of the Mining, Minerals and Sustainable Development Project History*, London: International Institute for Environment and Development and Berlin: Global Public Policy Institute. Available www.iied.org/mmsd/

George, Alexander L. and Bennett, Andrew (2005) *Case Studies and Theory Development in the Social Sciences*, Cambridge, MA: MIT Press.

Hall, Rodney B. and Biersteker, Thomas J. (2002) *The Emergence of Private Authority in Global Governance*, Cambridge: Cambridge University Press.

Keck, Margaret E. and Sikkink, Kathryn (1998) *Activists beyond Borders*, Ithaca, NY: Cornell University Press.

Kell, Georg and Ruggie, John Gerard (1999) "Global markets and social legitimacy: the case for the 'Global Compact'," *Transnational Corporations* 8,3 (December): 101–120.

Keohane, Robert O. and Nye, Joseph S., Jr. (eds.) (1972) *Transnational Relations and World Politics*, Cambridge, MA: Harvard University Press.

—— (2000) "Introduction," in Joseph S. Nye Jr. and John D. Donahue (eds.) *Governance in a Globalizing World*, Washington D.C.: Brookings Press.

—— (2003) "Redefining Accountability for Global Governance," in Miles Kahler and David A. Lake (eds.) *Governance in a Global Economy: Political Authority in Transition*, Princeton, NJ: Princeton University Press.

Khagram, Sanjeev, Sikkink, Kathryn, and Riker, James V. (2002) *Restructuring World Politics: Transnational Social Movements, Networks, and Norms* (Social Movements, Protest, and Contention, Vol. 14), Minneapolis, MN: University of Minnesota Press.

Krasner, Stephen D. (ed.) (1983) *International Regimes*, Ithaca, NY: Cornell University Press.

Witt, Jan Martin, Reinecke, Wolfgang H., and Benner, Thorsten (2000) "Beyond Multilateralism: Global Policy Networks," *International Politics and Society* 2.

Meyer, John W., Boli, John, Thomas, George M., and Ramirez, Francisco O. (1997) "World Society and the Nation-State," *American Journal of Sociology* 103,1 (July): 144–181.

Milner, Helen (1992) *Resisting Protectionism: Global Industries and the Politics of International Trade*, Princeton, NJ: Princeton University Press.

Oye, Kenneth A. (ed.) (1986) *Cooperation Under Anarchy*, Princeton, NJ: Princeton University Press.

Polanyi, Karl (1944) *The Great Transformation*, New York: Farrar & Rinehart, Inc.

Reinecke, Wolfgang H. and Deng, Francis M. (2000) *Critical Choices: The United Nations, Networks, and the Future of Global Governance*, Toronto: IDRC.

Rhodes, R.A.W. (1997) *Understanding Governance: Policy Networks, Governance, Reflexivity, and Accountability*, Buckingham: Open University Press.

Risse-Kappen, Thomas (ed.) (1995) *Bringing Transnational Relations Back in: Non-state Actors, Domestic Structures, and International Institutions*, Cambridge: Cambridge University Press.

Rittberger, Volker (ed.) (1995) *Our Global Neighborhood: Regime Theory and International Relations*, Oxford: Clarendon Press.

Ruggie, John Gerard (1982) "International regimes, transactions, and change: Embedded liberalism in the postwar economic order," *International Organization* 36: 379–415.

—— (1998) *Constructing the World Polity: Essays on International Institutionalization*, New York: Routledge Press.

—— (2002) "The Theory and Practice of Learning Networks: Corporate Social Responsibility and the Global Compact," *Journal of Corporate Citizenship* 5 (Spring): 27–36.

Simmons, P.J. and Oudraat, Chantal de Jonge (eds.) (2001) *Managing Global Issues: Lessons Learned*, New York: Carnegie Endowment for International Peace.

Sklair, Leslie (2000) *The Transnational Capitalist Class*, Oxford: Blackwell Publishers.

Waddell, Steve (2003) "Global Action Networks: A Global Invention to Make Globalisation Work for All," *Journal of Corporate Citizenship* 12 (Winter): 27–42.

Waltz, Kenneth (1979) *The Theory of International Relations*, Reading, MA: Addison Wesley.

Wendt, Alexander (1999) *Social Theory of International Politics*, Cambridge: Cambridge University Press.

—— (2003) "Why a World State is Inevitable: Teleology and the Logic of Anarchy," *European Journal of International Relations* 9,4: 491–542.

Wendt, Alexander and Fearon, James (2002) "Rationalism and Constructivism in International Relations Theory," in Walter Carlsnaes, Thomas Risse, and Beth Simmons (eds.) *Handbook of International Relations*, New York: Sage.

Woods, Ngaire (1999) "Good Governance in International Organizations," *Global Governance* 5,1: 39–61.

—— (2002) *Governing Globalization*, Cambridge: Polity Press.

9 "Stakeholders" and the politics of environmental policymaking

Darrell Whitman

Introduction

Environmental policymaking is a multi-layered process that not only identifies issues and makes choices, but also identifies decision-makers and defines key terms and concepts. The politics of policymaking are similarly multi-layered, and include personal, institutional, and ideological politics. In practice, there is no bright line between these forms of politics, with personal and institutional politics mixing with ideological assumptions to shape both processes and outcomes. Conventional policy studies tend to focus on institutional politics, primarily because policymaking derives its authority from government and choices are reduced to rules, regulations, and laws (see, e.g., Susskind and Ozawa 1992). There is, however, another way of thinking about policymaking that gives more importance to personal and ideological politics, and which generally falls within forms of critical thinking such as critical policy studies (see, e.g., Wagenaar and Cook 2003). This chapter is something of a hybrid: it recognizes the importance of institutional influences on policymaking but also interrogates policymaking from a critical view that gives considerable weight to its more normative aspects, and particularly to how ideas, values, and processes are shaped by policymaking discourses.

The specific focus of this critical inquiry into environmental policymaking is on what have become known as "stakeholder" processes. These have appeared widely in many public policy practices in recent years, but have rarely been analyzed for their political influence. As the following discussion will demonstrate, the stakeholder processes used in environmental policymaking are not benign or democratic, but have developed through a fairly recent history as part of a business management theory that has developed them for purposes of better controlling internal and external business relations. As such, they are disconnected from the idea that policy deliberations ought to be open and inclusive, or that environmental policy should somehow prioritize ecological sustainability. The central problem with stakeholder policymaking is that it acts discursively to interpose corporate economic values into deliberative policy processes. This occurs because these corporate-inspired formats come with their own set of assumptions about who can be authorized to participate and what can be deliberated, and because the key terms of policymaking are defined *before* designated stakeholders are allowed a voice.

In keeping with the theme of this book, this chapter also offers a way forward in gaining some democratic leverage over environmental stakeholder policymaking by redefining it to be more inclusive and with a greater potential for representing marginalized human and natural constituencies. The means to accomplish this goal are present in an alternate but far more powerful stakeholder discourse that has a much longer and deeply equitable history in law. Ironically, this alternate discourse is also rooted in business practices, but in a manner that acts to limit predatory economic interests to ensure that *absent interests* are recognized and protected when rights and duties are decided. The history of this alternate discourse is punctuated with many of the issues that are now excluded from environmental policymaking, such as the interests of future generations and the non-economic values of nature itself, based on claims that it is impractical to try to include them in policymaking.

The importance of discourse in environmental policymaking

Environmental policymaking occurs within a political culture and employs specialized language that is significantly different from that found in general society. One the one hand, environmental issues are most commonly articulated in the language of science, which tends to marginalize participation by requiring that it be interpreted: when science-knowledge dominates the debate, only those with adequate interpreters will be able to offer any meaningful comment. This reliance serves policymakers because it gives policy deliberations an aura of objectivity that obscures the essentially political nature of the choices that are made. This obfuscation also serves policymakers by creating ambiguities that allow participants to make claims about policy that can satisfy their separate and often conflicted constituencies. This is not so much a conspiracy as it is a necessity in gaining agreement among diverse groups that stand behind the policy process. Yet, at the same time, an overabundance of obfuscation also acts to promote antidemocratically a reliance on specialists and experts to give meaning to policy choices. The decline in public confidence in environmental policymaking at the end of the twentieth century has been said to follow from its inability to be clear, consistent, and democratic (see, e.g. Dowie 1995). Thus, the language used in environmental policymaking has a heightened importance over that which might appear with a subject that is more easily accessed.

The importance of language in environmental policymaking has become of increasing interest as part of a general trend in critical politics toward cultural forms. Anyone who has participated in discussions about an environmental issue of importance will quickly find that there is an array of opinion that, on closer inspection, reflects different personal histories and cultures. Policymakers, even the institutional ones, also have personal histories and bring these histories and cultures with them into policy deliberations (see, e. g., Hajer 2003). The "playing field" for these deliberations thus becomes littered with cultural landmines in the form of different understandings and conflicted interpretations of key terms. The ability to select or impose particular discourses and define key terms thus is a form of power that goes far beyond formal agendas and policy documents. This power becomes particularly important where deliberations occur in a multicultural context, as does global environmental policymaking and policymaking that extends beyond merely local issues.

The interest in language that has appeared in politics and environmental policymaking has been pursued as an art in business and business management. It is most visible in the huge investments that business has made in advertising, but it also exists within business management where it has been refined as a tool to maintain control and advance business interests. It should be understood that language in this case is more than written and spoken words. As Umberto Eco observes, we are awash in visual images and audio communications that use autosuggestion as a way of associating these images and communications with ideas and impressions, often without the conscious knowledge of those affected by them (Eco 1999). Thus, merely looking at text language, or even spoken language, does not fully account for how words are used to convey more than given meanings and how the control over words and definitions is more than formal pronouncements.

The concern in this chapter for the use of the term "stakeholder" is based on the discursive turn that has taken place in general society, which gives this term ideational as well as organizational power. What constitutes a recognized stakeholder in the current corporate-inspired use takes on economic and political meaning that comes from how business management values participation. Further, the term itself carries with it hidden values that reinforce a business-oriented agenda based on concepts of profit, property rights, and the resource value of nature. None of this necessarily appears on the surface, and may not be acknowledged or even known by business and government participants. But the lack of acknowledgment and recognition only means that they become more powerful as subliminal forms of communication.

Environmental policymaking has a second feature that also relies substantially on a discursive turn as an expressed interest in efficiency. As a dynamic entity, nature waits for no one, and environmental issues are often addressed in mid-stream with a sense of urgency. This gives rise to a renewed emphasis on "doing something," with the consequence that policy processes are often measured against the timeliness with which they produce a policy choice. The adoption of stakeholder processes can often be traced to these circumstances, because they are seen to be less confrontational and able to move more quickly toward an agreement than are publicly conducted open political discussions (see, e.g., Burroughs 1999). Whatever the merit of this claim, efficiency is almost always gained as a compromise that reduces participation and disciplines it to choices that are preferred by the most powerful. This is where language acts powerfully to make a claim of efficiency compelling and exclusive, and obscures how power relationships are at work in forming and articulating that claim. For this reason, judgments about issues, processes, and goals in policymaking should always be measured against the discourse that is producing them.

Why definitions matter

Discourses are made up of words in different forms, and words' individual histories of how meaning became imparted to them. Finding a definition for terms is, therefore, a bit of historiography that pits different constructions against one another, with meaning constructed according to the sense of history that emerges. This will seem self-evident to anyone who has struggled to communicate in a "foreign" language, but is often overlooked when we use language that appears to be familiar. Political philosophers, and particularly the more recent generation of discourse theorists, are much concerned with how words have come to have a particular meaning, and how those meanings become political tools (see, e.g., Habermas 1987; Foucault 1991). In a practical sense, this means that there is both a power in discourse—that the process of definition is one where power is exercised, and a power of discourse, which is the power of language to shape relationships and define values (Holzcheiter 2003).

In a normative sense, language is a repository of ideology that confirms our identification with particular language forms. But in the instrumental sense, language is also the medium through which meaning is negotiated and in some cases redefined. For example, as Douglas Torgerson observed in *Democracy's Dilemma*, "The word *policy* has acquired such strong technocratic overtones that the idea of pursuing democracy through policy discourse may seem puzzling, if not inherently contradictory" (Torgerson 2003: 113). He then goes on to argue that policymaking can be a vehicle for democratic participation if and when debates can be accessed democratically and policy discourses are open and creative enterprises. There are several key terms in this observation, including democracy. What democratic participation means in traditional liberal terms is *representative* democracy, or that a democratic claim can be made based on the ability of those present to represent those who are absent. This interpretation is rarely spelled out, because it is assumed from a Euro-American perspective to be understood. Other interpretations are possible, even in Euro-American culture, which might recognize democracy only in the purist terms as full and open access. Using the term democracy without explication in other cultural contexts would be problematic as it would be without clear meaning for many people. As is evident, supplying the definition is a way of defining participation.

The ability to define also matters in a normative sense because a common understanding clarifies the extent to which there is a common agreement. Simply opening doors to new voices is not enough, if those voices cannot be heard and understood. This leads to the question of what is required as a *meaningful* opportunity to be heard in a policy process. Once a policy process has been defined, it will carry its own definition of what "meaningful opportunity" means, and the institutional inertia of that already defined process will make it difficult to reform or expand that definition. However, that is not the whole story, because policymaking remains a human-centred process and humans are capable of, and often engage in, reinterpretation of terms through interaction with other policymakers (Innes and Booher 2003). The extent to which they exercise this discretion depends partly on how a definition was determined and the strength of the definition itself. If a definition is central to the process, such as an explicit declaration that participation is limited to those with a direct financial interest, then it will be far more difficult to dislodge than a more general declaration that *should* be limited to one or another group or that the identity of participants is peripheral to policy outcomes. Getting into the definition business early in policymaking allows for considerable influence over the subsequent agenda.

The definition of "stakeholder" in environmental policymaking has only rarely acquired a specific meaning or been located as a central and controlling concept. Most often it has been associated with those that have an "interest" in the policy issue at hand, which is commonly assumed to be an economic interest in policy choices (see, e.g., Jones 1997). But these also are broad terms with multiple meanings, which arguably open the door to further definition during policymaking. It becomes possible, then, to argue economic interests and impacts broadly, and to force open the door to other participants with a political argument that policy choices will not be seen as legitimate, and will not achieve full implementation, unless those initially left outside are invited in. This has been a popular strategy, particularly in Third World communities, where stakeholder processes have invariably been created from outside by international agencies or corporate entities with little knowledge of local communities.

The limits to reforming environmental policymaking after the fact

While it does not preclude reform, waiting until a policymaking process is in place and operational seriously limits the democratic potential that might arise if the process itself is democratically formed. Environmental policymaking has trended away from direct government regulation, and thus away from open political forums, because governments are increasingly reluctant to be held directly accountable for policy outcomes (Hay 1992). This reflects an increase in the political transaction costs of policymaking that is imposed by the contentious nature of environmental issues (see, e.g., Dryzek 1990). In its place have appeared various forms of alternative dispute resolution processes, such as mediation, arbitration, and public–private consultations, which were designed to serve business and now serve government by relocating policy deliberations away from the public eye. In some cases, these processes have their own set of rules, such as those created by the American Arbitration Association, that come with quasi-legal powers. But all of them limit participation to some degree in the interest of protecting existing arrangements of power, and once these processes are in place they are difficult to reform.

There are deep ideological reasons why this shift in policymaking occurred, which can be traced to the decline of liberalism and the rise of neoliberalism during the late 1970s and early 1980s. The principal features of this new ideology became a retreat of the state, a preference for business-based solutions, and hostility toward broad democratic participation in policymaking (Dryzek 1996).[1] The evolution of these new policymaking forms began with these ideological assumptions and prejudices, which have left them with considerable ideological baggage that resists reform, particularly by popular acclaim. This introduces a new and powerful layer of politics that is embedded in policymaking even before it becomes applied to particular environmental issues.

The principal counterpoint to neoliberal ideology and its influence over environmental policymaking is the underlying requirement that policy choices gain wide popular support. This is widely understood by both business and government policymakers and, for reasons that will be discussed below, stakeholder processes have become popular with these groups because they have been effective in creating an appearance of democracy but without any actual transfer of power over policymaking. This can be seen in the way that environmental policy is increasingly sold after-the-fact much as any commercial product, by bypassing questions of democratic public participation with a recasting of it as a consumer product. This is made all the easier by the sad state of environmental nongovernmental organizations—many of whom have fallen into a pattern of relying on subscription membership and corporate financial sponsorship—that can be enticed into endorsing policies in exchange for access to policymaking as "stakeholders." This provides an appearance of democracy sufficient to cast the policy as authoritative and legitimate.

To the extent that environmental policymaking is rooted in corporate-inspired and -controlled policy processes, it is subordinate to the basic laws of capitalist economics, or as Milton Friedman candidly observed, "the social responsibility of business is to increase its profits" (Friedman 1970: 26).[2] Thus, regardless of the professed intentions of participants, or the nobility with which policy choices are presented, these policy formats inevitably serve business and not environmental purposes. The truth of this argument can be found by closely examining the contradictory history of "stakeholder" from its historic roots, through its refinement in law, and to its separate life as a business management concept. It always has carried a certain economic quality with it, because "stake" has always been defined in monetary terms. However, its legal and business history move through opposite values and concepts, and arrive at very different conclusions about what stakeholders are and how they should be treated in public life.

The contradictory history of "stakeholder"

The irony of the definition of "stakeholder" used in contemporary business management theory is that it is the opposite of the definition that has developed elsewhere, and particularly in Anglo-American law. This divergence stems from two very different etiologies: the historical-legal definition grew out of an attempt to broaden the power of absent parties by creating authorized representatives, while the business management version grew out of attempts to divide potential parties and control them by privileging one group over another. The historical-legal definition is much older, having evolved from a seventeenth-century context in association with the British Crown, while the business management version is quite new with roots reaching back only to the 1960s and primarily to American business practices. As is evident, the historical-legal definition is a democratic and empowering concept, while the business management definition is an antidemocratic and controlling concept.

This divergence offers some intriguing possibilities for environmental policymaking, which because of its essential public interest purpose walks a fine line between private and public interests and which, at least in the United States, exists in the shadow of a legal-juridical state. One the one hand, the widespread use of corporate-inspired stakeholder processes has popularized its definition through an uncritical acceptance and use of the term by government and nongovernmental organizations that have been offered a place at the table. This popularized definition has gained political power because it is rarely offered in any meaningful detail, which has allowed it to take on an *assumed* ideological meaning rather than an openly negotiated one. On the other hand, the historical-legal definition has institutional power because it has been used narrowly and precisely, and because it carries the weight of a legal opinion that authorizes and legitimizes the modern state itself. These competing definitions have yet to be tested against one another, but if that testing were to occur it would take place in a legal forum where the historical-legal definition would begin with an institutional advantage. Testing these competing definitions also would meet fierce resistance from the corporate sponsors of business management stakeholder theory, which would have to be part of the political calculus in moving to conduct the test. Yet, the separate histories and logics of these definitions argue that such a test should be done, if for no other reason than that the weight of equity behind the historical-legal concept of "stakeholder" is far more democratic and ultimately representative.

The equitable roots of "stakeholder" as a historical-legal concept

The Anglo-Saxon legal history of "stakeholder" extends from King James I, who became the first stakeholder on record by sponsoring a lottery to support the Virginia Colony in North America, down through the present as an equitable concept in US insurance law. The common thread that runs through this history is an effort to fashion rights and duties to protect parties who cannot individually represent themselves for a variety of reasons, but whose rights and duties must be considered to achieve justice through law. This concept reflects considerations of risk of loss, which are also prominently present in most environmental issues, and circumstances where institutionally powerful parties claim rights and duties based on the personal interests of much weaker parties who have little or no access to legal process.

The concept of "equity," which is deeply embedded in Anglo-American legal theory as a balancing of statutory rights and duties against a sense that the law delivers "just" outcomes, has an enduring history as that which gives legal process a democratic claim. In the days of James I, equity had a decidedly theological twist, with the argument that the decrees of the monarch must be balanced against the morality of the church to give both the Crown and the church legitimacy in the eyes of the common people. This seems remarkably close to many of the more important facets of modern environmental policymaking, where the broad public interest is difficult to compose in a limited policy forum, but where a sense of justice is required to gain public acceptance for policy choices.

James I created his role as the first stakeholder in this history by chairing the Crown lottery commission, which collected funds against a lottery draw in an effort to provide financial support for American colonists. This left open many questions about what precisely the King's duties were in these circumstances. Most obviously, he became what we would now recognize as a trustee and acquired what we now commonly call a fiduciary duty to the ticket holders to preserve the funds, properly identify the lottery winner, and promptly deliver the money to the winner. As the most powerful figure in England, it was assumed that he could be trusted to faithfully carry out this duty, but it also came with a caveat that the King should not consider the money to be in any way his personal property. Thus, his *lack of interest*, not his direct personal interest, was what made him a stakeholder under these circumstances.

A second important feature of this first stakeholder arrangement was that it involved a future rather than a present interest. The right to the money was not known at the time when the stake was created in the form of money from purchased lottery tickets, and any premature suggestion of right would destroy the integrity of the lottery. This raised a whole series of equitable problems because the owner of a winning lottery ticket might die or disappear before the lottery was held, or ownership of the ticket might be disputed, or the ticket itself might be forged. Determining potentially competing claims on the basis of fairness and equity thus became an implied quality of a stakeholder and laid the foundation for the persistence of stakeholder as a common law concept.

Applying these concepts to stakeholders in modern environmental policymaking would require that they meet several equitable qualities. First, they could not have any direct interest of their own in policy choices. Rather, they could only act to protect the rights of others, such as those imagined by Andrew Dobson and others as "future" rights that would potentially vest in those who could not themselves participate in the process (Dobson 1999). Additionally, the identification of stakeholders would be measured by their ability to protect those interests as surrogates of the unrepresented. Implicitly, this would provide a protected place for the very young, very old, poor, educationally and politically disadvantaged, and distant citizens of planet Earth directly within policymaking, where they would be properly represented by those who would have to meet a test of representativeness.

"Stakeholder" in modern common law

The seventeenth-century equitable definition of "stakeholder" continued and expanded in modern common law after its introduction by James I. Its survival can be attributed, at least in part, to the free-market capitalism that reigned with little restraint until the early twentieth century. To take advantage of growing markets, merchants and producers required capital from private financers and banks, which required both interest and security in exchange for the risk that they assumed. This early form of "risk management" was not itself free from risk, as there was little in the way of public regulation or protection against poor management, unforeseen events, or outright fraud. The need to offer yet another form of protection against possible loss gave rise to insurance as one of the great capitalist inventions of the late eighteenth century, with insurers assuming the role of protector of the equities as institutional stakeholders.

The rapid expansion of insurance and its evolution into complex arrangements that protected both business and personal property confronted many of the same questions that arose with the Crown lottery. By definition, insurance companies acted to protect funds for clients, who in many instances were acting to provide protection to beneficiaries other than themselves. In some cases, as with life insurance, the potential beneficiary might not exist at the time the policy was written; even where they did, contentious disputes about entitlement often arose that required an equitable determination of right by the insurance company. In turn, these determinations would open the door to legal disputes and litigation, with the role of insurance company left in legal limbo.

The problem was solved in the United States in a 1934 Supreme Court case titled *Sanders v. Armour Fertilizer Works, et al.* (292 U.S. 190), which reaffirmed the equitable definition of the term "stakeholder" by holding that insurance companies could appear in court on behalf of their policy-holders as an equitable matter.[3] Elaborating, the Court confirmed that stake-holders could only be *disinterested* agents acting to protect the rights of others, and that those rights represented *future* rather than present interests. The *Sanders* decision became the primary precedent, or controlling legal opinion, thereafter and continues to represent current legal thinking in the United States.[4] Thereafter, when required to address "stakeholders," other courts reaffirmed and expanded the equitable view of stakeholder by applying the *Sanders* definition to a wide range of circumstances.[5] This view of "stakeholder" has become sufficiently settled in law to allow the *Sanders* definition to appear formally in Black's Law Dictionary as a "third-party [that holds] money or property [or] an interest or concern in a business or enterprise, but is not the owner," with one court going so far as to declare that the term "'stakeholder' has a definite place ... and is not to be varied ... by either circumlocution or the splitting of the essential word" (*State v. Dudley*, 21 A.2d 209).

What is remarkable about the legal discourse of "stakeholder" is that it has consistently refused to apply to a party that has a personal interest in the proceedings, but only allows its use when it can be applied as an equitable matter to avoid injustice being done to someone that could not appear in court on their own behalf. Many of the arguments and much of the reasoning that led to these conclusions are similar to those that appear in environmental policy debates. By their nature, these debates cannot be reduced to collections of mere things that can be owned and controlled by one party for their exclusive interests: if that were the case, they would not be public policy debates but private property rights. Rather, they become public policy because they have broad implications for collective interests, which in turn have indefinite temporal and spatial boundaries. The historical-legal doctrine of "stakeholder" more accurately reflects these circumstances by recognizing interests as broad representations of relationships and effects that cannot be subordinated to narrow economic and political power.

Business management theory and stakeholder processes

The evolution of stakeholder processes in business management theory took place outside of public policy and legal forums but inside a general shift in the organization of business itself during the 1950s and 1960s. The purpose of this shift was to accommodate changes in general society that had differentiated management functions to an extent that a new "managerial class" had formed to challenge control by traditional ownership (see, e.g., Burnham 1941; Galbraith 1979). These changes, which began during the 1930s, accelerated during the 1950s and 1960s along with the rapid expansion of national economies and introduction of new technologies. This formed the basis for what is now recognized as knowledge/information-based economics. Rather than relying on raw economic power and political power, which could be concentrated and controlled by a capitalist elite, this new form of economics disbursed power and control to those who possessed the knowledge and information necessary to make it function. Managers moved from being mere representatives of corporate authority to authorities over corporate production, with interests and ambitions that conflicted with old-line corporate management.

The development of corporate-inspired stakeholder processes, which emerged during the mid-1960s, was preceded by a rethinking of corporate governance in response to a growing demand for participation in corporate decision-making by workers and managers. The combination of economic depression and war had reshaped Euro-American social and political structures, producing expectations of democratic reformation and engagement throughout societies. The labor unions that formed before the war laid an ideological claim to be a part of this social revolution, producing a series of sharp and influential critiques of business organization and management (see, e.g., Whyte 1957; Hacker 1964; Mills 2002). In response, pro-business social theorists evolved a series of responses that argued that a reformation of management that offered a graduated entry to higher level business managers could succeed in inducing an increased corporate loyalty among this group, while splitting it away from any potential identity with its blue-collar associates (see Parsons 1967). The two most important elements of this new management theory advanced the argument that human society was an economic rather than political organism (Friedman 1957), and that conflict within and with corporations was largely the result of dysfunctional organizations (Parsons 1967). The corporate stakeholder process was born into this new cauldron of business management theory and over time became refined into a business management discourse of its own.

The fundamental assumptions of stakeholder processes are that they are effective tools in the conservation of management resources and the promotion of institutional goals. Thus, business management theory advances stakeholder processes for the purpose of achieving more efficient management by reducing conflict and the need to negotiate potentially contentious issues, and to promote business profitability by "socializing" economic and political relations. The classic confrontation between powerful corporations and organized workers, and the traditional role of government in regulating business to preclude its worst excesses, has been replaced with "processes" that obscure underlying conflicts of interest and seductively invite external parties to forums that are maintained and controlled discursively for business purposes. Talcott Parsons, one of the major theoretical architects of this strategy, gave this new management theory its rationale by arguing that complex organizational structures could be made more efficient by employing discourses that would promote a closer identification between the organization, its members, and national society (Parsons 1967), something which was later observed as borrowed from 1930s German propaganda (Holton and Turner 1986).[6]

The term "stakeholder" first appeared within modern business management theory as a corruption of the term "shareholder," and was applied to middle-level managers in the late 1950s in an effort to create a stronger corporate identity among them (Likert 1961). In practice, the term was applied to intra-corporate relations and involved offering "perks," such as stock options and transportation subsidies, to managers who might believe themselves included in higher management circles. At this stage there was no effort to apply it to public management, which remained firmly rooted in a liberal-institutional model. However, with the decline of liberal ideology during the 1960s, and the growing influence of business on public management, the wall between business management theory and public policymaking practice began to come down. The age of neoliberalism that followed in the 1970s and grew in power during the 1980s provided the ideological support for extending business management theory and influence throughout government agencies, particularly where these agencies were engaged in regulatory and management functions of interest to business.

What distinguished emerging neoliberalism from old-fashioned liberalism was its attack on government management and its pro-business affection for "market-based" policymaking (Barry 2002). This appeared discursively as "cost-benefit" analysis, which in environmental policy meant that choice was reduced to an economic formula that gave priority to business and market ideology (Bailey 1998). But it also appeared structurally as a privatization of policymaking itself, under the rubric of "alternative dispute resolution" (ADR) mechanisms in the 1980s that provided for private negotiations in the place of public litigation.[7] This offered an ideological discourse coupled with an institutional reform that substantially marginalized the public nature of environmental policymaking, which made it far more efficient in the eyes of business but far less democratically accountable.

The two faces of business management stakeholder theory

The development of new management strategies in the mid-1960s followed two separate but parallel tracks that have continued to compete for attention as the true face of business management stakeholder theory. The first face, identified as "instrumental stakeholder theory" (see, e.g., Berman 2000), generally argued that business existed in a socio-political milieu which required that management adopt practices incorporating value discourses that went beyond merely ordering relationships and actions. This analysis reflected a Weberian/Parsonian view that society was composed of individual private rights and preferences, and that organizational participation carried with it many embedded expressions of those rights and preferences as forms of "rational choice" (Buchanan and Tullock 1962). In this view, stakeholders could be identified by their economic interests as consumers and employees, and stakeholder processes could contribute to more effective management by accommodating those interests and directing them toward business goals. It fit nicely with the reconstitution of national capitalist economies as consumer/producer systems and the emergence of neoliberal concepts of public–private partnerships.

The second face, which emerged in strength during the 1980s, viewed stakeholder processes as normative structures that allowed business to extend its influence out from its corporate form and into general society as a vehicle for its socio-political values (see, e.g., Gibson 2000). While the theoretical emphasis in normative stakeholder theory differs from instrumental stakeholder theory, the underlying purpose remains substantially unchanged, with stakeholder processes continuing to be generated in an effort to secure and/or enhance business profitability through better internal and external business management (Freeman 1984). The politics of each theory, however, is fundamentally different, in that instrumental theory is very transparent in its purpose and intent, while normative theory conceals its purpose and intent in a thick discourse that draws on the democratic language and preferences found in general society. It is this second, normative face of stakeholder theory that is most commonly found in environmental policymaking.

These two faces of stakeholder theory reflect the historical circumstances in which they developed. Modern capitalism was self-assured and rapidly expanding during the 1950s and 1960s, and the new management theories it created were openly directed at promoting corporate culture as modern and desirable. With postwar economic growth consistently marching ahead under a corporate banner, companies felt confident in sharing business perks and power with employees, and in selling these new management arrangements to their shareholders as models of efficiency, profitability, and civic responsibility. The discourse that instrumental stakeholder processes generated thus reinforced existing ideological assumptions, which made their incorporation into public–private environmental policymaking during the 1970s all the easier.[8]

The development of the normative face of business management stakeholder theory appears to reflect the economic and environmental crises of the late 1970s and early 1980s, which called into question the benign effect of unregulated business practices. The hyperinflation and sharp economic recession of this period combined with a series of high-profile environmental disasters to undermine public confidence in claims that profitability alone was the measure of good business practices. The demand for public participation in environmental policymaking, which had been diverted into neoliberal alternative public–private consultations, reappeared in reinvigorated form as alliances of nongovernmental organizations with expanded technical expertise. The membership of these organizations were better informed and more technically sophisticated, and were not so easily marginalized in policymaking. Merely claiming that a practice was efficient would not by itself provide it with legitimacy, and business management began to rally to the idea that public good will was itself a valuable financial asset.

If recognized as a discursive shift rather than a fundamental change in management philosophy, normative stakeholder theory begins to appear as what Jurgen Habermas describes as a "Legitimation Crisis," where discourses are adjusted to redefine the nature and substance of an issue in an effort to deflect accountability (Habermas 1976). The neoliberalism of the period, which had offered government the means to shift responsibility for environmental management to public–private partnerships, was as invested in economic growth as the liberal-institutional ideology that preceded it (Barry 2002). But the viability of this arrangement rested on the assumption that business could more effectively absorb the political costs where policies failed. With government and business management both placed in doubt, a third strategy was required that could effectively draw public participation into policymaking, but without sacrificing ultimate control over policy goals. Normative stakeholder theory provided one answer by discursively recasting the purpose of public–private partnerships and environmental policymaking as a form of democratic participation.

Stakeholder processes as business management tools

With the understanding that business management stakeholder theory has always been about securing business goals, stakeholder processes can be seen as tools for the maintenance of corporate power over environmental policy. This was in evidence from the beginning, when the term was borrowed as a corruption of "shareholder" in an effort to convey an illusion rather than an actual carrier of power (Ansoff 1965). Thus, linking the term to ceremonial acts, such as symbolic awards and gratuities, gave an appearance that stakeholders had actual status when they did not. But it was very effective in muting potential conflicts by discursively arguing that there was a mutually beneficial relationship between a company and stakeholders that only required a system of shared management. As an early business writer observed, stakeholders could be defined as "individuals or groups which depend on the company for the realization of their personal goals and on whom the company is dependent. ... They place demands on the company and the company has claims on them" (Rhenman 1968: 25). Without actual power, however, stakeholders assumed accountability for management but with little opportunity to secure any interests or goals that did not serve the company itself.

Business stakeholder processes are an extension of what has generally been identified as the "shareholder value theory of corporate governance," which argues that in corporate politics shareholders rather than corporate boards are the source of governance (McCahery *et al.* 2002). In theory, these corporate shareholders hold the power to shape corporate policy and practice by appointing and recalling directors and demanding accountability for the action of corporate boards.[9] In practice, however, corporate board members are almost always shareholders with major holding in the company, with the remaining stock spread widely among smaller shareholders. Thus, voting control of a corporation generally remains with the board, which can exercise power with only a minority share of stock. Further, corporation law, at least in the United States, imposes a fiduciary duty on corporate boards to always act in the financial interests of the shareholders, and even a single shareholder has the legal power to call boards to account where they fail to protect the value of their stock. Claims that a corporation can be "greened," or made to be environmentally responsible, through a shift in corporate culture and values must always be tested against the institutional reality of corporations as legal entities (see, e.g., Robbins 2001).

That said, present corporate normative management strategies are substantially directed as creating the appearance of environmental responsibility—Chevron's longstanding public relations campaign claiming that "companies do care" about the environment and British Petroleum's recreation of itself as "Beyond Petroleum" and its internal emissions reduction program are both examples of how this works discursively. But perhaps more insidiously, businesses have become primary promoters of stakeholder processes because they offer opportunities to capture the legitimacy of participating individuals and organizations within a management regime that is designed to serve business. This allows these companies to point to these participants as endorsers of their environmental credentials, and argue that policy outcomes are democratically determined. A brief visit to R.E. Freeman's 1984 book, *Strategic Management: A Stakeholder Approach*, illustrates the point.

The use of stakeholder processes up through the early 1980s had always assumed that they were purely instrumental management tools, and that their most effective use was in intra-corporate relations. This changed with the crisis in corporate governance of the early 1980s because businesses became painfully aware that their public image could have a profound impact on their independence from regulation and their corporate competitiveness. R.E. Freeman, a business management theorist, addressed this crisis by arguing that stakeholder processes could be extended outside of the corporation as a new public relations tool. His use of the term "strategic management" gives away the nature of this move, which he envisioned as an instrumental trade-off between limited, short-term management choices and long-term corporate objectives. In his analysis, stakeholders had no recognized interests separate from the corporation, and their relationship to the corporation would always be defined in terms of protecting long-term corporate profitability. This would apply equally to stakeholders as individuals or as groups, and to stakeholders inside and outside the corporation.

Freeman's treatise spawned a vigorous debate in business management literature about the identity and function of stakeholders, which has been bounded by the two faces of instrumental and normative stakeholder theory and by the underlying purpose of profitability. Those that follow the instrumentalist form generally assume that issues of equity and fairness merely relate to fostering a positive working relationship between the corporation and its stakeholders (see, e.g., Jones 1995). In contrast, normative theorists assume that there is a pre-existing relationship between a corporation and the communities that constructs a sense of duty and obligation between them (see, e.g., Hill and Jones 1992; Gibson 2000). Absent from both theories is any argument that community stakeholders have interests and identities that are not shared with the corporation, or that values and purposes might be redefined through interactions between community and corporate members.

There are other aspects of business management theory that also influence this stakeholder discourse, such as the idea of "corporate citizenship." Citizenship long has been claimed for corporations in a variety of settings but most effectively in law, where corporations currently enjoy greater rights than do private citizens (Bakan 2004). But this idea of corporate citizenship was popularized and became part of a general public relations campaign during the 1980s as a consequence of demands for more public corporate accountability. It began by characterizing corporate–community relations as forms of citizenships, based on the multiple roles that corporations play in organizing communities. But it moved beyond mere public relations as a system of corporate rights and responsibilities in community governance. This gave the corporation standing to intervene politically in the organization and conduct of a wide range of community affairs, such as promoting forms of education, community planning, and environmental management. Ultimately, corporate citizenship is a discourse aimed at supplanting broad community-based democratic participation with narrow and specialized forms of participation based on corporate values.[10]

Linking stakeholder processes to claims of corporate citizenship involves a heavy investment in a reconstruction of political and property rights. Rather than placing personal and corporate community membership on an equal footing, it subordinates personal community membership to the corporation's power to define community relationships, values, and practices through its disproportionate economic influence. However, it also raises questions about whether a corporation can actually possess the essential qualities of citizenship, which include *reciprocal* rights and responsibilities (Held 1984; Altman 2000). Under these circumstances, policy choices do not reflect the history of a community, or the special qualities of its relationship with nature. Rather, they simply ratify disparities of power between the corporation and other citizens, and insulate policy choices against democratic claims of injustice and inequality (Short and Winter 1999). Further, these sort of stakeholder processes act discursively to impose a burden of accountability on the community without a concomitant power to manage policy outcomes.[11]

Gains and losses: can we recover stakeholder processes for democratic policymaking?

The practical benefits and ideological justification for the importation of stakeholder processes into environmental policymaking have become a large part of the stakeholder discourse itself. Motives for using these processes are complex, and many enter into them simply as a way to gain a voice in what appears to be limited policymaking access. With business gaining substantial control over environmental policymaking in the wake of a decline of direct regulation by governments, stakeholder processes arguably may be the only game in town. Yet, at the same time, the ideological roots of these corporate-inspired processes raise a cautionary note about how they are designed as a "crisis displacement strategy" that insulates responsible parties from accountability for environmental problems (Hay 1992; Benson 1996). Moreover, the private character of these processes means that participation is predetermined and restricted based on a corporate-economic agenda (Rosenau and Czempiel 1992). Thus, the potential for making these processes work in other, more democratic ways, appears to be limited and fraught with losses as well as gains.

Taking a closer look, however, there are cracks that, if properly understood and exploited, might revitalize stakeholder processes as democratic tools. As with policymaking generally, stakeholder processes are conducted not theoretically but practically, by the people who participate in them. Possibilities abound for participants to reshape the policy process, including definitions and goals, as part of the deliberative process (Wagenaar and Cook 2003; Allen 2004). The key points where this might occur are where stakeholders are identified (Kaler 2002), stakeholder motives are assessed (Richards *et al.* 2003), and policy choices are framed (Jones 1997; Mahanty and Russell 2002; McGlashan and Williams 2003). Here, the very character of what is at issue can be redefined, and the flow of power reversed in favor of community rather than corporate governance. A recently reported stakeholder process offers an example of how this might work.

During the late 1990s, the State of Rhode Island created a stakeholder process to facilitate the management of water quality in Narragansett Bay (Burroughs 1999). The problem at issue was that raw sewage discharges into the bay had seriously impacted water quality and the bay's ecosystem. This decline had caused a shutdown in shellfishing and denial of public access to beaches. Before the stakeholder process, the State's Department of Environmental Management operated under a "consent agreement" with the federal government, which allowed for continuing sewage discharges as a matter of public interest. Two plans emerged to rectify the situation: one, which was characterized as a "command and control" system of direct regulation, relied on conventional state management with limited public engagement; the other, which became the stakeholder process, was based on direct public participation in the management process. Both plans, however, were organized in response to federal mandates that water discharges into the bay could only continue where they conformed to federal technical standards for water discharges.

Public participation in the first plan was limited to three public meetings, one organized as a public hearing and the other two organized as advisory meetings, with participation limited to 27 "invitees" consisting primarily of public officials (56 percent) and a few nongovernmental organizations (19 percent).[12] No federal officials were involved, and citizen input was limited to comments offered on a plan developed by outside consultants. Ultimately, state and federal officials rejected this first plan, in part because federal guidelines had changed in the interim to mandate greater public involvement, and in part because the proposal was considered too costly.

The second "stakeholder" plan was organized to reflect new and more elaborate federal regulations concerning water quality management. Nineteen "stakeholder" meetings were held over a period of 18 months, with participation distributed between public officials (51 percent), nongovernmental organizations (34 percent), and business interests (15 percent). The plan's author represents that stakeholder "concerns dominated the discussions" (Burroughs 1999: 802), but in fact those concerns were themselves conditioned by a technical discourse concerning federal water quality standards and limited to choices pre-designed by the EPA. The stakeholders, however, were allowed to choose from among 16 control technologies and were given information about their economic impacts on residences and businesses, such as sewer rates and operation and maintenance costs. The principal tool of evaluation in this process was a cost–benefit analysis, with environmental benefits not valued in economic terms. The final decision was based on technological considerations and operating costs, which were approximately 65 percent lower than those presented by the first plan.

In the author's analysis, the stakeholder process resulted in "better dissemination and use of information, as well as much greater motivation for public involvement," which he attributes to "high levels of responsibility" (Burroughs 1999: 803). But he also admits that much of the plan reflected not stakeholder initiatives, but stakeholder acquiescence to pre-existing federal conditions and economic goals. What is clear is that these stakeholders had no opportunity to question the conditions that degraded water quality, to make connections with other social, political, and/or environmental circumstances, to solicit independent scientific, technical, or political advice, or to critically examine the policy process itself. The distribution of participation, while engaging larger numbers, appears to have varied little from that of the first plan: government officials participated proportionately, nongovernmental participation increased—but we do not know the identities or agenda of these organizations—and business gained an official representation. There is no indication of actual conflict, undoubtedly because there was little room for negotiation, and the final product seems to have greatly pleased the government organizers of the process.

The author of this analysis seems quite comfortable with this process, because the stakeholders produced a plan that was "consistent with national goals for the environment," "reduced costs," represented "a major process change away from public hearings and toward partnership in solving problems," and represented a power shift away from public agencies. Of course the stakeholder processes *appeared* to be more democratic than the regulatory plan, and there is undeniable merit in sharing knowledge with community members. However, embedded in these conclusions are arguments favoring centralized power, technological fixes, economic prioritization, and the privatization of public policy. At an even deeper level, the evidence is that this process empowered only the individuals privileged to participate and not the community. There are no tests applied to whether these stakeholders represented the broad community, or whether their participation extended the deliberative process to outside community members.

How might this stakeholder process be made more democratic and community based? The circumstances that favored the outcomes identified above included a process that was initiated by government for government purposes; a design that left key issues, such as who was qualified to participate, and what constituted proper subjects for deliberation, to the government organizers; a deliberative process that was episodic and did not engage with the community as a community over time; and a policy choice that left further inquiry and policymaking in the hands of institutional actors. Democratic deliberation was absent from the beginning, primarily because democratic organization around this issue was either weak or absent, which tells us that democracy must pre-exist policymaking and be broadly rooted in the community before it can become an effective part of a policy process. If adequately developed, it would provide both the initiative and the organization for a more inclusive process. Further, the pre-existence of a democratic base in this community would have insulated it against discourses and definitions that were democratically hostile. Under conditions of active democracy, the whole of the ecosystem, including non-economic community values, would have been considered, and the policy choice necessarily would have recognized the importance of continuing community engagement.

This narrow example has potentially broad implications for better understanding how stakeholder processes do and might work. The organization and design issues that it presents are typical of most stakeholder processes, including those generated directly by corporate and business interests. As you can imagine, reforming a process like this one is as much a matter of social and political organization as it is a consequence of any particular environmental issue. However, it also is possible to radically recast stakeholder processes, and institutionalize them as vehicles for democratic participation, by abandoning the dominant business management definition of stakeholder and redirecting it to its historical-legal root.

Reforming "stakeholder" as an equitable legal rerm

Law and legal process play a powerful role in modern society because as legal-juridical entities modern states rely on law for their authority and legitimacy. Environmental policymaking has long been a creature of law, at least in the United States, where it is composed of a dense web of laws, rules, and regulations. Anglo-American common law also acts as a political mediator, preserving long-term historical values and relationships with regard to defining rights and obligations by carefully constructing definitions for key terms that affect rights and obligations. As previously discussed, the term "stakeholder" has a well-established historical-legal definition, which gives it an equitable rather than proprietary function where it is applied. Because this form of the term has never been tested in environmental policymaking, the possibility remains that what is a stakeholder in environmental policymaking might be reformed in such a manner that stakeholder processes can come to be important ways for giving broad effect to democratic participation.

Public policy and law enjoy a curious relationship: policymakers identify and shape issues, and lawyers engage in constructing the issues as systems of laws, regulations, and rules, with both believing that they are working toward a common end. But policymakers and lawyers actually work with different discourses of power: policymakers use a political discourse that is fluid, dynamic, negotiated, and oft-times ambiguous, while lawyers use a legal discourse that is precise, rationally reasoned, conservative, and historically fixed. Also, policymakers generally admit to a normative quality in their discourse, but lawyers resist characterizations of law as anything but instrumental.

In practice, the differences between policymaking and law making are much smaller. Law serves many normative functions, and is ideologically dependent on the modern state and the modern political economy of capitalism (Weber 1953). At the national level, law making is concerned with ideas about human relationships and social norms (Conley and O'Barr 1998), and legal pronouncement has a dual purpose in legitimating state policy and regulating human relationships (Habermas 1996). In modern times, with the globalization of commerce and culture, Anglo-American law has taken on an international role in determining uniform practices among states (Falk 2002). This includes not only providing for a formal body of international law covering environmental regimes, but also the interpenetration of national legal systems by Anglo-American legal concepts and practices. Thus, Anglo-American innovations in law are spread and adopted far beyond England and the United States, with the power to reshape thinking and behavior.

The export of Anglo-American common law has not been without its contests. Nations that do not have an "English" history have generally adopted various forms of civil law, which are much more historically based and much more policy oriented. Where they collide, the differences are commonly negotiated and accommodated. But these negotiations are usually limited to areas of conflict that must be addressed for commercial/financial purposes, with other issues left for national law to determine. At this point, and in recognition that the United States has been the source of most environmental law during the last half century, common law appears to have the greater influence in national and international environmental policymaking, based on the comparative strength of environmental policy-making in the United States and the United Kingdom.

Common law contains two doctrines of importance to stakeholder processes. The first involves the framing of issues as legal problems, with common law following the rule of *stare decisis*, or preference to the thinking of earlier courts and particularly higher courts concerning the same or a similar issue. In this way, common law becomes a seamless web of rules and concepts that interplay with one another across areas of legal practice and through time. The second is the legal practice of balancing of strict interpretations of law against its equitable effect.[13] In this way, common law provides a court with power to modify the plain language of the law where doing so promotes a sense of "justice." The court used this equitable power when it determined the definition of "stakeholder" to ensure that affected parties would not be excluded from legal deliberations. These two rules fall into what is described as procedural law, which acts as the door through which access to the law can be made, and which defines the nature of the legal rights and obligations that can be considered.

Both civil law and common law reflect an archive of environmental values, because they offer the clearest expression of what the environment contains and how human-nature relationships are managed. In this way, they reflect deeply embedded ideational and ideological concepts that have evolved over time and now condition environmental policymaking. For example, the history of water in the American West is a narrative about its value as a scarce resource, which then became articulated in a system of laws about water, how it was defined, and who had rights and obligations concerning water (Worster 1985). Subsequent legal conflicts over water in the American West have reflected that history and its embedded values.

The power of law lies in its recognition of the importance of history and precision in language. Law thus represents a microcosm of how people have thought about an issue and their relationship to it in a particular place and time. The fact that law changes only ponderously and with great attention to detail provides the certainty that rights and obligations will be deeply rooted and equally applied. Rules or norms that might be adopted in practice, but without the benefit of legal definition, are limited in power to those who accept them under those conditions. If and when they are tested at law, they will survive or fall depending on how they fit into the overall legal thinking of that time and place. The existence of a parallel but not legally confirmed stakeholder discourse in business management theory has the authority only of discursive persuasion, which is of questionable legitimacy where it directly contradicts the equities of the legal doctrine of stakeholder. Reforming stakeholders as an equitable legal concept can be argued from the points of law already laid down by US courts.

While the 1934 US Supreme Court case *Sanders* was argued from the circumstances and history of insurance practices, its arguments and conclusions more broadly addressed stakeholders from a historical view as equitable agents. The issues in *Sanders* parallel those in environmental management: how to represent and protect the interests of those who will be affected but are absent from the deliberative process, and whose rights and obligations have yet to be determined. In finding that stakeholders must be parties that are themselves *disinterested* in the outcome, the court carved out a place where issues and outcomes would have to be constructed with sufficient breadth that justice would not be denied because of an inability to actively participate in and defend personal interests. The case remains good law in the United States, and other courts have elaborated on *Sanders* to substantially expand how and when its definition of stakeholder might be applied. Thus, a stakeholder relationship has been found to exist where real estate brokers hold deposits for purchasers (*Shaper v. Gilkison*, Tex.Civ. App., 217 S.W.2nd 878), banks hold rents for landlords (*Simon v. State Mutual Life Assurance Co*mpany, Tex.Civ.Appl., 126 S.W.2nd 682), record companies manage royalties for musicians (*Priority Records, Inc. v. Bridge-port Music, Inc.* (1995) 907 F.Supp. 725), and brokerage firms receive and hold stock dividends for investors (*Merrill Lynch, Pierce, Fenner & Smith, Inc. v. Cavicchia* (DCNY 1970) 366 F.Supp.149). In each case, the court reconfirmed the basic idea that a stakeholder can have no identifiable interest of their own in the matter, and that they can never appear as advocates on their own behalf (*Midlands National Life Insurance Company. v. Emerson*, 174 S.E.2nd 211). This legal definition is settled to the extent that it now appears formally in Black's Law Dictionary, which defines "stakeholder" as a "third-party [that holds] money or property [or] an interest or concern in a business or enterprise, but is not the owner."

By linking the term "stakeholder" to the legal doctrine of *interpleader*, the court in *Sanders* also gave it special meaning. This procedural law rule was fashioned explicitly for the purpose of expanding participation in legal proceedings where other rules and practices might unnecessarily and inequitably limit it. Thus, the use of the term "stakeholder" in legal form carries a weight that it would not have in casual use or in a management discourse.[15] This is important, considering how the legal definition of "stakeholder" might be measured against a business management definition that is far less precise, implicitly argued against rather than for broad participation, and resting on an assumption of a direct economic interest held by a putative stakeholder.

When they arrive in court, stakeholder processes will encounter three tests that are designed to give them a legal identity and authority. The first test asks whether the legal or the conventional use best reflects legislative intent, which then becomes an issue of political right to participate. Although it may exist somewhere in an obscure policy passage, the term has rarely if ever been defined as a matter of legislative intent. Even where it might appear, legislative intent almost always is presented in broad politically acceptable terms that draw on the democratic discourse, such as expressions of intent to promote broad-based participation and an open agenda in the service of more effective policymaking. This construction opens the door for a creative interpretation of the term that can place it within a broad constitutional mandate for political representation. Arguments that business management stakeholder processes achieve this intent by promoting efficiencies and/or economies simply cannot measure up to a legal standard because they lack equitable concerns that are firmly attached to the legal version.

The second test, whether a particular definition is "fair" to the parties, similarly presents an opportunity to attack the ambiguity of a business management stakeholder definition because the fairness at issue is not simply a matter of property rights or economic efficiencies. Rather, while a court might be sympathetic to business interests, it will as a matter of legal tradition focus on a "balancing of the equities" that does not tilt unnecessarily toward one party, but gives recognition to the rights of all interested parties, which is what the *Sanders* court did with regard to insurance beneficiaries. Also, the court would have to limit any desire to protect the narrow interests of one business that would undermine the political legitimacy of a deliberative process.

However, it is with the third test that the legal discourse of stakeholders gains its greatest authority. Measured against legal doctrines of equity and fairness that are reflected in a legal definition of stakeholder, business management stakeholder processes utterly fail to protect the process from bias and a compromised sense of justice. The ruling in *Sanders* was quite clear on this point: defining stakeholders as proxy representatives was necessary to protect parties whose interests could not otherwise be protected. If, as the business management stakeholder model argues, stakeholders merely represent their own interests, they are by definition incapable of defending the interests of others and the deliberative process is thus narrowed, not expanded. At the heart of this argument lies *public purpose*, or the ability to embrace the largest practicable participation to ensure that a stakeholder process contributes to rather than undermines a sense of justice in policy choices. If only present interests are represented, what of those that inevitably will exist as a consequence of policy? If only designated parties can participate on behalf of their own interests, where is the fairness to those excluded?

The legal definition of stakeholder also makes the stronger case for justice when it insists that a stakeholder can have no claim of its own, and act only to represent others. If they do not meet these tests, courts decertify them as stakeholders and require them to appear on their own behalf (*In re Trust Deeds of Smaltz*, 17 A.2d 455). The fairness in the legal definition resides in its preoccupation with "representativeness": whether or not the stakeholder has the capacity to represent the absent party(s), which is reaffirmed by its self-constructed identity, marshalling of appropriate resources, and uncompromised relationship to the issue. In a practical sense, this approach offers a way forward in expanding environmental policymaking to allow properly constituted representatives the opportunity to appear and participate on behalf of future generations, non-human interests, and the economically and culturally marginalized. Further, it would also allow for the representation of non-national interests in national courts, for example by designating appropriate stakeholders to represent indigenous communities, isolated ecosystems, and the disenfranchised in developing and less-developed countries.

The utility of a historical-legal definition of "stakeholder" in environmental policymaking becomes apparent when considering how current policymaking has become enslaved to economic concerns and corporate power, which produces an essentially anthropogenic view of nature and instrumental policy outcomes. As Arne Naess and other deep ecologists point out, this view has left much of nature, traditional relationships with nature, and people with other than an economic interest in nature as a resource outside of policymaking and traditional politics (Naess 1989). Further, there are solid arguments that broad-based deliberative processes are not just more democratic but also are more successful in addressing complex ecological issues (Fischer 2000), better reflect and incorporate a wider range of ecological values, including deep ecology (Gunderson 1995), are necessary to address the issues of intergenerational equity (Dobson 1999), achieve a higher level of environmental justice (Shrader-Frechette 2002), and become a more sustainable source of public commitment to effective policy implementation (Barry 1999).

There are other practical reasons for abandoning restrictive, corporate-inspired stakeholder processes and adopting a legally validated definition that are related to the need of states for political legitimacy (Held 1984; Habermas 1996). The law, and by extension the state that authorizes the law, acquires legitimacy by generating a sense of "justice," a belief that the law is fairly and equitably applied (Mondak 1993; Sarat 1993).[16] As an act that generates laws, rules, and regulations, environmental policymaking also must convey a sense of justice if it is to succeed in providing legitimacy and authority to the state. Thus, stakeholder processes must reach beyond particular issues and reflect actual community initiatives and interests to create a sense that they are representative and just (McSpadden 2000). This simply recognizes that policymaking is organized either directly or indirectly using the authority of a state institution, and that the state has an interest not just in policy outcomes and the management of power, but also in the legitimacy of the process.[17]

Some concluding observations

George Orwell once said "To think clearly is the first step toward political regeneration" (Orwell 1970: 156). Whether or not he is recognized as such, Orwell was an original discourse theorist because he linked politics to the construction of ideas through language. In Orwell's time, language was primarily transmitted by words or by texts, with its effect limited to those who could hear or read. At the beginning of the twenty-first century, forms of communication have changed and our understanding of how discourse structures politics has grown. Yet, our knowledge is imperfect and tends to lag behind changes in the world around us. We now live in a semiotic world where communications in the form of billboards, television advertisements, and pop-up messages on our computer screens bombard us, but often without our cognitive awareness of what they are saying. Propaganda is not new, but its forms are new and its effects in our time are ubiquitous.

We should not be surprised that a word like "stakeholder" comes with ideological baggage. If we inspect it closely, study how it developed and was used in the past, and compare that with how it is now used in policy discourses, we uncover its full character and potential. But even here, the discourse is not as simple as it appears. The texts used and images elicited by the stakeholder discourse are borrowed from around us, sometimes consciously and sometimes without regard. These argue for limits on participation, promote consumerism, privilege individuals, and prioritize short-term goals. They also tell us something about how the stakeholder discourse reflects and constructs power relationships in the politics of environmental policymaking. This is not a politics apart from the ordinary, but a politics that reflects the politics in society generally. The question that remains is not where the ideological politics are, but where we are in relationship to them.

This discussion has been offered as a study in the stakeholder discourse of environmental policymaking as representative of the way that our ideas and values are shaped through shared words and images. While its purpose has been broad, its focus was intended to illuminate how processes of deliberative democracy might be better fashioned in environmental policymaking. Between this broad purpose and the narrow focus lies a vast field of practical concerns about ecological sustainability, politically sustainable policymaking, and the current state of politics as various forms of neoliberal thinking. In this respect, the stakeholder discourse is representative of much of the market rhetoric and divisive politics that plague our time. Capitalism generally, and neoliberalism in particular, promote these fault lines and undermine our belief in deliberative democracy as collective decision-making. What it produces is not a debate, or public participation in the case of stakeholder processes, but a carefully choreographed presentation of issues and outcomes that are acceptably within the control of its political elites. However, this does not have to be the whole story.

We engage in political discourse either directly through participation, or indirectly by acquiescing to it: while silence is not necessarily consent, it is interpreted as consent where it stands alone. The current stakeholder discourse can be confronted and reformed, if we chose to engage it rather than acquiesce to it. The alternative stakeholder discourse in law is both powerful and offers promise for more politically and ecologically sustainable outcomes for environmental policymaking. It also offers opportunities to shift the discourse of environmental politics away from one dominated by Euro-American history and institutions and toward a more inclusive global community. The subdivisions in global environmental politics—between states, science and politics, politics and policymaking, policymaking and grassroots political action—are tied to problems with language that appear in innumerable discourses tainted by ideologies of which we are scarcely aware. Understanding the stakeholder discourse, and reforming it or not, is the politics of political practice. It is about creating a political space apart from the designed discourses and rediscovering how democratic deliberation actually works. Whether we collectively succeed in finding a way to live with nature depends in large part on our ability to think clearly about the words that we use.

Notes

1 Leading political theorists during the 1970s believed that the problem of liberal governance was that it produced a "democratic distemper" that diluted state control (Crozier, Watanuki, and Huntington 1975).
2 This is true regardless of whether business stakeholder theory is argued from either a normative or instrumental point of view (Van Buren and Paul 2000).
3 The Court drew on the *Interpleader Act* of 1926, which had substantially expanded the right to appear in federal court where a party had no direct interest in a dispute but might be affected by the outcome of the case.
4 The *Sanders* definition of "stakeholder" was recently reconfirmed in *Arizonians for Official English v. Arizona*, 520 U.S. 43.
5 For example, a stakeholder relationship was found to exist where real estate brokers shield deposits for purchasers (*Shaper v. Gilkison*, Tex.Civ.App., 217 S. W.2nd 878), banks hold rents for landlords (*Simon v. State Mutual Life Assurance Co*mpany, Tex.Civ.Appl., 126 S.W.2nd 682), record companies manage royalties for musicians (*Priority Records, Inc. v. Bridgeport Music, Inc.* (1995) 907 F. Supp. 725), and brokerage firms receive and hold stock dividends for investors (*Merrill Lynch, Pierce, Fenner & Smith, Inc. v. Cavicchia* (DCNY 1970) 366 F. Supp.149). In each case, the court drew on *Sanders* to reconfirm that the principal characteristic of a stakeholder is that it can have no identifiable interest in the interest that it holds. Thus, the legal treatment of "stakeholder" never applies the term to those who advocate on their own behalf (*Midlands National Life Insurance Company. v. Emerson*, 174 S.E.2nd 211).
6 Sigmund Freud and psychoanalytic studies of almost every feature of human behaviour dominated the 1930s. Thus, Parsons was not alone in his study of language as a means to shape organizations. Harold Lasswell, a well-known political scientist at the University of Chicago, made similar arguments about politics in his 1941 *Democracy Through Public Opinion*.
7 ADR was developed as a cost-effective alternative for disputes between business enterprises. It is structured to protect economic interests and operates under a system of rules and regulations developed and administered by the American Arbitration Association, a business-oriented supervisory organization.
8 Arguably, these instrumental-ideological concepts created the momentum for what emerged in Europe during the 1990s as "ecological modernization," which claims that environmental goals can be achieved only through more efficient management practices.
9 Of course, corporate board members are almost always shareholders, too, and voting control of a corporation rarely requires more than a minority share of stock because of the dilution of power represented in the wide disbursement of share holding. Yet, because of the fiduciary duty that corporate boards owe to

shareholders under corporate law, even a single shareholder has the legal power to call boards to account where they fail to protect the value of their stock.

10 For a more developed business management argument of corporate citizenship, see Burke 2005.

11 Analyses of business management stakeholder processes reveal that when they emphasize stakeholder accountability they also require cooperation with business-sponsored agendas and limit deliberative processes (Coppola 1997; Jones 1997; Burroughs 1999).

12 There is no indication of who qualified as a "non-government organization."

13 The balancing of equities against strict legal applications in common law reflects the balancing of the absolute rule of monarchs against the moral authority of the church in feudal times. This primarily protected the aristocracy, and then the merchant class, against the exercise of arbitrary power, and further advanced the authority of the monarch as conditioned on a respect for religious authority.

15 A court has gone so far as to declare that the term "'stakeholder' has a definite place ... and is not to be varied ... by either circumlocution or the splitting of the essential word" (*State v. Dudley*, 21 A.2d 209).

16 In his book *Why People Obey the Law*, Tom Tyler (1990) argues that obedience to law rests on the law's ability to combine moral argument, rhetorical practice, and regulation into a sense of *justice*.

17 Direct authorization by a public agency is the most common approach (see, e.g., Burroughs 1999), but indirect authorization sometimes occurs where states mandate action but leave non-state parties to determine the form (see, e.g., Shackley and Deanwood 2001).

References

Allen, Barbara L. (2004) *Uneasy Alchemy: Citizens and Experts in Louisiana's Chemical Corridor Disputes*, Boston, MA: MIT Press.

Altman, Barbara W. (2000) "Defining 'community as stakeholder' and 'community Stakeholder management': a theory elaboration study," in *Research in Stakeholder Theory, 1997–1998*, Toronto: University of Toronto Press.

Ansoff, I. (1965) *Corporate Strategy*, New York: McGraw Hill.

Bailey, Christopher J. (1998) *Congress and Air Pollution: Environmental Politics in the U.S.*, Manchester: Manchester University Press.

Bakan, Joel (2004) *The Corporation: The Pathological Pursuit of Profit and Power*, New York: The Free Press.

Barry, John (1999) *Rethinking Green Politics*, London: Sage Publications.

Barry, Norman P. (2002) "The new liberalism," in Barry (ed.) *Liberalism: Critical Concepts in Political Theory*, London: Routledge.

Benson, Ted (1996) "Sustainable development and the accumulation of capital: reconciling the irreconcilable?" in A. Dobson (ed.) *Fairness & Futurity: Essays in Environmental Sustainability and Social Justice*, Oxford: Oxford University Press.

Berman, Shawn (2000) "Managerial opportunism and firm performance: an empirical test of instrumental stakeholder theory," in *Research in Stakeholder Theory, 1997–1998*, Toronto: University of Toronto Press.

Buchanan, James and Tullock, Gordon (1962) *The Calculus of Consent*, Ann Arbor: University of Michigan Press.

Burke, Edmund M. (2005) *Managing a Company in an Activist World: The Leadership Challenge of Corporate Citizenship*, New York: Praeger Publishers.

Burnham, James (1941) *The Managerial Revolution*, New York: Van Rees Press.

Burroughs, Richard (1999) "When stakeholders choose: process, knowledge, and motivation in water quality decisions," *Society & Natural Resources* 12,8: 797–810.

Conley, John, and O'Barr, William M. (1998) *Just Words: Law, Language, and Power*, Chicago: University of Chicago Press.

Coppola, Nancy W. (1997) "Rhetorical analysis of stakeholders in environmental communications: a model," *Technical Communications Quarterly* 6,1: 25.

Crozier, Michael, Watanuki, Joji and Huntington, Samuel (1975) *The Crisis of Democracy*, New York: The Trilateral Commission.

Dobson, Andrew (1999) *Fairness and Futurity: Essays in Environmental Sustainability and Social Justice*, Oxford: Oxford University Press.

Dowie, Mark (1995) *Losing Ground: American Environmentalism at the Close of the Twentieth Century*, Cambridge, MA: The MIT Press.

Dryzek, John S. (1990) *Discursive Democracy: Politics, Policy, and Political Science*, Cambridge: Cambridge University Press.

—— (1996) *Democracy in Capitalist Times*, Oxford: Oxford University Press.

Eco, Umberto (1999) *Kant and the Platypus: Essays*, New York: Harcourt.

Falk, Richard (2002) "Reframing the legal agenda of world order in the course of a turbulent century," in Richard Falk, Lester E.J. Ruiz, and R.B.J. Walker (eds.) *Reframing the International*, New York: Routledge.

Fischer, Frank (2000) *Citizens, Experts, and the Environment: the Politics of Local Knowledge*, Durham: Duke University Press.

Foucault, Michel (1991) *Discipline and Punish*, London: Penguin Books.

Freeman, R.E. (1984) *Strategic Management: A stakeholder approach*, Boston, MA: Pitman.

Friedman, Milton (1957) *A Theory of the Consumption Function*, Princeton, NJ: Princeton University Press.

—— (1970) "The social responsibility of business is to increase its profits," *New York Times Magazine*, September 13.

Galbraith, John K. (1979) *The Great Crash 1929*, New York: Houghton Mifflin.

Gibson, Kevin (2000) "The moral basis of stakeholder theory," *Journal of Business Ethics* 26: 245–257.

Gunderson, Adolf G. (1995) *The Environmental Promise of Democratic Deliberation*, Madison, WN: University of Wisconsin Press.

Habermas, Jürgen (1976) *Legitimation Crisis* (tr. T. McCarthy), London: Heinemann.

—— (1987) *The Theory of Communicative Action, Volume Two* (tr. T. McCarthy). Cambridge: Polity Press.

—— (1996) *Between Facts and Norms: Contributions to a Discourse Theory of Law and Democracy*, Cambridge, MA: MIT Press.

Hacker, Andrew (ed.) (1964) *The Corporation Takeover*, New York: Ayers Publishing Co.

Hajer, Maarten A. (2003) "A frame in the fields: policymaking and the reinvention of politics," in Maarten Hajer and Hendrik Wagenaar (eds.) (2003) *Deliberative Policy Analysis: Understanding Governance in the Network Society*, Cambridge: Cambridge University Press.

Hay, Colin (1992) "Environmental security and state legitimacy," in Martin O'Connor (ed.) *Is Capitalism Sustainable?* New York: The Guilford Press.

Held, David (1984) *Political Theory and the Modern State*, Stanford, CA: Stanford University Press.

Hill, C.W.L. and Jones, T.M. (1992) "Stakeholder agency theory," *The Journal of Management Studies* 20,2: 134.

Holton, Robert J. and Turner, Bryan S. (1986) *Talcott Parsons on Economy and Society*, London: Routledge & Kegan Paul.

Holzcheiter, Anna (2003) *Discourse and Global Governance: From the Power of Discourse to the Power in Discourse*, unpublished thesis, University of Cambridge.

Innes, Judith E. and Booher, David E. (2003) "Collaborative policymaking: governance through dialogue," in Maarten Hajer and Hendrik Wagenaar (eds.) *Deliberative Policy Analysis: Understanding Governance in the Network Society*, Cambridge: Cambridge University Press.

Jones, Murray (1997) "The role of stakeholder participation: linkages to stakeholder impacts," *Greener Management International* 19: 87–98.

Jones, T.M. (1995) "Instrumental stakeholder theory: a synthesis of ethics and economics," *Academy of Management Review* 20,2: 404–437.

Kaler, John (2002) "Morality and strategy in stakeholder identification," *Journal of Business Ethics* 39: 91–99.

Lasswell, H.D. (1941) *Democracy Through Public Opinion*, Menasha, WN: Georgia Banta.

—— (1979) *The Signature of Power*, New Brunswick, NJ: Transaction Publishers.

Likert, R. (1961) *New Patterns of Management*, New York: McGraw Hill.

Mahanty, Sango and Russell, Diane (2002) "High stakes: lessons from stakeholder groups in the biodiversity conservation network," *Society and Natural Resources* 15: 179–188.

McCahery, Joseph A., Moerland, Piet, Raaijmakers, Theo, and Renneboog, Luc (2002) *Corporate Governance: Convergence and Diversity*, Oxford: Oxford University Press.

McGlashan, Derek J. and Williams, Evan (2003) "Stakeholder involvement in coastal decision-making processes," *Local Environments* 8,1: 85–94.

McSpadden, Lettie (2000) "Environmental policy in the courts," in Norman J. Vig and Michael E. Kraft (eds.) *Environmental Policy, 4th Ed.*, Washington, D.C.: Congressional Quarterly Press.

Mills, C. Wright (2002) *White Collar*, Oxford: Oxford University Press.

Mondak, Jeffery J. (1993) "Institutional legitimacy and procedural justice: reexamining the question of causality," *Law & Society Review* 27,3: 599–609.

Naess, Arne (1989) *Ecology, Community and Lifestyle: Outline of an Ecosophy* (trs. and rev'd D. Rothenberg), Cambridge: Cambridge University Press.

Orwell, George (1970) "Politics and the English Language," in *George Orwell: A Collection of Essays*, New York: Harvest Books.

Parsons, Talcott (1967) *The Structure of Social Action*, New York: The Free Press.

Rhenman, E. (1968) *Industrial Democracy and Industrial Management*, London: Tavistock.

Richards, Michael, Davies, Jonathan, and Yaron, Gil (2003) *Stakeholder Incentives in Participatory Forest Management*, New York: Intermediate Technology.

Robbins, Peter Thayer (2001) *Greening the Corporation: Management Strategy and the Environmental Challenge*, London: Earthscan.

Rosenau, James N. and Czempiel, Ernst-Otto (1992) *Governance Without Government*, Cambridge: Cambridge University Press.

Sarat, Austin (1993) "Authority, anxiety, and procedural justice: moving from scientific detachment to critical engagement," *Law & Society Review* 27,3: 647–672.

Shackley, Simon and Deanwood, Robert (2002) "Stakeholder perceptions of climate change impacts at the regional scale: implications for the effectiveness of regional and local responses," *Journal of Environmental Planning and Management* 45,3: 381–402.

Short, Christopher and Winter, Michael (1999) "The problem of common land: towards stakeholder governance," *Journal of Environmental Planning & Management* 42,5: 613.

Shrader-Frechette, Kristen S. (2002) *Environmental Justice: Creating Equality, Reclaiming Democracy*, Oxford: Oxford University Press.

Susskind, Lawrence and Ozawa, Connie (1992) "Negotiating international agreements," in Andrew Hurrell and Benedict Kingsbury (eds.) *The International Politics of the Environment*, Oxford: Clarendon Press.

Torgerson, Douglas (2003) "Democracy through policy discourse," in *Deliberative Policy Analysis: Understanding Governance in the Network Society*, Cambridge: Cambridge University Press.

Tyler, Tom R. (1990) *Why People Obey the Law,* New Haven, CT: Yale University Press.

Van Buren, Harry J. III and Paul, Karen (2000) "Company reactions to socially responsible investing: an empirical analysis," in *Research in Stakeholder Theory, 1997–1998*, Toronto: University of Toronto Press.

Wagenaar, Hendrik and Cook, S.D. Noam (2003) "Understanding policy practices: action, dialectic and deliberation in policy analysis," in Maarten Hajer (ed.) *Deliberative Policy Analysis: Understanding Governance in the Network Society*, Cambridge: Cambridge University Press.

Weber, Max (1953) *The Theory of Economic and Social Organization*, Berkeley, CA: Hans Gerth.

Whyte, William H. (1957) *The Organization Man*, London: Jonathan Cape.

Worster, Donald (1985) *Rivers of Empire: Water, Aridity and the Growth of the American West,* New York: Pantheon Books.

Legal citations

United States Supreme Court

Arizonians for Official English v. Arizona, 520 U.S. 43.
Sanders v. Armour Fertilizer Works, et al. (1934) 292 U.S. 190.

United States Federal Courts

Merrill Lynch, Pierce, Fenner & Smith, Inc. v. Cavicchia (DCNY 1970) 366 F. Supp.149.
Priority Records, Inc. v. Bridgeport Music, Inc. (1995) 907 F.Supp. 725.

United States State Courts

Arizona Bank v. Wells Fargo Bank, N.A. 148 Ariz 136.
In re Trust Deeds of Smaltz, 17 A.2d 455.
Midlands Nat. Life Ins. Co. v. Emerson, 174 S.E.2nd 211.
Paul v. Harold Davis, Inc., 20 So.2d 795.
Porter v. Day, 37 N.W. 259.
Shaper v. Gilkison, Tex.Civ.App., 217 S.W.2nd 878.
Simon v. State Mut.Life Assur.Co., Tex.Civ.Appl., 126 S.W.2nd 682.
State v. Dudley, 21 A.2d 209.

10 Rethinking authority, territory, and knowledge

Transnational socio-ecological controversies and global environmental governance

Ken Conca

Introduction

This chapter uses the specific domain of water to trace the rise and fall of the dominant paradigm of global environmental governance during the Rio-to-Johannesburg period. The chapter also explores some possible post-Rio approaches to global environmental governance. Water was not a central theme at the 1992 UN Conference on Environment and Development (UNCED), but a wide array of post-UNCED initiatives to promote "sustainable water governance" illustrate the core assumptions and principal limitations of the Rio model in action. Water is also an arena in which alternative models have begun to emerge. These various approaches to governing water often embody dramatically different understandings of authority relations, and construct the transnational dimensions of the world's water challenges in dramatically different ways. As I will argue below, a principal flaw of the Rio model has been its failure to recognize and engage transnational socio-environmental controversies about "local" problems of natural resource management. As a result, approaches to governing water that recognize and engage such controversies as they spill across borders are of particular interest.

The chapter begins with a general discussion of the Rio model and its limitations. In doing so, I pay particular attention to the model's depoliticized and increasingly obsolete framework of incremental national policy adjustments linked through sovereign international diplomacy, and to the inability of that approach to contain or manage transnational socio-ecological controversies. The chapter then turns to the specific domain of global water governance, within which there are several high-profile initiatives that usefully illustrate the Rio model's presumptions and limitations. The chapter concludes by examining efforts to manage transnational conflicts around water, with particular attention to socio-ecological controversies related to large dams, water privatization initiatives, and the idea of water as a human right.

The Rio model

As suggested in Chapter One, the earth summits of Rio de Janeiro (1992) and Johannesburg (2002) bracketed an era that was dominated by a particular paradigm of how best to create and deepen global environmental governance. For simplicity, this approach will be referred to hereafter as the "Rio model," but it should be stressed that the approach to global environmental governance to which I am referring extends well beyond the 1992 Earth Summit and should not be considered primarily as an outcome of the conference itself. Rather, it spans an era that began with the rise of the Brundtland Commission in the early 1980s. Similarly, while the near-total lack of environmental content at the 2002 Johannesburg summit offers a tempting symbolic marker for the death of the Rio model, important elements linger on. They endure because they have been woven into the institutional fabric of international environmental diplomacy, the standard operating procedures of international NGOs and national ministries, and international funding mechanisms such as the Global Environment Facility (GEF).

Similarly, it should be stressed that the term "model" is used here not to refer narrowly to the specific blueprint documents surrounding UNCED, such as the Brundtland Commission report, the Rio Declaration, or Agenda 21, although these documents are exemplars of the sort of thinking to which the term refers. Rather, I use the term in the broader, paradigmatic sense, to refer to a particular understanding of global environmental problems, solutions, and the pathways to achieving those solutions. This understanding was embraced enthusiastically by many liberal internationalists in western NGOs, academia, intergovernmental organizations, and the media, and somewhat more circumspectly by many of the governments in attendance at the Rio summit.

Viewed in hindsight, the Rio model had four core components: a regulatory strategy of international environmental regimes, a technological strategy of ecological modernization, a participatory strategy based on stakeholder dialogue, and a political strategy of global bargaining across the North–South divide in world politics. International environmental regimes would provide issue-specific, institutionalized sets of rules that would in turn generate the capacity, incentives, and momentum to change national-level behavior, with particular attention to a handful of high-profile challenges that agenda-setters took to be the most pressing. Ecological modernization of production systems would promote more sustainable patterns of resource consumption, pollution, and material throughput. Stakeholder models of participation would defuse social conflict on international controversies and incorporate a sufficiently wide array of participants to allow for effective and legitimate policy making and implementation. Providing the political will and resources to make it all work would be the job of a grand diplomatic "global bargain," with rich countries bringing financing and technology to the table and poor countries committing to alter their economic and demographic trajectories toward more sustainable pathways.

Limits of the Rio model

More than 15 years after its occurrence, the 1992 Rio summit remains an ambiguous event. It has alternately been portrayed as a dramatic paradigm shift with regard to environment development linkages, an irrelevancy that rehashed ground already well covered 20 years earlier at the Stockholm conference, and a hijacking of good intentions by actors with narrow or hidden agendas (Conca and Dabelko 1998). My purpose here is not to go back over that well-traveled ground but, rather, to point out some of the problematic conceptual underpinnings of what came to be a sort of "grand strategy" of liberal international environmentalism from that era.

Viewed with the benefit of hindsight, it is clear that the Rio model lacked an effective political strategy. Its boosters overestimated the breadth and depth of commitment among many key governments and failed to articulate a coherent political strategy for engaging an increasingly rejectionist United States. Their efforts to craft a global North–South bargain on environment and development quickly ran aground on the distributive politics of funding for green development assistance; negotiations for even weak global regulatory regimes on climate and forests faltered over time; and the United States has swung from being a frequent supporter of international environmental initiatives to the most consistent and consequential opponent.

Beyond the question of political strategy, several of the chapters in this volume have pointed to critical underlying limitations of the Rio model's specific regulatory, technological, socio-political, and grand-strategic elements. These include its failure to grapple with the transnational effects of global commodity chains, its privileging of corporate power and private goods, its skirting of central questions related to consumption and throughput, and its affinity for top-down, one-way approaches to political bargaining and stakeholder dialogue.

To this list we can add a critically important conceptual failure with regard to the transnational dimensions of environmental problems. The model was doomed by its failure to engage, or even acknowledge, economic globalization—or, rather, the particular neoliberal trajectory of global economic adjustment that began in the late 1970s and accelerated dramatically after the Cold War.

Rooted in a paradigm of cooperation and collective action among distinct sovereign entities, the model instead parsed nature into neatly separable domestic and international constituents. It then prescribed a dramatically different approach to problems in each domain (Conca 2002). Domestic problems—that is, those physical manifestations of environmental harm that appeared within the territorially bounded space of individual countries—would remain the purview of sovereign states, albeit supported by international expertise and development assistance. International problems—meaning problems with a physically apparent border-crossing aspect—would become the purview of collective action through diplomatic bargaining.

In other words, the Rio model understood environmental problems in physical-spatial terms, with "international" referring to problems that either spilled over sovereign borders in a direct physical sense (acid rain, shared rivers, migratory fish stocks) or sat outside sovereign control entirely as a "commons" (global climate, stratospheric ozone, the oceans). The fundamental misunderstanding of the Rio model was the assumption that ecological globalization had proceeded more rapidly than social globalization, such that those aspects of international nature, which would not "sit still" for domestic governance, required conventional international cooperation in the form of treaty-based agreements, foreign aid, technology transfer, and the like. What the model failed to grasp is that—despite the power of the imagery of "lifeboat Earth" and the blue planet seen from space—processes of social and economic globalization have outstripped our geophysical and ecological interconnectedness, such that even the seemingly localized, domestic aspects of environmental problems refuse to sit still for sovereign governance. In an increasingly globalized world economy, neither the causes nor the consequences of the insults remain at the local level.

A second and equally important ramification of globalization is the transnationalization of social-movement activism and advocacy, which has dragged many "local" socio-ecological conflicts squarely into the global realm. These conflicts often pit local communities against developmentally minded (or merely clientelistic) states and their international partners. Examples include the construction of large water infrastructure projects, the transformation of coastal mangrove forests into production zones for shrimp aquaculture, the replacement of traditional forest livelihoods with modernized forestry systems ("sustainable" or otherwise), and the creation of national parks, nature preserves, and sites for (eco)tourism. The modernizing logic on one side of these conflicts has long had a transnational dimension; increasingly, so does the resistance.

The Rio model steered away from making these "domestic" problems the subject of a serious global response. Instead, they were tucked into an Agenda 21 wish list of best practices for governments to pursue in their domestic policies. The role of the international community in Agenda 21 was limited primarily to providing international expertise and foreign aid. This response ignored both the powerful transnational linkages underpinning these "local" problems and the growing capacity of locals to carry their objections into the international realm.

As I have argued in detail elsewhere, the world's largest environment-development challenge is not the management of pollution across borders, but what I have referred to as "protecting the planet's places": addressing the cumulative toll of localized insults to the world's forests, coastlines, watersheds, wetlands, soils, settlements, and landscapes (Conca 2006). The

Rio model's conception of global environmental governance as the domestic sanctity of coherently sovereign vessels, complemented by international collective action, had little chance of effective response to emergent transnational socio-ecological controversies surrounding these problems. The technological strategy of ecological modernization had little hope of keeping pace in a world of rapid economic globalization, awash in ever-cheaper consumerist opportunities for the middle classes and the explosion of consumer desires in emerging economies. The narrow understanding of "stakeholder dialogue" as tripartite consultation among governments, businesses, and a select group of well-heeled NGOs had equally little hope of containing the white-hot socio-ecological controversies occurring when local resource bases and livelihoods were pitted against the commodity value of a stand of timber, a stretch of coastal mangroves, or a tourist vista. Simply put, in a world of socio-economic globalization and transnationalized socio-ecological controversy, the traditional tools of law and science had little hope of crafting effective cooperative arrangements for Rio's list of "international" problems or of capacitating sovereign governments to make "domestic" nature sit still for governance.

The point is not to suggest that Rio should have embraced a "global governance" model that downplayed the role of local authority in favor of more interventionist practices. Controversies that will not sit still for disciplining by national governments are just as unlikely to be containable from Washington, Brussels, Tokyo, or Geneva. The political challenge of global environmental governance is not to hand over these controversies to the management authority of a global neoliberal order any more than it is to consign them, as Rio did, to the solo flights of developmental states or the incapacity of failed ones. Rather, the challenge is to develop new mechanisms to acknowledge, understand, and engage socio-ecological controversies that fit poorly within the existing institutional apparatus at both the domestic and international levels. The failure to push the world creatively in this direction remains the Rio model's principal deficit.

Water and the Rio model

Water was a late-arriving theme at UNCED. International water experts were appalled when the Brundtland Commission's manifesto, *Our Common Future*, made almost no mention of global water challenges (WCED 1987). A global conference of freshwater experts and advocates, meeting in Dublin shortly before the Rio summit, helped to raise the salience of water, which received its own chapter in the voluminous Agenda 21 blueprint. But there were no significant diplomatic initiatives on water issues at Rio and water was not one of the original themes of the Global Environment Facility (the international funding mechanism for sustainable development created in the wake of UNCED).

Despite this slow start, water became a significant item on the international policy agenda in the 1990s. The growing political salience of water came from several sources. Among these were fears about "water wars" in an increasingly scarce world, the growing power of an emergent network of water experts promoting integrated water resource management, and the failure of UN initiatives dating to the 1970s to make a significant dent in global water deprivation. As water began to take center stage in the 1990s, it did so in ways that reflected the powerful hold of the Rio model on political imagination and the limitations of that model in practice.

The international problem: cooperation in shared river basins

Reflecting the parsing of nature into its domestic and international expressions, the dominant frame that emerged for the international side of the water problem was that of promoting cooperation in the world's internationally shared river basins. One driver for this focus on shared basins was mounting fear of scarcity-induced water conflicts or "water wars." Despite its overwhelmingly domestic focus, Agenda 21 called for the "harmonization" of national water strategies and development plans in those instances where neighboring states shared river basins (UNCED1992: ch. 18, section 18.12.o.c). The World Bank also weighed in, making it clear that loans for development projects in shared basins would be contingent on having a cooperative basin-level agreement in place with neighboring states that might be affected by the project. The immediate post-UNCED period saw a surge in the number of international agreements on shared rivers (Conca, Wu, and Mei 2006).

Central to this pulse of international river diplomacy was the UN Watercourses Convention (United Nations 1997). The convention, which emphasized the principles that should govern cooperation on internationally shared rivers, stressed not only environmental protection and sustainability but also peaceful dispute resolution, avoiding significant harm to other riparian states, equitable use of shared water supplies, and sovereign equality. The impetus for the convention predated the Brundtland Commission, UNCED, and the rise of sustainability discourse; work on the convention began in the UN International Law Commission (ILC) in the late 1960s, and several of the convention's key principles had roots in earlier soft-law formulations on water such as the Helsinki Principles. By the time draft articles were approved by the ILC in 1991 and sent to the General Assembly, however, the convention reflected a much greater concern for issues of environment and sustainability, containing several clauses on the specific obligations of states to protect the environment. Indeed, the most legally progressive aspects of the agreement were its stronger and more detailed emphasis on environmental protection and its promotion of a responsibility to avoid harm to other riparian states (concern for which would provide an important entry point for environmental concerns in downstream states).

In addition to reflecting the impetus to solve environmental problems by writing problem-specific framework treaties, the Watercourses Convention also reflected the prevailing conceptualization of global environmental governance sketched above. The convention limited itself to transboundary watercourses, protecting states from any obligation to bring domestic waters into conformity with its provisions. Essentially, the management and governance of freshwater ecosystems—which involve complex watershed-scale interactions among land-based and aquatic systems and processes—are reduced to the problem of sharing border-crossing water conduits, which are to be divided in an agreed-upon manner. The convention makes very strong presumptions about the domestic capacity of states to manage these transboundary spillovers. These presumptions, moreover, apply to states and only states: efforts to create an entry point for NGOs and citizen's groups were beaten back, and a draft provision in the articles produced by the ILC that might have afforded citizens standing in the legal systems of treaty-partner states was dropped as too politically controversial.

Like many of the international environmental conventions of the 1990s, the Watercourses Convention has failed to catalyze a robust process of institutionalized cooperation. Although it passed the General Assembly by a vote of 103–3, many important states abstained and the convention fell far short of the requisite number of ratifications. As a framework convention intended to establish principles for specific treaties negotiated at the level of individual river basins, one could argue that the main significance of the convention is as a model articulating best international practices, for which formal ratification is a lesser consideration (McCaffrey 2001). However, analysis of trends in basin-level agreements on shared rivers shows the limited extent to which the bulk of the convention's core principles have been taken up, even rhetorically, by states in practice (Conca, Wu, and Mei 2006).

The domestic challenge: integrated water resources management

If the international problem of water expressed itself as the need to institutionalize cooperation in shared river basins, the domestic problem came to be framed as failure to manage water resources properly. Several factors combined to create space for new thinking about water problems and water policy. These include the growth of environmental concerns, the general perception that water issues could not be solved exclusively through enhanced supply, and the failure of many governments to meet expanding requirements for drinking water and sanitation. A growing community of water experts, linked by an increasingly dense array of networks, conferences, journals, and professional associations, took advantage of that space, using their growing voice and standing in the late 1980s and early 1990s to champion the idea of integrated water resources management (IWRM) (Conca 2005a).

Although there are many ways of defining and conceiving IWRM, its foundations include a handful of widely shared premises: water must be managed for all of its competing economic, social, and ecological uses; water must be managed as close to the source as possible; water management must involve the wide participation of diverse actors in society as well as government. The water chapter in Agenda 21 took IWRM as its point of departure:

> The widespread scarcity, gradual destruction and aggravated pollution of freshwater resources in many world regions, along with the progressive encroachment of incompatible activities, demand integrated water resources planning and management. Such integration must cover all types of interrelated freshwater bodies, including both surface water and groundwater, and duly consider water quantity and quality aspects. The multisectoral nature of water resources development in the context of socio-economic development must be recognized, as well as the multi-interest utilization of water resources for water supply and sanitation, agriculture, industry, urban development, hydropower generation, inland fisheries, transportation, recreation, low and flat lands management and other activities.
>
> (UNCED 1992: ch. 18, para. 18.3.)

Riding the momentum that Rio gave to the idea of sustainability, IWRM had emerged by the late 1990s as the predominant language of international water debates and policy forums. The rise of IWRM to near-hegemonic status as a framework for thinking about water problems brought with it some welcome new emphases: the importance of demand management, the importance of ecological functions and attention to the health of freshwater ecosystems, and the need for greatly broadened social participation in water governance. However, when married to the intersovereign framework at the heart of the Rio model, these new themes fell back into a comfortably old understanding of national policy frameworks complemented by international funding and technical expertise. As a result, what has come to be institutionalized internationally is a familiar picture to students of the machinery of international development: exhortation for greater funding, the championing of domestic examples of "best practices" as universal models from which governments should learn, and networks that make international expertise available for domestic consumption. Central institutional developments in this regard include the formation of organizations such as the World Water Council and the Global Water Partnership, and the emergence of the World Water Forum as a periodic gathering place and advocacy platform for the world's water experts, advocates, and stakeholders.

The idea of creating a world water council was launched at the 1992 Dublin water conference and subsequently promoted by the International Water Resources Association, a membership organization for water professionals (Grover and Biswas 1993). The World Water Council (WWC) was created in 1996. Its founding institutions were the Egyptian Ministry of Public Works and Water Resources, the Canadian International Development Agency, and the French firm Suez-Lyonnaise des Eaux, backed by a group of ten inter-governmental and international professional organizations active in the water arena. Institutionally, the WWC represents an intersection of water elites from national and international development agencies, the private sector, and inter-national professional-technical associations related to the building of water infrastructure. The council grew quickly to include more than 300 organi-zations, with membership largely reflecting its combined governmental, inter-governmental, professional, and corporate genesis.

1996 was also the year in which the World Bank, the Swedish Interna-tional Development Agency (SIDA), and the UN Development Programme (UNDP) came together to launch the Global Water Partnership (GWP). Although it maintains a small secretariat and staff in Stockholm, GWP consists principally of a set of regional networks linking organizations that embrace IWRM approaches to water management, governance, and adminis-tration. The organization's mandate is to mobilize legal, financial, technical, and administrative resources to help countries implement policies that will promote water sustainability.

Although the division of labor between the two groups has not always been clear, WWC has tended more toward vision statements, policy advo-cacy, and organizing global water summits every four years under the billing of the World Water Forum, while GWP has focused more on regional-level dialogues and project implementation. The two groups came together to present a framework for global water sustainability at the second World Water Forum in 2000. The framework emphasized "the gloomy arithmetic of water" as growing populations and booming urban, agricultural, and industrial demand were not being met by adequate levels of public invest-ment in expanding water supplies, improved water quality, and enhanced water efficiency (World Water Commission 2000: 15; Cosgrove and Rijs-berman 2000). Projections foresaw a world of 2025 in which a business-as-usual scenario would condemn four billion people to live under conditions of water stress (Cosgrove and Rijsberman 2000). The two organizations' call to action at the forum included measures intended to improve water effi-ciency, reform water management practices for efficiency and accountability, promote "full-cost pricing" of water to promote efficiency and conservation, expand private-sector investment in water infrastructure and water supply, and enhance stakeholder involvement in decision making.

Whether the World Water Council's elite global advocacy and the Global Water Partnership's regional initiatives have altered the trajectory of water-related policies and practices is debatable. What is clear, however, is that IWRM with its expert-based, sovereignty-conforming, universalistic, and technical-rational framework has been an inadequate platform from which to engage transnational socio-ecological controversies surrounding water. As I have argued in detail elsewhere, even as IWRM-based expert networks came to take on an increasingly influential role in framing the discourse on water, they have also become subject to increasing cleavage and fragmentation on social controversies for which IWRM provides little guidance (Conca 2005a).

One such controversy involves questions of participation, authority, and stakeholders. The growing popularity of the idea of stakeholder governance has been much in evidence in the domain of water. The importance of incorporating stakeholders into decision processes and implementation mechanisms became a foundational principle of the idea of integrated water resources management. Scratching below the surface of generalized stakeholder rhetoric, however, one finds a particular understanding of the relevant stakeholders and the main purposes of stakeholder consultation. As is the case with the UN Global Compact, the result is a tripartite framework with states and corporations holding down two of the poles, and the wide array of actors with civic, environmental, gender-related, or labor concerns crowded onto the third rail of "civil society." This approach was in evidence during the "consultation" process leading up to the crafting of the World Water Vision for the second World Water Forum, which NGOs and independent observers widely decried as being tightly controlled by governmental, intergovernmental, and corporate actors (Dubash *et al.* 2001).

The point is not that all actors embracing IWRM frameworks have this elite, top-down perspective on authority and participation, for this is certainly not the case. Rather, it is to suggest that technical-rational models such as IWRM, which seek to mobilize international assistance for domestic policies, have been hamstrung when it comes to incorporating a sufficiently broad participatory base to make those policies actually work. The need to broaden the participatory base is seen in the growth of social conflict around water, including controversies over the construction of large dams and water infrastructure projects; struggles related to water marketization and the role of private-sector participation in the provisioning of water as a public good; social conflicts and violence surrounding the impacts of shrimp aquaculture on coastal mangrove forests, estuaries, and the associated traditional livelihood resources of local communities; and the struggle to have water recognized as a human right, both legally and in practice. The Rio model in general and its specific water-related expressions have been largely silent on these issues, which proved to be too contentious for the model's conventional international diplomacy and too inconvenient for its domestic emphasis on developmental-state agendas.

Beyond the Rio model

The period since the Brundtland Commission report and the Earth Summit has also seen the emergence of approaches to transnational governance growing out of the very conflicts that the Rio model failed to recognize or proved unable to address. Although scholarly attention in the study of international relations has been drawn inordinately to cooperative diplomacy as the source of global institution building, social conflict can also be generative of newly institutionalized practices. The resulting institutions may have little in common with the conventional products of diplomacy.

One such controversy involves the construction of large dams. Dam building around the world has been a transnational enterprise since the time of the Roman Empire. In the modern era, international financing mechanisms such as World Bank loans, the global reach of large dam-building firms, and the global-market rationale for many such projects (in support of export agri-culture, aluminum smelting, and the like) means that "local" disputes about whether and where to build a large dam are embedded in global commodity chains, authority relations, and expert networks. The new dimension to dam struggles is the ability of opponents to embed their activities in parallel (if looser and weaker) linkages. This has been done by building networks that join site-specific dam protests and local mobilization to a wide array of extra-local resources for dam opponents: international human rights acti-vism, national and transnational environmental networks, campaigns against the practices of multilateral development banks and export credit schemes, and the international indigenous peoples movement.

Another such controversy involves water marketization (or what is more commonly referred to as privatization).[1] Spurred by the pressures of neo-liberal structural adjustment and trade liberalization, many municipalities around the world have come under intense pressure to allow various forms of "private sector participation" in the supply of water and sanitation services. In many ways, opponents of water privatization face a different struggle than opponents of large dams. Dams are the legacy of a traditional model of state-supplied public goods of water and power, whereas water market-ization (or at least its most extreme variants) envisions a brave new world in which water is a private commodity rather than a public good. In practice, however, there are common elements: for dams, "state-supplied" often means radically subsidized, and the recipients often constitute a thin and particular segment of the public; for commodified water, "market prices" often mean publicly financed risk guarantees for private investors and the steering of services toward those most able to pay. More importantly, the water mar-ketization controversy reflects a similar dynamic in which grassroots mobi-lization by labor, the poor, and other opponents has been occurring in the growing trans-local linkages. In both cases, social, economic, and political globalization has meant that the controversy has spilled outside of domestic dispute resolution mechanisms, be they coercive or deliberative and situated in either democratic or authoritarian states.

A second important shared feature in these cases is institutionalization. Activists in either domain would laugh at the notion that either struggle has been won in some definitive sense. However, in both cases, new norms are emerging that have become increasingly difficult to ignore. One such norm speaks directly to Rio's static understanding of nature as either domestic terri-tory (governable by the state) or international commons (governable only by the international community of states). Transnationalized socio-ecological controversies around water start with a very different premise: that these physically localized controversies, played out on the scale of a watershed or a municipality, are the normal and proper business of a transnational community of concern. This norm is validated not only by activists, but by the powerful actors who sit down with them in increasingly routinized arguments.

A second emergent norm, which also speaks directly to a failed premise of Rio, involves who sits where in these arguments, or the question of authority. As suggested previously, the Brundtland/Rio notion of stakeholders translated too often in practice into tripartite bargaining sessions in which the triangle of discussion was decidedly not equilateral, and in which dialogue often proved to be a decidedly one-sided affair of giving society its marching orders. I have argued elsewhere that what we are seeing in transnational contentious environmental politics is more akin to the "hybridization" of authority (Conca 2005b). States of course remain powerful actors; but they have enjoyed no particular pride of place in settings such as the World Commission on Dams (WCD) or the "stakeholder dialogue" on private-sector participation. Nonstate actors in these processes perform some surprisingly state-like functions, not simply of agenda setting but also political bargaining. In doing so, they draw upon legitimacy rooted in expertise, a compelling moral claim, or the credible threat to put protesters in the streets. States, too, perform new functions often thought of as reserved for societal forces. In the dams case, states' reactions to the WCD deliberations and output played a legitimizing (or in some cases, delegitimizing) role akin to the (in)validating role of societal responses to interstate bargaining initiatives. The point here is certainly not to project some sort of role reversal, but rather to note a process of blending and blurring.

A third emergent norm that challenges the confines of Rio involves knowledge. Knowledge is a critical element in the legitimization strategies of actors on all sides of these struggles, and expertise thus a powerful gatekeeper of effective participation. Struggles to define the good and bad effects of dams, or to estimate the "true" price of water, are efforts to stabilize the knowledge that informs (and legitimizes) governance. As such, while they may be more overtly politicized, these knowledge struggles are not unlike the mechanisms by which expert networks and "epistemic communities" shape interstate treaty negotiations. However, one difference between treaty negotiations and the politics of transnationalized socio-ecological controversies is that the latter must contend with actors who may bring to the table radically different "ways of knowing" than those marking modern international science. The stabilized body of knowledge (perhaps negotiated, perhaps imposed) that seems to be a central target of traditional environmental diplomacy may simple be unavailable, and an epistemology of local contingency, uncertainty, precaution and surprise, the context in which knowledge struggles play out.

The point is not to argue that these new normative frameworks for understanding territory, authority, and knowledge have somehow shoved aside or supplanted Westphalia, the modern project, or the logic of contemporary capitalism. The point is that these latter vessels are failing to contain transnational socio-ecological controversies in an era of notable socio-economic and ideational globalization. Perhaps the key, then, is a more explicit focus on the social contentiousness of these issues, in settings that can accommodate more hybridized forms of authority; trans-local, non-territorial, and networked understandings of place; and contingent approaches to the quest for stabilized knowledge.

Conclusion

Some critics have argued that the Rio model understood global neoliberalism all too well. In this view, mainstream environmentalism of the late twentieth century had become little more than a new regime of social regulation in line with a new mode of accumulation. In other words, the global shift toward post-Fordist forms of economic organization—stressing global-scale production systems, niche markets, flexible specialization, trade liberalization, and transnational investment—created pressure for a parallel shift in the character of the regulatory state. For the industrialized countries, this meant a move away from the welfare-state model of national compacts between capital and labor and toward the more "flexible" arrangements of Thatcherism. In this view, the rise of sustainability as the mantra of mainstream environmentalism was an effort to soften the increasingly apparent contradictions of modern systems of production, consumption, and exchange without tackling those contradictions head-on.

Such an interpretation sheds some important light on several trends within environmentalism over the past few decades: the growing bifurcation between the institutionalized, NGO-based mainstream and the more activist grassroots, the rise of economics as a central language of environmentalism, and the growing emphasis on the right-thinking environmental citizen as savvy consumer. It may also explain what the elite architects of Rio had in mind and how the Rio model fits in with other institutional developments of the same era, such as the UN-based Global Compact (Chatterjee and Finger 1994).

When it comes to what the Rio model actually accomplished, however, we must be careful not to overstate the extent to which this model succeeded in bringing about the requisite adjustments for a neoliberal order. The fact is that the *governance* model embedded in Rio fits the new terrain of neoliberal economic globalization quite poorly, and has come up woefully short as a mode of social regulation consistent with the increasingly dominant mode of accumulation. In other words, making the environmental world safe for global capitalism would require a set of national-level policy adjustments and international-level accords that Rio's political strategy proved unable to deliver.

It seems doubtful that the moderate, adjust-around-the-edges view embedded in the Rio model would have been adequate to put the world on a substantially more sustainable trajectory. But the question is largely academic at this point, given the manifest failure of the model to deliver even those incremental adjustments. In the search for a better way, we must recognize that the central challenge of global environmental governance is to find ways to address transnationalized socio-ecological controversies that are socially just and ecologically effective. Our mounting body of experience with these controversies points the way toward new understandings of territory, authority, and knowledge that will have to be central elements.

Note

1 I use the term marketization to refer to the process of turning water into a marketized commodity, a process that may or may not involve an expanded role for the private sector as connoted by the term privatization.

References

Chatterjee, Pratap and Finger, Matthias (1994) *The Earth Brokers*, London: Routledge.

Conca, Ken (2002) "The World Commission on Dams and Trends in Global Environmental Governance," *Politics and the Life Sciences* 21,1 (March): 67–70.

—— (2005a) "Growth and Fragmentation in Expert Networks: The Elusive Quest for Integrated Water Resources Management," in Peter Dauvergne (ed.) *International Handbook of Environmental Politics*, Cheltenham: Edward Elgar.

—— (2005b) "Old States in New Bottles? The Hybridization of Authority in Global Environmental Governance," in John Barry and Robyn Eckersley (eds.) *The State and the Global Ecological Crisis*, Cambridge, MA: MIT Press.

—— (2006) *Governing Water: Contentious Transnational Politic and Global Institution Building*, Cambridge, MA: MIT Press.

Conca, Ken and Dabelko, Geoffrey D. (1998) "The Earth Summit: Reflections on an Ambiguous Event," in Ken Conca and Geoffrey D. Dabelko (eds.) *Green Planet Blues: Environmental Politics from Stockholm to Kyoto*, Boulder, CO: Westview Press.

Conca, Ken, Wu, Fengshi, and Mei, Ciqi (2006) "Global Regime Formation or Complex Institution Building? The Principled Content of International River Agreements," *International Studies Quarterly* 50 (June): 263–285.

Cosgrove, William J. and Rijsberman, Frank R. (2000) *World Water Vision: Making Water Everybody's Business*, London: Earthscan.

Dubash, Navroz K., Dupar, Mairi, Kothari, Smitu, and Lissu, Tundu (2001) *A Watershed in Global Governance? An Independent Assessment of the World Commission on Dams*, Washington: World Resources Institute.

Grover, Brian and Asit K. Biswas (1993) "It's Time for a World Water Council," *Water International* 18 (1993): 81–83.

McCaffrey, Stephen (2001) "The contribution of the UN Convention on the law of the non-navigational uses of international watercourses," *International Journal of Global Environmental Issues* 1,3–4: 250–263.

United Nations (1997) *Convention on the Law of the Non-Navigational Uses of International Watercourses*, United Nations General Assembly document A/51/869, April 11, 1997.

United Nations Conference on Environment and Development (UNCED) (1992) *Agenda 21*, adopted by the UN Conference on Environment and Development, June 14, 1992.

World Commission on Environment and Development (WCED) (1987) *Our Common Future*, New York: Oxford University Press.

World Water Commission (2000) *A Water Secure World: Vision for Water, Life, and the Environment*, Paris: World Water Commission.

Index

eBooks